# Wars of Words

# WARS OF WORDS

## The Politics of Language
## in Ireland 1537–2004

TONY CROWLEY

OXFORD
UNIVERSITY PRESS

# OXFORD
## UNIVERSITY PRESS

Great Clarendon Street, Oxford OX2 6DP

Oxford University Press is a department of the University of Oxford.
It furthers the University's objective of excellence in research, scholarship,
and education by publishing worldwide in

Oxford New York

Auckland Cape Town Dar es Salaam Hong Kong Karachi
Kuala Lumpur Madrid Melbourne Mexico City Nairobi
New Delhi Shanghai Taipei Toronto

With offices in

Argentina Austria Brazil Chile Czech Republic France Greece
Guatemala Hungary Italy Japan Poland Portugal
Singapore South Korea Switzerland Thailand Turkey Ukraine Vietnam

Oxford is a registered trade mark of Oxford University Press
in the UK and in certain other countries

Published in the United States
by Oxford University Press Inc., New York

© Tony Crowley 2005

The moral rights of the author have been asserted
Database right Oxford University Press (maker)

First published 2005

British Library Cataloguing in Publication Data

Data available

Library of Congress Cataloging in Publication Data

Data available

Typeset by Kolam Information Services Pvt. Ltd, Pondicherry, India
Printed in Great Britain
on acid-free paper by
Biddles Ltd, King's Lynn, Norfolk

ISBN 0-19-927343-X   978-0-19-927343-0
1 3 5 7 9 10 8 6 4 2

*For*
*ANGELA POINGDESTRE*
*and*
*STEPHEN SHEEDY*

# Acknowledgements

Institutional acknowledgements are easiest to make, so I will begin with them. I am indebted to the staff at Leabharlann Náisiúnta na hÉireann/ National Library of Ireland and at Trinity College Dublin Library, particularly in the Early Printed Books Reading Room. They made my research trips easy, productive, and pleasant. I am very grateful to my colleagues at the John Rylands University Library Manchester, particularly the Deansgate staff. A special thank-you is due to Janet Wallwork for an introduction to the Cassedy Collection of Irish texts and manuscripts, and to John Hodgson for facilitating access to it. Stella Halkyard's professionalism, enthusiasm, and energy have been invaluable; this project could not have been completed without her support.

I would like to thank the Leverhulme Trust for a Research Fellowship in 1993; John Rylands University Library Manchester for a research award in 1997; the British Academy for a small research grant in 2001; the University of Manchester for sabbatical leave in Autumn 2003; and the Arts and Humanities Research Board for a research leave award in Spring 2004. I am grateful to the American Conference for Irish Studies, the University of Barcelona, the Canadian Association for Irish Studies, Ionad an Léinn Éireannaigh (the Centre for Irish Studies) at the University of Galway, and the Keogh Institute for Irish Studies at the University of Notre Dame for opportunities to present and discuss research included in this book. The Centre for Cultural Studies at the University of California, Santa Cruz gave me the space and time to work on the very last stages of this text; I extend particular gratitude to the co-directors Chris Connery and Gail Hershatter for their generosity and kindness.

I am grateful too for the kind permission of Gallery Press to reproduce Nuala Ní Dhomhnaill's 'Ceist na Teanga' and its translation, 'The Language Issue' by Paul Muldoon. And for the permission of Cumann na Sgríbeann nGaedhilge (Irish Texts Society) to quote from 'Nach ait an nós', 'Iomda scéim ar chur na cluana', 'Cathréim an Dara Séamuis', *Duanaire Dáibhí Ó Bruadair*, Pts I and III, and 'An Mileadh d'imthigh ar

Mhór-Schleachtaibh na hÉireann', 'Tarngaireacht dhuinn fhírinne', and *Dánta Aodhagáin Uí Rathaille*.

I happily own a debt of gratitude to the undergraduate and post-graduate students with whom I have worked over a number of years at Manchester University.

While writing this book I have been fortunate to have benefited from the help and encouragement of friends and colleagues: Emily Cuming, Terry Eagleton, Tadhg Foley, Rachael Gilmour, Rosa Gonzalez, Paul Hamilton, Richard Hogg, Anne McKee, Peter McKee, Andrew McNeillie, Bernard O'Donoghue, Heather O'Donoghue, Gearóid Ó Tuathaigh, Louis de Paor, Bruce Robbins, Alan Shelston, Helen Small, Tolly Taylor, and Paul Young. I thank them all.

Thanks are due to the editors at OUP: Jacqueline Baker, Sophie Goldsworthy, Tom Perridge, and Elizabeth Prochaska.

And a very special mention to Jack, Ellie, Rory, Erin, Roisín, Tom, Matt, and Helen.

This book is dedicated to Angela Poingdestre and Stephen Sheedy, for their support, friendship, and love over a very long time.

# Contents

# *Abbreviations*

| | |
|---|---|
| *Cal. S. P. Ire* | Calendar of the state papers relating to Ireland |
| *Cal. Carew MSS* | Calendar of the Carew manuscripts preserved in the archiepiscopal library at Lambeth |
| *Cal. pat rolls Ire* | Calendar of the patent and close Rolls of Chancery in Ireland 18th to 45th of Queen Elizabeth |
| *H. M. C. rep. 10* | Historical Manuscripts Commission tenth report |
| *S. P. Hen VIII* | State Papers, Henry VIII |
| *Stat. Ire* | The statutes at large passed in the parliaments held in Ireland |

CHAPTER ONE

# *Introduction: Language Acquisition*

'His language, so familiar and so foreign, will always be for me an
acquired speech'
James Joyce, *A Portrait of the Artist as a Young Man*, 1916.

In 'A New Look at the Language Question', Tom Paulin begins by
asserting that 'the history of a language is often a story of possession and
dispossession, territorial struggle and the establishment or imposition of
a culture'. He continues: 'arguments about the "evolution" or the
"purity" of a language can be based on a simplistic notion of progress
or on a doctrine of racial stereotypes' (Paulin 1984: 178). Several of the
themes with which this text will be concerned are outlined here: proprietorship, sovereignty, cultural struggle, progress, purity, racial identity, authenticity; there are others of course, not least the highly
significant factor of religion. What this means is that the history which
will be set out in this account is often highly complex, and that is an
important starting point because the history has suffered greatly in the
past from simplification. The presentation of the complexities will
challenge the simplicity of certain received versions of this history,
and my argument is that this will be useful not just because the more
complicated account is more accurate, but because the simplified versions are misleading and therefore dangerous. For example, in what was
for a long time a standard account of the issue, 'The Spoken Languages
of Medieval Ireland', Ireland's leading early twentieth-century historian
declared baldly that 'the native cause had always been identical in the
minds of the Gaelic race with the Irish language' (Curtis 1919: 252).
There is in fact little if any evidence for this linkage between language
and 'the native cause'; the claim is quite anachronistic, although the
political implications of such a relationship for understanding national
identity at the time the claim was made (pre-independence) were clear.
Pride in a language, and by corollary defensiveness about a language,

occur usually in contexts of cultural and political threat and danger, and there was little if any sense of that until a considerable way into the colonial occupation of Ireland. Scattered evidence can be found, however, for the argument that after the Anglo-Norman conquest of 1169 there appears to be a sense of distinctiveness (and distinction on the Irish side) with regard to Irish identity and the language. For example, in the late 1270s the Anglicized citizens of Cork protested to Edward I against the appointment of a Gaelic-speaking Irishman as a customs collector on the grounds that Irish speakers were enemies to the king and his subjects (*'Hybernica lingua vobis et vestris sit inimica'*) (Watt 1987*b*: 346). And in 1285 an English governmental commission recommended that none of the Gaelic Irish ever be appointed to the ecclesiastical hierarchy on the grounds that they,

semper predicant contra Regem, et prouisiones faciunt in ecclesiis suis semper de Hibernis . . . ita quod eleccio episcoporum possit fieri de Hibernis, ad sustinendam Linguam suam . . . Similiter fratres predicatorum et minores de Lingua illa faciunt multa (Watt 1961: 151).

(always preach against the King and always furnish their churches with Irishmen . . . so that the election of bishops shall be of Irishmen in order to maintain their own language . . . Likewise the Dominicans and Franciscans make a lot of that language).

A proper clarification needs to be made here however, since what is signified is a sense of nationality, based on culture, rather than nationalism, based on political cause, and again it is anachronistic to read it otherwise.[1] The complexity of the cultural situation at the time is demonstrated in that some twelve years later a term which was to become central in later debates is first used to describe those amongst the colonists who had been Gaelicized. They were described as *quasi degeneres* in parliamentary legislation in 1297, a concept which was to reappear in Renaissance ideas of English degeneration in Ireland, meaning the process by which the colonizers had fallen away from their original stock or race and whereby their Englishness had decayed. The fact that this concept is found so early in the colonizing process indicates that questions of the propriety and status of identity were crucial to it from the very beginning.

---

[1] For a discussion of the literature concerned with ethnicity and nationalism see the introduction to Kidd 1999; another useful account is 'The Idea of Nationality; Terminology and Historical Background' in Leerssen 1996: 15–31.

There are contradictions and complexities throughout this history then, but there are also many positions and viewpoints which are to be expected. Colonialism is of course a central strand in the story. Legislation by the colonizing power was first passed against the use of Gaelic in 1366, and then again in 1665, 1695, and 1733. But the anti-Irish story proper has to start with the work of Giraldus Cambrensis (Gerald of Wales) and his account of the Irish and their culture in *Topographia Hibernica* (1188). Despite the fact that he had little to say on the language of the Irish, apart from a few speculative observations on its origins and the etymologies of names, Giraldus's attitude to Irish culture was extremely influential in the centuries which followed, particularly amongst the late sixteenth-century Anglo-Irish chroniclers.[2] Typical of his account was his description of the Irish as 'so barbarous that they cannot be said to have any culture'. 'A wild and inhospitable people' who live like beasts, they are, he opined, 'devoted to laziness', barbarian (though 'incomparably skilled' in music), treacherous, and vicious. Their coronation ritual, outlined in detail, stood as a cipher for their civilization: the King copulates with a white mare which is then slaughtered and boiled; the King bathes in that water and he and his people eat the horseflesh and drink the broth (O'Meara 1982: 110). In fact one of the Anglo-Irish chroniclers, Richard Stanihurst, built directly on the antipathy of Giraldus in his account of the Gaelic language, *A Treatise Containing a Plain and Perfect Description of Ireland* (1577). Noting a report of a woman babbler in Rome, Stanihurst informed the reader that she could speak any language but Irish, since Irish was so difficult that 'the very devil was gravelled therewith' (Stanihurst 1587: 7). Such deprecation was not of course ignored, or at least not after the intensification of linguistic colonialism in the mid to late sixteenth century when the dangers of what was happening first seem to have become notably apparent to native Irish commentators. Seathrún Céitinn (Geoffrey Keating) was one of the first to reject the attack on Irish language, history, and culture. In *Foras Feasa Ar Éirinn* (A Basis of Knowledge about Ireland) (1634) Céitinn dismissed the 'worthlessness of the

---

[2] Though the texts are known as the Anglo-Irish Chronicles, they were in fact composed by authors from very different backgrounds and in certain cases from opposing viewpoints. Thus Richard Stanihurst, writer of *A Treatise Containing a Plain and Perfect Description of Ireland* (1577), was a representative of the Old English faction (Anglo-Norman families, or those settled before the English Reformation). However, Edmund Spenser's *A View of the State of Ireland* (1596) was written as a polemic for the New English (English Protestant settlers after the Reformation).

testimony' of Stanihurst on the grounds that Stanihurst 'had so great an hatred for the Irish' that he had simply misread history. For Céitinn, any conquest which attempted to extinguish the language of the conquered was by that criterion alone a pagan rather than a Christian exercise (Céitinn 1902: 31). His refutation of the attacks on Gaelic orchestrated by the chroniclers was echoed a little later in the century by Gratianus Lucius (John Lynch) in *Cambrensis Eversus* (1662), an influential text for later Irish nationalists.

There appears to be a fairly simple opposition here between the colonists and their apologists on one side, and the native defenders on the other. Yet again the real historical picture is more complicated as an example can illustrate. The first piece of colonial prohibition passed against the Irish language of any real note was included in the Statute of Kilkenny (1366), a legislative effort to codify various attempts to resolve colonial problems, which was maintained in theory until the early seventeenth century. It began by means of historical and cultural contrast:

> whereas at the conquest of the land of Ireland, and for a long time after, the English of the said land used the English language, mode of riding and apparel, and were governed and ruled, both they and their subjects called Betaghes, according to the English law...now many of the said land, forsaking the English language, manners, mode of riding, laws and usages, live and govern themselves according to the manners, fashion, and language of the Irish enemies (Irish Archaeological Society 1843: 3, 5).

The consequence was that 'the said land, and the liege people thereof, the English language, the allegiance due our lord the king, and the English laws there, are put in subjection and decayed, and the Irish enemies exalted and raised up, contrary to reason'. Part of the response to the evident corruption of the Irish dominion was an ordinance primarily relating to language:

> Also, it is ordained and established, that every Englishman do use the English language, and be named by an English name, leaving off entirely the manner of naming used by the Irish; and that every Englishman use the English custom, fashion, mode of riding and apparel, according to his estate; and if any English, or Irish living amongst the English, use the Irish language amongst themselves, contrary to this ordinance, and thereof be attainted, his lands and tenements, if he have any, shall be seized into the hands of his immediate lord (Irish Archaeological Society 1843: 11, 13).

This seems to be an early and paradigmatic piece of colonial legislation: proscription of the native language in favour of the language of the colonizer, with harsh penalties for disobedience, including loss of land and imprisonment. It seems to be an example of colonial practice which Spenser's pronouncement in the 1590s later summarized: 'it hath ever beene the use of the Conquerour to despise the language of the conquered, and to force him by all meanes to learne his' (Spenser 1633: 47). In fact, however, the issue is historically more complex and therefore interesting, since this was not legislation primarily directed towards the native Gaelic population, but towards the colonists. It was not an essay in the eradication of the Gaelic language, but an order to uphold the use of the English language; not so much an attempt to establish an anglophone Ireland as to preserve English linguistic, cultural, and political identity. Beyond the Pale (a term first used in the 1490s—based on the pale at Calais—to signify that small area of Ireland in which the English monarch's writ ran), the Irish were more or less free to use their own language, follow their own cultural customs, and practise their own Brehon code of law. The Statute of Kilkenny was intended to govern the English in Ireland, to ensure that they remained English, to prevent them from going native; that is to say, from being Gaelicized. And the reason for this is that for two centuries following the initial conquest in 1169 this was precisely what had happened: English order had not been imposed across Ireland; rather the colonizers had been acculturated to Gaelic ways. This is significant because what it indicates, not for the last time in such debates, is not a confident, dominating master-culture exercising control over its colonial subjects, but a fearful and anxious one which was forced to threaten its own English subjects with dire penalties in order to have them conform to its norms. One of the more ironic things to notice about the statute moreover is the language in which it was written. Though it defended the use of 'English', the statute itself was composed, as we would expect since it is a legal document, in Norman-French. The text which begins the statute, rendered above in modern English, is in the original: 'Come a la conquest de la terre Dirland et long temps apres les Englois de la dit terre userent la lang morture et vesture Engleis . . .' (Irish Archaeological Society 1843: 2).

If the Statute of Kilkenny reveals one complication of Irish history, then there are other examples which show that any simplified opposition between colonists and colonizers hinders rather than enables historical understanding (one instance is the omission of any account of Gaedhil versus Gaedhil antagonism in favour of Gaedhil versus Gaill struggle in the earlier period). Likewise the familiar antagonism between Protestant and Catholic takes surprising form in language debates. The mid to late eighteenth-century revival of interest in Irish antiquity for example was largely led and certainly funded by Protestant patriotism; Charles Vallancey, a key figure in the movement was a British military officer; Charlotte Brooke, the first collector of modern Irish poetry and an early Irish literary critic, was the daughter of a unionist who was a Protestant supporter of the Penal laws (though he later changed his mind). Moreover the early nineteenth-century Catholic Church turned its back on Gaelic, unsurprisingly since Maynooth, instituted in 1795 as its premier intellectual focus, used English; Protestant proselytizers in Ireland at the same time stressed the need for preaching in Irish. In the 1840s, Thomas Davis, Young Irelander and middle-class Protestant, declared that 'a people without a language of its own is only half a nation' and described Irish as 'a surer barrier, and more important frontier, than fortress or river' (Davis, 1914: 98). His contemporary, the great Irish nationalist political leader Daniel O'Connell, a Catholic and native Gaelic speaker, was reported to have declared that he could 'witness without a sigh the gradual disuse of the Irish' (Daunt 1848: 15). Towards the end of the nineteenth century the poverty-stricken Irish-speaking peasantry of the western seaboard were repeatedly recorded as being ashamed of their language and as desperately wanting English for their children. And at precisely the same time Douglas Hyde, an adherent of the Protestant Church of Ireland and leader of the Gaelic League, argued passionately the case for 'the necessity for de-Anglicising Ireland' and for the restoration of Ireland to its true Gaelic nature. Adding to the strange complexity was the appearance of the Language Freedom Movement in the Republic of Ireland in the 1960s; the group was dedicated to attacking the compulsory teaching of Irish in schools, removing its status as prerequisite for the Civil Service, and diminishing the spending of public monies on its restoration. And in the terrible days of war in the mid 1970s we find the striking assertion in a journal of one of the Loyalist groups engaged in paramilitary activity in Northern Ireland, that with regard to language, 'the truth of the matter is, Ulster Protestants have as much claim, if not more in some cases, to the Gaelic culture as the Roman Catholic population' (Ó Glaisne 1981: 870). Members of the Ulster Volunteer Force not only studied Irish in the

Northern Irish prisons, they gained the Gaelic League's Fáinne (commemorative badge) to demonstrate their proficiency in the language. Yet perhaps most striking of all when viewed historically are the language specifications in the section devoted to 'Rights, Safeguards and Equality of Opportunity: Economic, Social and Cultural Issues' in *The Belfast Agreement* (1998), the ambitious attempt to bring the central historical conflict on the island of Ireland to a peaceful and lasting resolution. Under the agreement, all signatories promised 'to recognise the importance of respect, understanding and tolerance in relation to linguistic diversity, including in Northern Ireland, the Irish language, Ulster-Scots and the languages of the various ethnic communities, all of which are part of the cultural wealth of the island of Ireland' (*Belfast Agreement* 1998: 19). The British government specifically committed itself to taking 'resolute action to promote the language', including the encouragement of the use of Irish in private and public life, the removal of restrictions upon the language, statutory facilitation of Irish medium education, and the stimulation of financial support for Irish language film and television production in Northern Ireland. It was a remarkable turn around; Gaelic street names had previously been outlawed and it was an offence to give your name and address in Irish if arrested by the police or army.

Of course it is necessary to draw attention back to the fact that Irish history has largely been a colonial history, and therefore that the linguistic history of Ireland and the politics of language in Ireland have been underpinned by the experience of the processes of colonialism, anti-colonialism, and post-colonialism, with all of the attendant difficulty, violence, and bitterness that has entailed. The period under consideration did after all witness the near-death of a language (though there are contemporary signs of a revival). But there is more to this narrative than just an account of the effects of colonialism on the Irish language; there is a fuller, more complicated and interesting story to be told. It may, however, be worth saying at this point what this book is not: it is not an attempt to render a precise history of the development of the Gaelic and English languages in Ireland, nor does it seek to sketch the history of the literatures in the two languages, nor is it in any sense a philological study of the languages. What the book does try to achieve is to work within the broad confines of the field of the politics of language in order to study the roles of language in history in a particular space over a given time; roles which are linked to issues such as identity, legitimacy, proprietorship, cultural struggle, and memory to mention but a few. It intends to tell an extraordinary story of apparently inevitable attraction and repugnance, hatred and fascination, generosity and bitterness, miserable dereliction and soaring achievement, great joy and awful sadness. It will use materials which range from colonial state papers to the writings of Irish revolutionaries; from Irish priest-historians to contemporary loyalists; from English attempts to make the Irish speak and dress according to English fashion to Irish attempts to make them speak Gaelic and dress only in Irish cloth; from Gaelic dictionary makers to lexicographers of Ulster-Scots. And it will tell a story in which at various times Irish was described as foreign and English as familiar; and in which at other times English was described as foreign and Irish as familiar. A story in which English was the language of the rational intellect, Irish the language of the immaterial soul; Irish the language of history, English the language of everyday modern business; English a hybrid and impure language, Irish the pure language of Eden; English the language of poetry, Irish the language of philosophy; Irish a fetter on Irish hopes, English the language of better prospects; English the defence against the superstitions of paganism, Irish the guarantor of Ireland's religious freedom; English the language which could be used to save the Catholic flock, Irish the key to the Protestant reformation of Ireland; English the language of oppressive colonialism, Irish the language of the anti-colonial struggle ... It is a story whose contradictions are encapsulated by the contrasting thoughts of one young man, Joyce's Stephen Dedalus in *A Portrait of the Artist as a Young Man* (1916). After a colonial encounter with one of his English university tutors and a disagreement over the use of the word 'tundish', Stephen thinks to himself: 'the language in which we are speaking is his before it is mine ... His language, so familiar and so foreign, will always be for me an acquired speech' (Joyce 1992: 205). Later, however, after discovering something of the word's origins and history, Stephen explodes: 'Damn the dean of studies ... What did he come here for to teach us his own language or to learn it from us?' (Joyce 1992: 274).[3] Viewed historically, it is an interesting question.

---

[3] The dean of studies implies that 'tundish' is a word used in Ireland, thereby making Stephen's usage provincial—hence Stephen's reaction of hurt and dismay. In fact 'tundish', as Stephen discovers when he looks it up, is a late medieval English word, or as he puts it, 'English and good old blunt English too' (Joyce 1992: 274).

CHAPTER TWO

# *Reforming the Word and the words of the Irish, 1537–1607*

'The sword alone without the word is not sufficient, but unless they be forced they will not come once to hear the word preached'
Archbishop Loftus to Lord Burghley, 1590.

Medieval Ireland was a complex place, a site of contact between a number of languages and cultures. As Cronin has argued with regard to the historically significant processes of translation, 'the cultural reality for many medieval scholars was not monolingual but plurilingual' (Cronin 1996: 39). Such a stress on historical diversity, however, has not always been the received view; an older account saw this period simply in terms of a ceaseless contest between two separate and antagonistic cultures which resulted from the Anglo-Norman invasion in 1169. But just to take the example of the Gaelic and colonial cultures, if direct confrontation were the only result of colonization, an endless warring between Gaedhil and Gaill, then how can we explain the perceived need on the part of the colonizers to pass the linguistic prescriptions of the Statute of Kilkenny some two centuries after the invasion? Why in 1366 would Irish need to be banned in the Pale? And why would intermarriage or the fostering of children require proscription? The statute's provisions are only explicable if it is understood that there was more to the relations between the two major cultures in medieval Ireland than unrelieved hostility. As Watt has pointed out, 'the two cultures did not merely collide, they also interpenetrated: each nation assimilated people from the other. Each culture, of course in different degrees and to unequal extents, was affected by the other' (Watt 1987a: 308). What can be seen are the processes of assimilation and acculturation typical of border cultures: cultural formations which exist in close proximity and which are connected by regular interchange.

Such exchanges, evidently, often do not take place in a comfortable or consensual manner and they are sometimes the result of brute imposition, sometimes of necessary co-operation, often a mixture of both; but the interrelations do take place, and the effects in medieval Ireland were notable, particularly for the colonists.

Initially the linguistic situation after the invasion was confused; the colonizers brought with them to Gaelic Ireland not just their own Norman language (which as the ruling class they also used in England) but also the various languages of their soldiery, including Flemish, Welsh, and Anglo-Norman. Flemish and Welsh soon dropped out of view and the real contest of languages took place between Irish, Latin (the language of learning, international communication, and power in medieval Christendom), French, and English. French and Latin were the languages of bureaucracy and administration; French was used in acts of parliament between 1310 and 1472, and French and Latin alternated in the municipal records of the major towns. There is, however, little evidence that French spread at all as a vernacular, and in so far as it remained it was as the language of the aristocratic rulers. In England much the same process took place, and it was not until the reign of Edward I that the language of the Anglo-Saxon population became the second language of the English monarchy and aristocracy (Curtis 1919: 236–7). English only became the language of the courts and of the opening of parliament after 1362 (Anderson 1983: 45). Gradually, however, French was displaced by English as the main rival to Irish in Ireland, as evinced by the Statute of Kilkenny, which was drawn up in Norman-French (since it was a legal document) but which addressed in part the problem of the adoption by the colonists of the Irish language at the expense of English. Thus, although English was not used in acts of parliament in Ireland until 1472 (it was used in the municipal records of Waterford from as early as 1365), it emerged gradually as the language of commerce, traffic, and eventually power within the boundaries of English rule; which is to say that it became the language of the towns. Gaelic on the other hand was the vernacular language of the native Irish—from chieftain to the lowest follower—within the area of their own culture and order; which is to say that it was the language of the greatest part of the country. Again, however, it is necessary to point out that this was not a situation in which wholly distinct cultures were hermetically sealed from each other. There were regular economic, political, and cultural contacts, and the immediate historical consequence of such relations was the limited development of Anglicization and the incremental spread of Gaelicization. This prompted a colonial concern which recurred frequently over a long period: how to stop the English from becoming Irish, and as a central part of that process, how to elevate the English language at the expense of Gaelic. For in the medieval period, even in the major towns themselves, complaints were often heard about the use of Irish within the walls, which is unsurprising given the influx of the peasantry in search of work. Thus, although in the thirteenth century the future appeared to belong to the colonists, at least economically and politically, the Gaelic revival in the fourteenth century and the effect which it wrought on colonial culture meant that the later prospects for the native culture were much brighter (Watt 1987*a*: 307). This was despite the fact that the causes of the revival itself were more to do with the weakness of crown rule, limited resources, and irresolute central government, rather than a concerted effort by the largely disunited Gaels to reverse the conquest (Ellis 1998: 18–19).

By the beginning of the fourteenth century an important cultural distinction was being made between the English in England and the English in Ireland (sometimes described as 'the middle nation'), or the English by birth and the English by blood (Watt 1987*c*: 352). The historical appearance of a new form of cultural distinction is of course often deeply disturbing, as it challenges received notions of identity and otherness. In this specific context the sense that a new hybrid breed was appearing in Ireland (later to be called the 'Old English'), neither fully English nor Irish, was evidently problematic to the colony and there are repeated attempts in both the fourteenth and fifteenth centuries to bring the cultural miscreants back to their proper natures.[1] For example in 1465 the Irish Parliament passed 'An act that the Irishmen dwelling in the counties of Dublin, Myeth, Vriel, and Kildare, shall go apparelled like Englishmen, and wear their Beards after the English Maner, swear Allegiance, and take English surname'. It was an edict which combined cultural, political, and linguistic prescription for the Irish living in the Pale. And it demonstrated the political significance of cultural activities: shaving in a particular manner was to be accompanied by, and was formally equivalent to, declaring allegiance to the English authorities.

---

[1] The phrase 'Old English' was first used by Spenser in *A View of the State of Ireland* in 1596. Stanihurst called them 'Anglo-Hiberni' in *De Rebus in Hibernia Gestis* (1584); in Moryson's *Itinerary* (1617) he termed them the 'English-Irish'.

With regard to the crucial issue of naming, the heads of families were ordered to take

> an English surname of one town, as Sutton, Chester, Trim, Skryne, Cork, Kinsale: or colour, as white blacke, browne: or arte or science, as smith or carpenter: or office, as cooke, butler, and that he and his issue shall use this name, under payne of forfeyting of his good yearely, till the premisses be done (*Stat. Ire* 1786: 5 E 4. c. 3).

The unsuccessful nature of these efforts to prevent hybridization was to have long-lasting cultural and historical repercussions which will be explored later; the problem of identity, how to understand it and how to render it, will be a central theme in this text.

It is clear that at the end of the fifteenth century Gaelic language and culture were still dominant throughout the colony; beyond parts of Leinster and the major towns the population was apparently irredeemably monoglot Irish. So much so that when the Statutes of Kilkenny were confirmed again in 1495, all articles were re-affirmed with the significant exception of 'those that speaketh of the Irish language' (*Stat. Ire* 1786: 10 H7. c. 8). The cultural compromise forced on the colonizers is also demonstrated in evidence from the municipal archives of Waterford in 1492–3 regarding legal proceedings. An edict established that no one 'shall enpleade nor defende in Yrish tong ayeneste ony man in the court, but that all they that ony maters shall have in courte to be mynstred shall have a man that can spek English to declare his matier'. The rule, however, was subject to an important condition: 'excepte one party be of the countre; then every such dueller shalbe att liberte to speke Yrish (*H. M. C. rep. 10* 1885: 323). Furthermore, an account of the state of Ireland in 1515 asserted that there were large parts of the country in which 'all thEnglyshe folke of the said countyes ben of Iryshe habyt, of Iryshe langage, and of Iryshe condytions, except the cyties and the wallyd tounes'. Even within the small lands subject to crown rule, 'all the comyn peoplle of the said halff countyes, that obeyeth the Kinges lawes, for the more parts ben of Iryshe birth, of Iryshe habyte, and of Iryshe langage' (*S. P. Hen VIII*, ii, 6–8). This was the situation which faced Henry VIII in the immediate aftermath of his succession: a politically unreliable, culturally and linguistically divided colony in which many of the English settlers appeared to have gone native.

Henry's concern with Ireland was undertaken in earnest after the break with Rome and the passing of the Act of Supremacy in the Irish parliament (1537) confirming the king and his successors as supreme Head of the Church of Ireland. This new era in Anglo-Irish relations saw a more interventionist stance by a monarch whose entire political strategy was based upon centralization of power. Henry addressed the citizens of Galway in 1536, instructing them to use English and send their children to school to learn the language; his most notable ordinance, however, was the 'Act for the English Order, Habit and Language' (1537). Based on the principles of the knowledge of God and the inculcation of political obedience, Henry ordered all of his subjects to conform to English manners, dress, and language since difference in these areas, it was argued, created other more telling divisions:

> there is again nothing which doth more contain and keep many of his subjects of this his said land, in a certain savage and wild kind and manner of living, than the diversity that is betwixt them in tongue, language, order and habit, which by the eye deceiveth the multitude, and persuadeth unto them, that they should be as it were of sundry sorts, or rather of sundry countries, where indeed they be wholly together one body, whereof his highness is the only head under God (*Stat. Ire* 1786: 28 H 8. c.xv.).

Cultural difference, to which linguistic difference was considered central, created political division, and was thus an important hindrance to Henry's plan to incorporate all the inhabitants of Ireland as subjects of the crown. But what was most significant in the act was the implicit recognition of the relationship between language and national identity. Though the text argued explicitly for a constitutional definition of the nation there was a tacit acknowledgement of the problematic potency of linguistic difference to persuade people that they should be of 'sundry countries'.[2]

Henry ordained that the Kilkenny Statute be executed (a reflex repeated in the following centuries) and that his own act be passed by the Irish parliament with harsh penalties for disobedience:

> his Majesty doth hereby intimate unto all his said subjects of this land, of all degrees, that whosoever shall, for any respect, at any time, decline from the order and purpose of this law, touching the increase of the English tongue, habit, and order, or shall suffer any within his family or rule, to use the Irish habit, or not to use themselves to the English tongue, his Majesty will repute

---

[2] The tension between political and ethnic definitions of the nation, particularly with regard to the language question, is one which recurs in Irish history. Its significance in the twentieth century is discussed in Chapter seven.

them in his noble heart . . . whatsoever they shall at other times pretend in words and countenance, to be persons of another sort and inclination than becometh the true and faithful subjects (*Stat. Ire* 1786: 28 H 8. c.xv.)

In other words, conforming to cultural Englishness was to be the proper test of political and religious loyalty for 'true and faithful subjects'; the use of Irish was to be taken as a sign of treachery.

In a significant move Henry targeted the education of the children of Ireland as a particularly important component of the project of cultural colonialism. Heads of families were ordered to bring up the children in places where they 'may have occasion to learn the English tongue, language, order and condition'. The clergy were instructed to 'bid the beads in the English tongue, and preach the word of God in English', and to keep schools in their parishes for the teaching of the English language to children. The centrality of the educational project to the whole reform programme, partly explained by its central place in Renaissance Humanism's theory of the social order, can also be seen later in the sixteenth century. An 'Act for the Erection of Free Schools' was passed in 1570 under Elizabeth and echoed Henrician rhetoric. Aimed at curing the rude and barbarous state of the native Irish by bringing them to knowledge of God's prohibition of their daily heinous offences and to the 'due and humble obedience' towards their rulers which had been intended by scripture, the act ordained that there should be 'a free school within every diocesse of this realm of Ireland, and that the schoolmaster shall be an Englishman, or of the English birth of this realm' (*Stat. Ire* 1786: 12 E 1 c.1). The address of James Stanihurst, Speaker to the Irish House of Commons, reaffirmed the point; it was appended to Edmund Campion's *A Historie of Ireland* (1571), which was itself little more than an appeal for the effectiveness of education. Arguing for free grammar schools, Stanihurst proposed that this would,

foster a young frye, likely to prove good members of this commonwealth, and desirous to traine their children the same way. Neither were it a small help to the assurance of the Crowne of England, when Babes from their Craddles should be inured under learned Schoole-masters, with a pure English tongue, habite, fashion, discipline; and in time utterly forget the affinity of their unbroken borderers (Campion 1633: 132).

Using the common metaphor of cultural contact as an infection which required inoculation (Irishness as a malaise in need of a good dose of Englishness), Stanihurst invoked the Humanist medium of the school as

the way to a reformed society. Tudor reformers, like their Jesuit counterparts, believed in the merits of catching their subjects early. The
Tudor project for educating Irish children was finally effectively realized
in the National School system instigated in 1831.

The noise in these debates was often more impressive than the
practical results which ensued; in the same year as Henry's act, and as
evidence of its necessity, a commentator noted that 'all the English
March borderers use Irish apparel and the Irish tongue' in the Pale as
well as elsewhere (*Cal. S. P. Ire* 1509–73: 32). Perhaps the best indication
of the reality facing these Tudor cultural reformers, and, more tellingly,
of their somewhat pragmatic attitude towards it in practice, is given by
the events surrounding Henry's 'Act for Kingly Title' in 1541. Henry's
declaration of his kingship over Ireland (voluntarily offered by the Irish
nobility) was proclaimed in English to the Irish Lords and Commons.[3]
Yet despite the fact that the membership of both houses was almost
exclusively made up of descendants of the Anglo-Normans (the Old
English), the Speaker's address had to be translated into Irish by the
Earl of Ormond for the benefit of the listeners.[4] This was four years
after the language had effectively been proscribed by the state. A sign of
the realism of Tudor attitudes towards Gaelic was the institution of the
official post of Interpreter of the Irish Tongue to the Dublin Lord
Deputy, a key crown functionary (Jackson 1973: 24); complaints about
the use of Irish even within the Pale were to continue long after Henry's
declaration of intent to Anglicize Ireland.

Religion was of course a central issue in Anglo-Irish relations; it was
enormously problematic and complex, and the language question was
central to it. For Protestantism one of the central doctrines was access
to the Bible in the vernacular tongue, a prerequisite for the right of the
individual to read the sacred text directly and to make up their own mind
(though of course given literacy rates and church practices this was of
more theoretical than practical concern). In Ireland this presented
particular difficulties, since the overwhelming majority of the population was composed of monoglot Gaelic speakers (literacy in Irish was

---

[3] Before the assertion of sovereignty in 1541 Henry had, like his predecessors, been Lord of
Ireland; for a discussion of the constitutional significance of the change see Hayes-McCoy
1976.
[4] Ó Cuív notes that after the 1541 parliament the next record of a parliamentary assembly in
which Irish was used as the medium of business was the inaugural session of the revolutionary
Dáil Éireann in 1919 (Ó Cuív 1996: 413).

essentially confined to the bardic class), and the English reformers had little access to the language. In 1538 George Browne, the Archbishop of Dublin appointed to prosecute the early Reformation, promulgated the official English versions of the Lord's Prayer, the Creed, the Hail Mary, and the Ten Commandments, and ordered the clergy to teach them to their flocks (Ellis 1998: 208). But this was of little practical use and a sign of the problems evident in the early Elizabethan period was the passing of the 'Act for the Uniformity of Common Prayer and Service in the Church, and the Administration of the Sacraments' (1560). Given the lack of English ministers who spoke Irish, or willing Irish speakers prepared to translate for them, the Irish parliament sought permission to use the old Catholic language of Latin in Gaelic areas, a request which had significant theological implications. Another manifestation of the troubles faced by the established church was the pitiful petition in 1562 of Craik, 'to be disburdened of the bishoprick of Kildare, as he cannot understand the Irish language' (*Cal. S. P. Ire* 1509–73: 208).

Irish Protestantism was at one and the same time typical and anomalous with regard to the methods and practices of European Protestantism. As Anderson has pointed out, in Europe 'Protestantism was always fundamentally on the offensive, precisely because it knew how to make use of the expanding vernacular print market being created by capitalism' (Anderson 1983: 43). But if the alliance between Protestantism and print-capitalism was highly effective in Europe, including England, its efficacy in Ireland, given the specific linguistic and economic conditions which prevailed there, was necessarily more limited. The first book printed in Irish was in part a response to the problems of language and religion: Seon Carsuel's ( John Carswell) *Foirm na nUrrnuidheadh* (Book of Common Order) (1567) was a translation of Knox's revision of the 1552 prayer book. Published in Edinburgh (Carsuel was the Bishop of the Isles) it was printed, in roman characters, in the standard literary language common to Ireland and Scotland at the time; appearing in the same year as the Welsh New Testament and Prayer Book (authorized by Elizabeth in 1563) the text was embarrassing for the established Irish church. In the Epistle Dedicatory Carsuel made a cultural and religious attack on the 'supporters of the Gaelic, in that they prefer and practise the framing of vain, hurtful, lying earthly stories about the Tuath de Dhanond, and about the sons of Milesius, and about the heroes and Fionn Mac Cumhail' rather than the 'faithful words of God and the perfect way of truth' (Carsuel 1873: 19). But this criticism was considerably undermined in its political effect simply by the fact that it was addressed to a common Gaeldom, the 'Gael of Alban and Eireand', at a time when the centralizing English administration was attempting to cut Ulster's traditional and military links to Scotland for its own political ends. This was not the only cause of embarrassment: Carsuel's comment that 'the Holy Bible has never been printed in Gaelic as it has been printed in Latin and English' (Carsuel 1873: 18) unwittingly drew attention to the fact that the Act for the Uniformity of Common Prayer had granted the Irish parliament's request for Latin to be used in certain circumstances in Gaelic Ireland even though English was prescribed in the Englishry. Most important of all, the far from latent Presbyterianism of the text composed a serious challenge to the Protestantism of the established church (and this was an antagonism which would reappear) (Ellis 1998: 235–6). In this context, and prompted by Elizabeth's annoyance at the delay in publishing an Irish Bible (in 1567 she threatened to demand the return of her advance of £66 13s 4d if there was no immediate progress) the Church of Ireland published the first book printed in Ireland itself, Seán Ó Cearnaigh's (John Kearney) *Aibidil Gaoidheilge & Caiticiosma* (Gaelic Alphabet and Catechism) in 1571. Paid for by William Ussher and printed on the Gaelic font provided by Elizabeth, it contained translations from the catechism in the Book of Common Prayer, Parker's twelve articles of religion, prayers from Carsuel's text, and a brief introduction to the orthography and pronunciation of Irish. Ó Cearnaigh's work pre-dates the first Catholic text printed in Irish by forty years, though its circulation and the extent of its use is open to doubt.

In a letter to the Queen in 1576, Sir Henry Sidney lamented the 'deformed and as cruelly crushed' state of the church in Ireland and in particular the lack of Irish-speaking ministers. He recommended that the monarch search the universities and the reformed church in Scotland for candidates, adding helpfully that though this would prove expensive in the first instance (cost was paramount for the Tudors), 'you shall find it returned with gain before three year be expired' (*Cal. S. P. Ire* 1574–85: 93). There are also repeated references in the state papers to planters translating religious texts for the benefit of the native population. Sir William Herbert, for example, commented that divine worship (according to his definition) was not practised in Cork in the late 1580s and he registered the fact that he had 'taken order that public prayers shall be said in their own tongue and that they shall assemble themselves at their churches on Sundays'. He continued: 'I have caused the Lord's Prayer and the Ten Commandments, and the Articles of the Belief, to be translated into Irish, and this day the ministers of these parts repair unto me to have it in writing' (*Cal. S. P. Ire* 1586–8: 331). Such activities indicate that there was an important shift in crown policy towards the Gaelic language between the reigns of Henry and Elizabeth, despite the fact that the Queen lamented as late as 1593 that failure to enact Henry's initial language policy had 'engendered a great frowardness and perverseness and also diversity amongst our people in Ireland' (*Analecta Hibernica* 1931: 426). Be that as it may, Henrician pre- and pro-scription, threatening but largely unenforced, was succeeded by Elizabethan promotion not of the language per se, but of texts and practices in Irish which would enhance the Protestant Reformation. In fact Elizabeth's interest in the language became personal and prompted Christopher Nugent, Lord Delvin, to compose his *Primer of the Irish Language* (c.1584–5). Delvin took it as axiomatic that the Queen's endeavour 'to understand the language of your people' in Ireland was part of her reformation project and the primer consisted of the Irish alphabet, a glossary, idioms in Irish, Latin, and English, instructions for reading the language, and a brief introduction to the origins of the language and nation (Delvin 1882: pt. IV, vol I, p.xxxv). In this respect Elizabeth's attitude to Irish compared favourably to that of James I, though James himself was concerned that Trinity College Dublin (founded in 1592) fulfil its mission to train Irish-speaking clergy. Elizabeth persevered with her commission of the New Testament, which was reputedly translated in 1587 but not finally printed until 1602, a year before the queen's death. It was reported that when the chief translator of the New Testament and the Book of Common Prayer, Uilliam Ó Domhnaill (William Daniel) presented the texts to King James the king was pleased, until he asked the Archbishop the Gaelic for 'raw egg'. On being told, the king's response was said to have been: 'is that a language to put the word of God in? My dog Jowler can speak as good language as that' (Barnard 1993: 259).

The tone and content of Ó Domhnaill's preface to the New Testament rendered an illustration of the political and religious attitudes of the late Elizabethan period. Earlier Tudor political strategy had been characterized by persuasion and negotiation. Henry VIII for example, though undoubtedly a legal and constitutional absolutist, was, appearances notwithstanding, a political pragmatist and reformist rather than by temperament dogmatically authoritarian. Against his advisers' counsel of coercion against the Gaelic chiefs, Henry famously argued for the reduction of Ireland by 'sober ways, politic drifts and amiable persuasions founded in law and reason' (Ellis 1998: 122). The fact that Henry was otherwise engaged with internal and external political problems, and that he, like all the Tudor monarchs, was extremely wary of the expenditure required for military conquest, does not obscure the fact that he was something of a gradualist compromiser in Ireland, as is clear in the successful policy of surrender and regrant. Under this policy, which brought in the important Gaelic rebel Conn O'Neill, the Gaelic chiefs acknowledged English sovereignty in return for the re-granting of their lands and the bestowal of a peerage. They gave up their Gaelic patronymic in favour of an English title (O'Neill became first Earl of Tyrone, though ironically when he attended London to receive the title he thanked the King in Irish, which was then translated by his chaplain), and agreed to act with the English administration and to adopt English custom and language. While it lasted it was an effective means of extending royal power, centralizing the administration and spreading Anglicization without the costs of military conflict. Gradually, however, such policy grew less effective and Ireland became increasingly an apparently intractable problem for its rulers. Certainly by the time of Elizabeth's reign Ireland had become militarily difficult and, more significantly, highly expensive for the English crown. In fact 'Irish' had become another word for trouble; Archbishop Parker argued that without the appointment of suitable bishops, the north of England itself would be 'too much Irish and savage' (Ellis 1998: 48). By the 1580s it was clear that from the Crown's point of view earlier Tudor policy would no longer serve and that radical measures would need to be taken; the project of aggressive military colonialism began in earnest. A typical example of proposals for reform was Sir Henry Sidney's response to Elizabeth's request in 1583 for his opinion as to how 'Ireland might with the least charge be reclaimed from barbarism to a godly government'. His 'Discourse for the Reformation of Ireland' asserted that 'God's will and word must first be duly planted and idolatry extirped; next law must be established, and licentious customs abrogated' (*Cal. Carew MSS* 1575–88: 367–8). The proposed measures included cultural as well as religious stipulations: 'all brehons, carraghes, bards, rhymers, friars, monks, Jesuits, pardoners, nuns, and such like, to be executed by martial law', and 'Irish habits for men and women to be abolished, and the English tongue to be extended' (*Cal. Carew MSS* 1575–88: 369).[5]

Appearing at the end of the Nine Years War, Ó Domhnaill's preface to the New Testament (1602) reflected the bitterness of the day as well as the fact that a victory by the newly united Gaelic chieftains over English crown forces had been very narrowly avoided indeed, and was perhaps lost only by mistaken military strategy at the last. Ó Domhnaill's own Puritan standpoint also influenced the tone: this was not a proselytizing instrument intended to convert Catholics by persuasion, but a blunt introduction to the only possible means of salvation. The preface began with a common assertion of the equation of religious and social order: 'the quietness and peace of Kingdomes (most gratious Soveraigne) consisteth chiefly in the planting of true Religion and in the utter extirpation of ydolatrie and superstition'. The delivery of the Word, the means by which this was to take place, had been ordained by the Almighty himself:

And as in his heauenly wisedom he hath sanctified the preaching thereof to beget faith and repentance vnto saluation: so hath he in mercie given excellent blessings vnto the godly labours of such, as with iudgment, care and conscience have trauelled in deriuing of the saving light from the pure fountain of the original vnto the vulgar tongue (Ó Domhnaill 1602: Preface).

The lack of a vernacular translation of the sacred word, Ó Domhnaill proclaimed, meant that the mere (ethnically unmixed or Gaelic) Irish 'haue sit in darkness and in the shadow of death, without hope, without Christ, without God in the world'. Elizabeth's Bible project, allied to her system of English justice, had thus offered to the lost Irish a path to salvation, but despite that, 'yet hath Satan hitherto preuailed, and still they remain . . . through the ignorance of our Ministers, the carelessnesse of our Majistrates, and the subtiltie of AntiChrist and his vassals, the filthy frye of Romish seducers, the hellish firebrands of all our troubles' (Ó Domhnaill 1602: Preface). It is important not to underestimate the sincerity of the conviction expressed in Ó Domhnaill's writing since like many of his contemporaries he believed that Catholics were diabolic; similar, if exactly contrary, opinions were expressed by Catholic writers who called Luther 'Luitéir Mac Lucifer', Luther son of Lucifer. Yct in the preface, along with a tone of apparent absolute confidence it is

---

[5] Palmer discusses the various attempts to explain the shift from reform to conquest ideology, a matter of controversy among Irish historians (Palmer 2001: 15–19).

possible to read a certain defensiveness and anxiety: Satan has prevailed till now, Protestant ministers and magistrates have been ignorant and careless, and recent history has been chaotic and almost disastrous from the English point of view. It was very near to an admission that the Tudor Reformation had failed, with all of the implications that would have had. From its promising beginnings under Henry, the Reformation had hit a decisive crisis in the late sixteenth century. And while Ireland may have been subdued after the Battle of Kinsale (1601), it was hardly a willing recipient of the Protestant faith. In a similar sense and for related reasons, though it had made some headway in important areas, the English language was also very much the language of a small minority; Ireland remained stubbornly Gaelic-speaking.

In other ways too the certainty of English victory was called into question and one place where we perhaps unexpectedly find this is the set of political writings about Ireland, written during late Elizabethan and early Jacobean periods, known as the Anglo-Irish Chronicles. Essentially these were essays in justifying the colonial expropriation of Ireland and the imposition of Crown rule, together with analyses of the causes of the reluctance of the Irish to conform to this social order. Among the most significant of the late sixteenth-century chronicles were Edmund Campion's *Historie of Ireland* (1571), Richard Stanihurst's *A Treatise Containing a Plain and Perfect Description of Ireland* (1577) and, most famously, Spenser's *A View of the State of Ireland* (1596). Owing much to the work of Giraldus Cambrensis, and borrowing heavily from one another, the chronicles were significant for present purposes for a set of common themes: the origins of the Irish and their language, the use of Irish in Ireland, and the effect of the Irish language on the English colonists. Together they form a set of reflections on Irish and English cultural identity which reveals contemporary attitudes and which was important in influencing later opinions.

Campion and Stanihurst ascribed Biblical origins to Gaelic (the clan of Noah's son Japhet was thought to have brought one of the Babelic languages to Ireland), and traced the influences upon the language made by the later invaders—the Scythians, Greeks, Egyptians, Spaniards, and Danes (the Spaniards were considered particularly important).[6] The name Hibernia was said to derive from the Latin *hibernus*, wintry, or

---

[6] Hadfield 1993 presents a useful discussion of Tudor origin myths with regard to the Irish; Kidd offers an important account of figurations of ethnicity and nationhood in Ireland 1600–1800 (Kidd 1999: chapters 3, 7, 8).

from Hiberus, the name of a Spaniard, or from the name Iberia, meaning Spain itself. Spenser, the most rigorous and accurate of the chroniclers, as well as the most interesting and influential, denied the Spanish origins of the Irish and insisted instead on Scythian and Gaulish roots. The Irish language itself, Spenser stressed, bore testimony to this history, since in it there are 'surely very many words of the *Gaules* remaining and yet dayly used in Common speech'. In response to a request to identify Gaulish speech, Spenser provided an early example of comparative Celtic language-study:

The *Gaulish* speech, is the very *British*, the which was generally used here in all *Britainne* before the comming of the *Saxons*; and yet it is retained of the *Welshmen*, *Cornishmen*, and the *Brittaines* of *France*... there be many places, as havens, hills, townes and Castles which yet beare the names from the *Gaules* (Spenser 1633: 32).[7]

Campion's description of the Gaelic language was in general positive: 'sharpe and sententious, [it] offereth great occasion to quicke apothegms and proper allusions, wherefore their common Jesters, Bards, and Rymers, are said to delight passingly those that conceive the grace and propriety of the tongue'. He added, however, that 'the true Irish indeede differeth so much from that they commonly speake, that scarce one among five score, can either write, read, or understand it. Therefore it is prescribed among certaine their Poets, and other Students of Antiquitie' (Campion 1633: 12). The form which Campion referred to here is Classical Modern Irish (sometimes known as Early Modern Irish), the literary standard language which was maintained throughout the Gaeldom of Ireland and Scotland from around 1200 to the seventeenth century by the Bardic schools. This was indeed the preserve of a small élite, and by the end of the sixteenth century had long diverged from the popular spoken language. This difference between the medium of the bards and that of the common people was to provoke its own problems for Catholic devotional writers in the seventeenth century. Moreover the difficulty of the language was undoubted (bardic apprenticeship was long and arduous) and this theme was taken up by Stanihurst. Though he was later to argue for the copiousness and elegance of the Irish

---

[7] Draper's critical review of Spenser's acquaintance with Celtic philology makes clear that his detailed historical knowledge was weak, but then most historical language study at the time was pretty speculative and was based for the most part on Biblical suppositions or inaccurate history.

language in *De Rebus in Hibernia Gestis* (1584), in his description of
Ireland he made a point of relating a tale which mocked its complexity:

> And in veriey deed the language carrieth such difficultie with it, what for the
> strangenesse of the phrase, and the curious featnes of the pronuntiation, that a
> very few of the countrie can atteine to the perfection thereof, and much lesse a
> forrener or stranger. A gentleman of mine acquaintance reported, that he did
> see a woman in Rome, which was possessed with a babling spirit, that could
> have chatted anie language saving the Irish: and that it was so difficult, as the
> verie divell was gravelled therewith (Stanihurst 1587: 7).

The alternative explanation that the language is too holy for the devil is
dismissed by a bystander: 'the apostles in their copious mart of languages in Jerusalem' could not have managed Irish. Neither the divine
gift of tongues, nor the devil's cunning, could facilitate mastery of this
apparently mysterious, rebarbative language.[8]

The real interest of the chronicles, however, lies in their reiteration of
a theme which has already been noted and which goes as far back as
Giraldus. In *Topographia Hibernica* Giraldus warned against contact with
the native (mere) Irish on the ground of their innate treachery: 'to such
an extent are habits influenced by one's associates, and he who touches
pitch will be defiled by it;... foreigners coming to this country almost
inevitably are contaminated by this, as it were, inborn vice of the
country—a vice that is most contagious' (O'Meara 1982: 109). Communication with the Irish carried great danger: the disease of their culture
and their manners spreads and corrupts all those who come in contact
with it. This was the great cultural preoccupation which haunted English
colonialism in Ireland (not least because in many ways it was realized).
Irishness was infectious and it is this anxiety which lay behind the
Statute of Kilkenny and a great deal of other colonial legislation: how
to avoid the decay of Englishness and the malady of Irishness, and how
to prevent degeneration (the concept which had first been articulated in
1297). Central to this fear was concern about the role played by the Irish
language in the colony.

Distinguishing between the mere Irish and the Old English, Campion
asserted that the result of any interchange, or 'education' as he calls it, is

---

[8] In *De Rebus in Hibernia Gestis* (1584) Stanihurst rejects the charge that he 'disparaged
thoughtlessly a tongue of which I was ignorant'. Instead he admits 'on the authority of scholars
that the speech of the Irish is rich in vocabulary, elegance and wit'. He maintains, however, that
'it is not in the interests of our community for Irish (which our ancestors shunned as they
would rocky crags) to be spoken widely and freely' (Lennon 1981: 144).

rapidly apparent: the English, 'conversant with the brutish sort of that people, become degenerate in short space, and are quite altered into the worst sort of Irish rogues' (Campion 1633: 14). Yet the damage to the individual, harmful as it was, was as nothing compared to the corruption inflicted upon the whole of the English community in Ireland. Stanihurst argued that when the Pale had been self-enclosed and inhabited by the mere English, it was culturally and politically flourishing and tradition (in its conservative sense of the transmission of values from one generation to the next) was assured:

The inhabitants of the English Pale have beene in old time so much addicted to their civility, and so farre sequestered from barbarous savagenesse, as their onlelie mother toonge was English. And trulie, so long as these impaled dwellers did sunder themselves as well in land as in language from the Irish: rudeness was daie by daie in the countrie supplanted, civilitie ingrafted, good lawes established, loyaltie observed, rebellion suppressed, and in fine the coine of a young England was like to shoot in Ireland (Stanihurst 1587: 4).

Though safe in its insularity, English civility was under constant threat and communication with the Irish brought the disaster, to use the prevalent metaphor, of cultural sickness:

when their posteritie became not altogither so warie in keeping, as their ancestors were valiant in conquering, the Irish language was free dennized in the English Pale: this canker tooke such deep root, as the bodie that before was whole and sound, was by little and little festered, and in manner wholly putrified (Stanihurst 1587: 4).[9]

Stanihurst's conclusion, which was a general perception, was that linguistic intercourse with the uncivilized Irish spelt danger; contact engendered jumbled, bastardized forms of culture and language which were neither one thing nor the other. To illustrate, he cited the example of a state official sent to Wexford who thought that he could understand Irish after a short while in the county, whereas in fact he was listening to the confused English of the Wexfordians. Though Wexford was once a bastion of English purity, Stanihurst noted, by dint of close proximity and contact with the Irish the Wexfordians 'have made a mingle mangle or gallimaufrie of both languages, and have in such medleie or check-crwise so crabbedlie jimbled them both together, as commonlie the

---

[9] The concatenation of Ireland and disease imagery reappeared in the Famine period (Morash 1995: 23–5); I am grateful to Emily Cuming for drawing my attention to this point.

inhabitants of the meaner sort speak neither good English nor good Irish' (Stanihurst 1587: 4).[10] Once relations were established, unless great care were taken to protect English culture and language, dire consequences would follow. He reported the experience of the politically important planters of Ulster as evidence:

> neighborhood bred acquaintance, acquaintance waffed in the Irish toong, the Irish hooked with it attire, attire haled rudenesse, rudenesse ingendered ignorance, ignorance brought contempt of lawes, the contempt of lawes bred rebellion, rebellion raked thereto warres, and so consequentlie the utter decaie and desolation of that worthie country (Stanihurst 1587: 5).

As is clear from such opinions and the conviction with which they were expressed, there was a lot more at stake in the language debates than the question of the choice of language; the very future of English rule in Ireland was in play.

Remedies for the degeneration of the Old English before the 1580s tended to be geared towards bringing them back to their proper natures. The Lord Chancellor Gerrard, for example, wrote to the Privy Council in 1577–8 warning against taking harsh measures towards the English degenerates:

> Soche as affirme the swoord muste goe before to subdue thise, greatly erre. For can the swoord teache thim to speake Englishe, to use Englishe apparell, to restrayne them from Irishe exaccions and extorcions, and to shonne all the manners & orders of the Irishe? Noe it is the rodd of justice that muste scower out those blottes . . . justice without the sword may suffize to call all those to her presence . . . to defende the Englishe from all Irishe spottes, to settel thim in the quiett estate they were in before they so degenerated . . . to withstand all the force of the Irishe, and by consequent, save chardges at this daye spent (Gerrard 1931: 96).

Rather than attempting the coercion of the Gaelicized English, Gerrard's strategy was essentially a reformulation of the earlier Henrician policies towards the native Irish—'amiable persuasions founded in law and reason'. His cure also included the familiar recommendation of gathering all existing laws under one new statute, particularly those

---

[10]  In *De Rebus in Hibernia Gestis* Stanihurst praises 'the pure and pristine English' spoken by the Old English in Ireland and contrasts it with the English spoken in England (and by the New English): 'that borrowing from foreign languages which is so common among our contemporaries' which makes for 'strange and florid English' which is 'not English at all' (Lennon 1981: 144).

concerning relations between the English and the Irish ('the very cankers that devour the estate').

From the 1580s, however, particularly in the light of the Catholic Tridentine reform movement, a more antagonistic view was taken towards the Old English by the crown and its New English representatives. Old English attitudes had been set out in the Anglo-Irish Chronicles by writers such as Campion and Stanihurst.[11] For a representation of the New English viewpoint it is necessary to turn to Edmund Spenser, poet, planter, and colonial servant. Spenser began his *A View of the State of Ireland* in 1596 and registered it in 1598 (though it was not published till 1633); written in the middle of the Nine Years War, it bore all the bitterness of that conflict. By means of a dialogue between two characters, Eudoxus and Irenius, Spenser presents a wide-ranging account of Ireland, its past and present, its achievements and its failures, and the radical remedies needed to secure it for proper English sovereignty.[12] The aim of the essay was to offer a critique of, and answer to, the problems which were plaguing contemporary Ireland. The main targets of the piece were the Irish and the degenerate Old English.

During the dialogue Irenius touches on the history of the invasions of Ireland (a key theme in Gaelic historiography), and in a discussion of the Anglo-Norman invasion in the twelfth century he identifies it as the most significant in its establishment of an enduring colony which the Irish could not rout, though it consisted now only of those who 'remain English'. Spenser uses Eudoxus' puzzlement at the reference to those who 'remain' English to bring up the issue of corruption. Eudoxus asks: 'Why? are not they that were once *English*, *English* still?', and the response from Irenius is emphatic: 'No, for some of them are degenerated and growne almost meere Irish, yea, and more malitious to the *English* then the *Irish* themselves' (Spenser 1633: 34). In fact, he argues,

the cheifest abuses which are now in that Realme, are growne from the *English*, and some of them are now much more lawlesse and licentious then the very wilde *Irish*: so that as much care, as was then by them had to reforme the *Irish*, so and much more must now bee used to reforme them, so much time doth alter the manners of men (Spenser 1633: 44).

---

[11] Campion, English by birth, was executed in 1581 as a Jesuit traitor; Stanihurst ended his days in exile in Spain as a Jesuit. They met at Oxford.

[12] Canny offers a full discussion of the radicalism of Spenser's proposals and their long-term influence (Canny 2001: chapter 1).

Eudoxus' shock 'that men should so much degenerate from their first natures, as to grow wilde' is compounded when Irenius informs him that some of the English had renounced their English names and taken Irish names instead in order that they might be more completely Irish.

Spenser seized on a concern of the English authorities since before the Statute of Kilkenny: that political and linguistic corruption go hand in hand. In *Timber, or Discoveries* (1641) Ben Jonson depicted the relationship as one in which a wanton social order produced wayward language: 'wheresoever, manners, and fashions are corrupted, Language is. It imitates the publicke riot' (Jonson 1947: 593). Spenser, however, reverses the order as Irenius specifies the principal agent of degeneration: 'first, I have to finde fault with the abuse of language, that is, for the speaking of *Irish* among the *English*, which, as it is unnaturall that any people should love anothers language more then their owne, so it is very inconvenient, and the cause of many other evills' (Spenser 1633: 47). Citing the classical precept of Roman imperial practice in support of Irenius, Eudoxus renders a definition of linguistic colonialism which was to be taken up across the globe in later centuries: 'it hath ever beene the use of the Conquerour, to despise the language of the conquered, and to force him by all meanes to learne his. So did the *Romans* always use, insomuch that there is almost no Nation in the world, but is sprinckled with their language...'(Spenser 1633: 47). Small wonder that Spenser wrote to Gabriel Harvey demanding why the English, like the Greeks, should not 'have the kingdome of oure owne Language' (Palmer 2001: 111).

Spenser's account of how this process began, how the Irish were able to undertake the corruption of the English, was significant. He followed Stanihurst in arguing that the blame lay with the English themselves for their close relations with the Irish, particularly in interbreeding or the care of children, which bring about 'most dangerous infections'. Thus, Irenius concludes, 'are these evill customes of fostering and marrying with the *Irish*, most carefully to be restrayned: for of them two, the third evill that is the custome of language, (which I spake of) chiefly proceedeth' (Spenser 1633: 48). Spenser lit upon the use of Irish nurses for babies as especially pernicious since children imitate their first teachers, specifically with regard to language: 'the words are the image of the minde, so as they proceeding from the minde, the minde must needes be affected with the words. So that the speach being *Irish*, the heart must needes bee *Irish*: for out of the abundance of the heart the tongue speaketh' (Spenser 1633: 48). This was an important argument since Spenser was almost two centuries ahead of his time in his articulation of a link between speaking a language and feeling emotional identity with a nation. It was a belief which was to become enormously powerful later in European history and it was at the heart, so to speak, of many of the different forms of cultural nationalism which ranged from nineteenth-century Hungary to contemporary Catalunya; ironically it was the core principle of the late nineteenth and early twentieth century Irish cultural nationalists in their struggle against British rule in Ireland.

'Degeneration' was evidently a key term in these debates and its use was deeply influenced by the theological discourse of the fall of humanity from divine grace. Yet its historical significance and development bears more general analysis. Derived from the Latin *dēgenerāre*, from the root *de genus*, the definition offered for the adjective *degener* is succinct: 'that departs from its race or kind, degenerate, not genuine'. When it passed into English it retained this sense, the Oxford English Dictionary (*OED*) definition of the adjective being: 'having lost the qualities proper to the race or kind; having declined from a higher to a lower type; hence declined in character or qualities, debased'. 'Race' here is not to be confused with the 'scientific' and biological uses which attached to it in the late nineteenth century, but the potency of the term 'degenerate' is easily understood in Tudor debates, particularly with regard to the position of the English in Ireland. In fact 'degenerate' entered the language at precisely this point in history: though the first recorded use of the term is given as 1494 (around the time of the appearance of the phrase 'the Pale' in the English lexicon), its first adjectival uses are 1605 and 1611; the verbal form first referred to persons in 1553; the noun of process, 'degeneration', was first recorded in 1607; the noun 'degenerate' was first used in 1555. Amongst the earliest uses of these variants were, pointedly given the relation between the political representation of events and the vocabulary used to describe them, references to a Cornish revolt, Wyatt's rebellion, and the Scots; curiously there are no references in the *OED* to the various uses of the term by Spenser or any other of the Anglo-Irish chroniclers.

What does the appearance and use of this term signify? A helpful parallel may be made with the appearance and use of the term 'miscegenation' some three centuries later. Both terms, which have a common etymological root, point to a climate of cultural, political, and sexual anxiety. This might at first sight appear an unusual interpretation of the relations between England and Ireland at the time. After all, was this not the period in which Crown rule was being consolidated militarily, politically, and culturally, not least by means of confiscation of land, the plantation of English and Scottish settlers, and the final victory over the Gaelic chieftains at the Battle of Kinsale and their subsequent flight to Europe? This is of course true. And was this not also a period of political and cultural centralization within Britain, both as a result of Tudor policy and then in the body of James the First of England and the Sixth of Scotland? This too is true. But there is more to the story and a return to the specifics of linguistic history can help to demonstrate why degeneration, particularly linguistic degeneration, was such a key issue.

The late sixteenth and early seventeenth centuries have been described as the period of the 'triumph of the English language' (Jones 1953), the historical point at which the English vernacular threw off its slave (*verna*—a slave born in the house of the master) rank and achieved independence and status as a copious language in its own right. That remarkable flourishing of English creative writing which stretched the language in new ways, from Nashe to the King James Bible, from Shakespeare to the first dictionaries, is testimony to this achievement. But there is another view of this process since within it there were clear signs of tension and unease. One indication of cultural centralization and sensitivity to the issue of language and identity was Thomas Wilson's coinage of the phrase 'the King's English' in *The Arte of Rhetoric* in 1553 (the same decade as the appearance of a number of early uses of 'degenerate'). A related development was Puttenham's definition of the 'natural, pure and most usual' form of English as 'that usual speech of the court, and that of London and the shires lying about London, within lx miles and not much above' in *The Arte of English Poesie* in 1589 (Puttenham 1936: 144–5). From one perspective these appear to be nothing but the confident flourishes of a successful and dominant nation, terms and concepts which indicate a growing sense of national cultural identity. But there is another way of thinking about them. For accompanying centralization there is also marginalization; together with the idea of the legitimate language there is also the question of that which is excluded; for our purposes, along with an emergent sense of Englishness as a form of cultural identity, there is also the problem of Irishness in its various forms. It is this which lies at the heart of debates around 'degeneration': the cultural and political identity and loyalty of the Old English, the New English and the Gaelic Irish. Just as

Ó Domhnaill's preface to the New Testament bespoke both confidence *and* nervousness, the triumph of the English language and the new forms of cultural identity that accompanied it were at one and the same time brash and insecure.

One practical realization of these fraught issues was the stage Irishman, that early embodiment of Irishness for English audiences in plays such as Dekker's *Old Fortunatus* (1600), Peele's *Life and Death of Captain Thomas Stukeley* (1605), Beaumont and Fletcher's *The Coxcomb* (1609), and Jonson's *Irish Masque at Court* (1613). Many of the representations reflect prevailing attitudes and are therefore contemptuous and satirical. In *The Coxcomb* for example the protagonist Antonio disguises himself as an Irish servant and adopts an Irish form of the English language. His verdict on it is that 'this rebbell tonge sticks in my teeth worse than a toughe hen; sure it was nere knowne at Babell, for they soul'd no apples, and this was made for certaine at the first planting of Orchards, 'tis so crabbed' (Bowers 1966: 297).[13] And in Jonson's *Irish Masque at Court* a political fantasy was enacted in which the Irish characters fall over themselves before James to profess their loyalty in their own version of the King's (Irish) English:

Dermock: Vee be Irish men, and't please tee.
Donnell: Ty good shubshects of Ireland, an't please ty mayesty.
Dennise: Fo Connough, Leymster, Ulster, Munster. I mine one shelfe vash
        borne in te English payle, an't pleash ty Mayesty.
Dermock: Tou hasht very goot shubshects in Ireland.
Dennise: A great goot many, o' great goot shushects.
Donnell: Tat love ty mayesty heartily...
Donnell: Be not angry vit te honesh men, for te few rebelsh, and knavesh.
Patrick: Nor beleeve no tayles, king YAMISH.
Dermock: For, by got, tey love tee in Ireland (Jonson 1941: 400–1).[14]

But there was one significantly difficult dramatic representation of the Irishman, one of the earliest, which sheds light on the actual complexity

---

[13] The reference to apples and orchards is not without political significance since one of the common charges against the uncivilized Irish was that their agriculture was predominantly pastoral in contrast to the civilized arable system of the English; see Chapter three, note three. The planting of orchards, particularly in Ulster, was a sign of such civilization. Brian Friel's *Making History* (1989) utilizes this distinction for dramatic purposes, though recent historical research has demonstrated that agriculture in Gaelic Ireland was more mixed than previously recognized.

[14] The masque's political deceptiveness is demonstrated by the circumstance which prompted it: a delegation of Old English Catholics to London to protest James' Irish policies.

of the question of Irishness in the late sixteenth and early seventeenth centuries. Shakespeare's MacMorris in *Henry the Fifth* presents a highly ambivalent attitude to the Irish and Irishness; a wary, cautious, perhaps even confused approach. One which might represent an English English (so to speak) view rather than an Old or New English standpoint. This is part of the Irish soldier's speech at the siege of Harfleur:

By Chrish Law tish ill done: the Worke ish giue ouer, the Trompet sound the Retreat. By my Hand I sweare, and my fathers Soule, the Worke ish ill done: it ish giue ouer: I would haue blowed vp the Towne, so Chrish saue me law, in an houre. O tish ill done, tish ill done: by my Hand tish ill done... (Shakespeare 1623: 78).

As commentators have often noted, MacMorris appears to fit some of the stereotypes of the Irishman: bloodthirsty, excitable, ready for a fight, and of course, unable to pronounce the King's English properly. Yet he also has, as has likewise been pointed out, an important role in the battle as an engineer of the mines (Leerssen 1996: 85). And when the English forces are undermined by the French, MacMorris attempts to deflect the criticism of another of the soldiers, the Welshman Fluellen, by interrupting him brusquely:

It is no time to discourse, so Chrish saue me: the day is hot, and the Weather, and the Warres, and the King, and the Dukes: it is no time to discourse, the Town is beseech'd: and the Trompet call vs to the breech, and we talke, and be Chrish do nothing, tis shame for vs all: so God sa'me tis shame to stand still, it is shame by my hand: and there is Throats to be cut, and Workes to be done, and there ish nothing done, so Chrish sa'me law (Shakespeare 1623: 78).

This anxious bluster on the part of MacMorris can be interpreted as a desire to mask his incompetence by an act of violent bravado. But there may be more to this since it also presents an indication of a deeper anxiety about his role and identity in this English war, as the odd man out in the British quartet of whom the other members are the Welshman Fluellen, the Scot Jamy, and the Englishman Gower.[15]

---

[15] The play is set during the English war with France in 1415, but by Shakespeare's time such soldiers would effectively be British. The representation was particularly complex given that both the English and the Irish armies often contained significant numbers of ordinary soldiers 'on the wrong side'. Between a third and half of the successful English army in the decisive Nine Years War is believed to have been Irish (Palmer 2001: 194). Canny renders a study of the tension between the different political forces within England, Scotland, and Ireland engaged in the project of transforming Ireland from the late sixteenth to the mid seventeenth centuries (Canny 2001).

MacMorris is difficult to read (in both senses of the term) linguistically and the complexity of his representation was partly revealed by his
very name. In his *Discovery of the True Causes Why Ireland was Never Entirely
Subdued* (1612), Sir John Davies commented on 'the Irish customs which
the English colonies did embrace and use after they had rejected the
civil and honourable laws and customs of England, whereby they
became degenerate'. One important offence noted specifically by
Davies, which also caused Spenser's Eudoxus to be outraged, was that
the English in Ireland 'did not only forget the English language and
scorn the use thereof, but grew ashamed of their very English names,
though they were noble and of great antiquity, and took Irish surnames
and nicknames'. Dexcester, Davies noted, became MacJordan, Dangle
became MacCostelo, one of the Bourke branches became MacDavid,
and 'in Munster, of the great families of the Geraldines planted there,
one was called MacMorice' (Davies 1890: 298). MacMorris (Makmorrice
in the original Shakespearean spelling) is a hard character to read
precisely because he points to another aspect of the great fear which
haunts colonial rule at the time: cultural hybridity. He has an Irish name
but we know that many of the Old English took Gaelic names; he
speaks English yet he does so with clearly Irish pronunciation. And in
response to what he angrily understands as a charge against the Irish, or
at least the version of Irishness which he represents, he asks the
question which brings the issue to a head:

Of my Nation? What ish my Nation? Ish a Villaine and a Basterd, and a Knaue,
and a Rascall. What is my Nation? Who Talkes of my Nation? (Shakespeare
1623: 78).

There is a lot riding on that 'ish' and it prompts a series of questions.[16]
What is MacMorris? Who is MacMorris? What does he signify? Whom
does he represent? Why is he so angry at the mention of nationality?
What is his nation? All of these questions, which revolve around issues
of identity and loyalty, belonging and exclusion, were crucial precisely at
this historical and political juncture. Shakespeare's text, just as much as
Spenser's *View*, reflects a deep unease and sense of linguistic and cultural
anxiety.

[16] The question 'what ish my nation' returns in the work of later Irish writers. In *Ulysses*
Bloom is asked a variant—'what is your nation?'—by the Citizen, the Irish cultural nationalist
in Cyclops (Joyce 1992: 430). In Heaney's 'Traditions', in a direct reference to Shakespeare's
question, 'sensible Bloom' gives the same answer: 'Ireland....I was born here. Ireland'
(Heaney 1980: 69); see Chapter six.

Thus far the attitudes of the English (both the Old English and the New English) to the Gaelic language have been analysed, together with the political values which they embodied. But what of the attitudes of the Irish towards the English language? Did they also have an antipathy to the language of their cultural 'other'? In truth there is only relatively little evidence to be able to judge, which in itself tells us something of Irish opinions, at least those of the bardic class. For the bards hardly mentioned the English language at all and it appears that certainly until the late sixteenth century they were largely indifferent or unimpressed by the cultural events taking place around them (though this was to change quickly after the Flight of the Earls in 1607). But there are some indicators of Irish attitudes. Stanihurst, for example, indicated a difference between the English and the Irish with regard to their languages, a point which may reinforce the fragility of English in the eyes of at least some of its users. Of the English colonists, he demanded rhetorically, 'is it decent (thinke you) that their owne ancient native tonge shall be shrowded in oblivion, and suffer the enimies language, as it were a tettar or ringworme, to harbour it selfe within the jawes of the English conquerors?' (Stanihurst 1587: 5). In contrast, he asked why 'English-speaking [is] so much despised in Irish areas?' (Lennon 1981: 144–5) and cited as evidence of Irish antipathy to English the example of the rebel Shane O'Neill: 'One demanded merrilie whie O'Neile that last was would not frame himselfe to speake English? What (quoth the other) in a rage, thinkest thou that it standeth with O'Neile his honour to writh his mouth in clattering English?' (Stanihurst 1587: 6). A report in the State Papers (1598) confirmed that Shane inherited the prejudice from his father:

For language, they do so despise ours, as they think themselves the worse when they hear it. As did appear by old Con O'Neill, father to the now rebel who upon his deathbed, left his curse to any of his posterity, that would either learn English, sow wheat, or make any building in Ulster, saying that language bred conversation, and consequently their confusion, that wheat gave sustenance with like effect, and in building, they should do but as the crow doth, make her nest to be beaten out by the hawk (*Cal. S. P. Ire* 1598–9: 440).[17]

---

[17] In fact the rebel of the 1590s was Hugh O'Neill, son of Matthew, Conn O'Neill's heir; Shane O'Neill was Conn's son and legitimate heir. When Hugh O'Neill, Earl of Tyrone and leader of the Irish forces in the Nine Years War, submitted in 1603, he did so in English.

It is striking that O'Neill's warning adverted to precisely the same danger for the Ulster Irish in respect of communication with the English that Stanihurst had given to the Ulster colonists with regard to contact with the Irish ('neighborhood bred acquaintance, acquaintance waffed in the Irish tongue ...'). The issue of naming was also evidently as important to the Irish as it was to the New English. Though Spenser and Davies observed the tendency for the Old English to change their names, other New English commentators noted that the Irish maintained theirs:

none, with his good-will, will be called Henry, Edward, Richard, George, Francis, or such like English names, but rather Morrogh, Moriertagh, Tirlogh, and such harsh names, both for a difference to distinguish them from the English, and as a mark of their offspring, which they observe with as great care, as they joy wherein with great boast (*Cal. S. P. Ire* 1598–9: 440).

There is some evidence that at times of crisis the Irish regarded the English language as a sign of pro-English tendencies (as the English did vice versa with the Irish). Thus O'Sullivan Beare's *Historia Catholica Ibernia Compendium* (1621) reported that after the siege of Enniskillen during the Nine Years War, O'Donnell retaliated against Bingham's 'heretical tyranny' in Connacht by destroying English colonists, 'sparing no male between 15 and 60 years who did not know how to speak the Irish language' (O'Sullivan Beare 1903: 82). And the anonymous English atrocity text, *The Supplication of the Blood of the English Most lamentably Murdered in Ireland, Cryeng out of the Yearth for Revenge* (1598) claimed that the Irish 'have proclaymed in their campe deathe to speake Englishe'. It contrasted that with English attitudes: 'he that can speake no Irishe amongst them must dye: yet have wee no punishment at all for them, that disdayne the Englishe, that scorne that language, that loath to endeavore the practice of it' (Maley 1995: 65). In general, however, apart from these examples there is no significant indication that English permeated sufficiently into the everyday life of the great majority of the Gaelic-speaking population before the end of the sixteenth century for it to have seemed a serious threat and thus to have attracted widespread opprobrium or resistance. There was though a remarkable early testament to an awareness of the cultural changes which were starting to take place and the importance which they would have. The pre-Elizabethan poem 'Fúbún fúibh, a sluagh Gaoidheal' (*c.*1542–3) is an attack on those of the leading Gaelic families who had conformed to English political power and cultural practices (including no doubt those which had taken part in the surrender and regrant policy). It included the penultimate stanza:

> Fúbún fán ngunna ngallghlas,
> fúbún fán slabhra mbuidhe,
> fúbún fán gcúirt gan Bhéarla
> fúbún séana Mheic Mhuire
>
> (Shame on the grey foreign gun, shame on
> the golden chain, shame on the court without
> the language of the poets (Irish law?),
> shameful is the denial of Mary's son)
> (Caball 1998: 41)

The topical references to artillery promised by James V of Scotland to O'Donnell, and the gift of a gold chain to O'Neill at his submission in London, convey the contempt of the poet. Despite an argument which prefers to read it as an early seventeenth-century text (Canny 2001: 421), the real significance of the piece is the poet's idiosyncratic but acute political foresight with regard to the linguistic and cultural implications of the colonial dispensation for the Gaelic order. Caball's reading of 'Bhéarla' as the language of the bardic poets, though not uncontentious, makes sense in the context of the poem's admonitory intent. Even at this point there was a dawning recognition that Gaelic language and culture and the Catholic religion were under threat from England, English, and Protestantism. The seventeenth century saw the realization of the threat.

# CHAPTER THREE

# *Language, God, and the struggle for history: 1607–1690*

'Isn't that what history is, a kind of story-telling?'
Brian Friel, *Making History*, 1989.

The decisive events at the beginning of the seventeenth century in Ireland, which are often taken as signalling the beginning of the end of the Gaelic order, were the decisive defeat of the Irish forces at the Battle of Kinsale in 1601 and the subsequent Flight of the Earls in 1607. The self-exile of the Gaelic chieftains to Catholic Europe in particular was an act with serious cultural implications; given the dependence of bardic culture on the patronage of the chieftains, their absence was to prove highly damaging in both the short and long run. Ó Domhnaill, who was one of the first three Trinity graduates and received a Doctorate in Divinity for his translation work on the New Testament, recognized 1607 as a turning point which from his perspective promised hope for peace and stability in the Irish colony (Cronin 1996: 54). It is unsurprising therefore that the anti-Catholic rhetoric of his New Testament preface was extended in the foreword to the *Leabhar na nUrnaightheadh gComhchoidchiond* (Book of Common Prayer) published in 1608:

notwithstanding that since the time that Sathan was set at liberty, the smoke of the bottomless pit hath darkened the Sun and Aire, as well in this Kingdome, as in all other Christian Kingdomes of the World: Yet there is great hope that (Sathan being now tyed, the short time of his tyranny for deceiving universally being expired) this Kingdome may flourish in the same mercy that the neighbour Kingdomes doe (Ó Domhnaill 1608: i).

The end of the Nine Years War and the exile of the leaders who had brought unity to Gaelic Ireland and had been so uncomfortably close to victory over the Crown's forces, was taken by Ó Domhnaill as a demonstration of God's providential intentions for Ireland:

our gracious God having made the way plaine, by causing our warres to cease, the Lord having partly swallowed up in displeasure the disturbers of our peace, and partly spued them out into Straunge Countryes, craving better Inhabitants to enjoy her blessings (Ó Domhnaill 1608: ii).

In order to take advantage of such providence and to enhance the future of Ireland, Ó Domhnaill stressed the importance of the use of the sacred texts in the native language, based on the recognition that 'the liturgy of the Church comming in the cloud of an unknown tongue, can leave no blessing behind it'. Ó Domhnaill's argument for the vernacular, an interesting mix of an acknowledgement of ancient Irish learning and of Ireland's reputation as one of the cradles of western Christianity combined with a fiercely Protestant zeal, gained some influence. In 1634 the convocation of the Church of Ireland accepted canons which encouraged the use of Irish for religious purposes. William Bedell, the English Provost of Trinity College and one of the central figures in the debate, began his translation of the Old Testament into Gaelic in 1632; though completed in 1640, the text was eventually published through the efforts of the scientist Robert Boyle in 1685.

As well as vernacular proselytizing, education was another important element in the reform programme. Trinity College Dublin had been instituted in 1592 in order to supply Irish-speaking ministers and to combat Catholic recusancy. Elizabeth recorded its foundation and purpose as,

A College for learning whereby knowledge and civility might be encreased by the instruction of our people there, whereof many have usually heretofore used to travel into France, Italy or Spain to get learning in such foreign universities where they have been infected with popery and other ill qualities, and so become evil subjects (*Cal. pat rolls Ire* Eliz. 1862: 227).

In response O'Neill made education one of his standing points in negotiations with Elizabeth in 1600 and demanded that 'there be erected a University upon the Crown Rents of Ireland, wherein all sciences shall be taught according to the manner of the Catholic Church' (*Cal. S. P. Ire* 1599–1600: 280). The request was dismissed contemptuously by Cecil as 'Ewtopia'. But Trinity's early record in fulfilling its fundatory obligation was poor, a point which concerned James I when he noted that the 'rude

Irish' 'are kept in darkness, and apt and ready thereby to be misled into error, superstition and disobedience by the Popish priests, who abuse their simplicity and ignorance, which proceedeth from want of masters who could speak their own language' (*Cal. S. P. Ire* 1615–25: 276–7). James added that though Trinity had been 'plentifully endowed by us', there was little evidence as to practical results, and he rebuked the college governors for the abuse of both trust and revenues, instructing the university visitors to ensure that Irish speakers be trained in Protestant catechizing immediately. Despite Ó Domhnaill's best efforts, in 1623 the King had to order that the Gaelic New Testament and Book of Common Prayer be used in areas with large Irish-speaking populations; of the five hundred copies of the New Testament originally printed, a number remained undistributed a quarter of a century later (Cronin 1996: 55).[1] Nonetheless Ó Domhnaill, a representative of the state's opinions in this respect, saw Trinity and 'like Schools of good learning' as 'the chiefest means of reformation' of the barbarous Irish. It was not of course a new idea since Henry VIII had identified precisely this role for education, but it was certainly highly controversial. The Catholic response can be measured from the comments of Richard Conway, a Jesuit priest living in Dublin in 1612, on the effect of Protestant educational initiatives:

The greatest injury they have done, and one of the most serious consequences, was the prohibition of all Catholic schools in our nation … with the object of sinking our people to degradation, or filling the Universities of England with the children of those who had any means to educate them, where they might become more dependent on heretics, and contaminated with their errors (McDonald 1874: 204).

Such education as was offered to the native population conformed to Henry's strictures on the use of the language, as revealed in Conway's complaint that the Protestant educators 'have also taken singular care that all children be taught English, and they chastise them if they hear them speak their own native tongue'. Such efforts were not greatly effective in terms of religion and Catholics quickly began to organize their own response to Protestant methods, but the gradual introduction of the English language as the medium of learning had begun.

---

[1] Sir John Davies is recorded in State Papers as believing in 1606 that texts printed and taught in Irish would 'incredibly allure the common country people' (*Cal. S. P. Ire.*, 1603–6: 467); his prediction fell foul of the history which was to follow.

Victory in the Nine Years War and the blow to the Gaelic order suffered in 1607 led one of the more acute observers on Ireland in the period to pose a pertinent question. In his *Discovery of the True Causes Why Ireland was Never Entirely Subdued* (1612), Sir John Davies asked,

> why this kingdom, whereof our kings of England have borne the title of sovereign lords for the space of four hundred and odd years…was not in all that space of time thoroughly subdued and reduced to obedience of the Crown of England, though there hath been almost a continual war between the English and the Irish? (Davies 1890: 217–8).[2]

It was an important question posed at a critical time, a puzzling one in some respects, and one which was also potentially embarrassing in its implications. Put another way, Davies was asking what it was about English rule in Ireland that had made it so ineffective over such a long period? Why was it that the English could defeat the Irish militarily, but not bring them to orderly obedience? Was there something about Ireland which made it naturally resistant to English rule? Davies picked up even more disturbing questions from the Anglo-Irish chroniclers. Why was it that so many of the English who had gone to Ireland had become, in the famous phrase, *Hiberniores Hibernis ipsis* (more Irish than the Irish themselves)? Was Irishness contagious, or were the English just susceptible to cultural disease? What was it about Ireland which made the English forgo their ethnic identity, even to the extent of rejecting their native language and names in favour of Gaelic replacements, which 'they did in contempt and hatred of the English name and nation, whereof these degenerate families became more mortal enemies than the mere Irish'? (Davies 1890: 298).

Having reviewed Irish history, Davies gave his answer to the conundrum: 'the defects which hindered the perfection of the conquest of Ireland were of two kinds, and consisted, first, in the faint prosecution of the war, and next in the looseness of the civil government' (Davies 1890: 218). Using the significant metaphor of agricultural practice (viewed at the time as one of the distinguishing characteristics of English and Gaelic civilization) Davies argued that land must be broken,

---

[2] Davies was Solicitor General from 1603–6 and then Attorney General from 1606–19. As Lord Deputy Chichester's chief law officer he was involved in the revision of the settlement made by Mountjoy at the end of the Nine Years War; he recommended (and took advantage of) full scale plantation, particularly in Ulster.

manured, and then sown with good seed if a flourishing crop is to be gained.[3] Colonialism must act in a similar fashion:

So a barbarous country must first be broken by a war before it will be capable of good government: and when it is fully subdued and conquered, if it be not well planted and governed after the conquest, it will eftsoons return to the former barbarism . . . For that I call a perfect conquest of a country which doth reduce all people thereof to the condition of subjects; and those I call subjects which are governed by the ordinary laws and magistrates of the sovereign (Davies 1890: 218–19).

War to break the land and people, law to sustain them and keep them in good order, good new seeds to be planted in order to produce bounty. The crucial element, after the control of the land and the defeat of the Gaelic order, was the proper introduction of law and with it subject-hood: common law must replace totally Brehon law (the Gaelic code) and any remnants of March law (the compromise set of laws operative in the border areas between Gaelic and English rule). The spread of common law throughout Ireland had begun in effect with the surrender and regrant policy of the 1540s and was more or less complete by 1610; the Lord Deputy's proclamation of 1605 decreed that all were thereafter subjects of the King and were to take grievances to the justices of assize or the county governors. Davies' comment on the progress of such legal and cultural reform was a typical assertion of colonial optimism: 'here-tofore the neglect of the law made the English degenerate and become Irish; and now, on the other side, the execution of the law doth make the Irish grow civil and become English' (Davies 1890: 336).[4]

Such political confidence also extended to his assessment of the use of the English language by the native Irish. The spread of English law through the assizes and sessions, he argued, had already made an impact on Irish cultural practice with regard to dress, hairstyle, and, most particularly when the Irish appeared before the courts, language:

---

[3] Davies claimed that Irish agriculture, in its lack of planning for the future, was another sign of the general barbarity of the people: 'neither did any of them, in all this time, plant any gardens or orchards, enclose or improve their lands, live together in settled villages or towns, nor made any provision for posterity; which, being against all common sense and reason, must needs be imputed to those unreasonable customs, which made their estates so uncertain and transitory in their possessions' (Davies 1890: 292).

[4] His optimism, probably attributable to his office, was not widely shared; other commen-tators such as Fynes Moryson and Barnaby Riche were more sceptical of the extent to which common law had successfully been imposed.

because they find a great inconvenience in moving their suits by an interpreter, they do for the most part send their children to schools, especially to learn the English language; so as we may conceive an hope that the next generation will in tongue and heart and every way else become English, so as there will be no difference or distinction but the Irish sea betwixt us. And thus we see a good conversion and the Irish game turned again (Davies 1890: 335–6).[5]

His sanguinity, however, was premature: State Papers reported in 1613 that 'it is also very inconvenient that the judges are unacquainted with the Irish language, and cannot understand the witnesses that speak no English, whereby they cannot so well judge the cause' (*Cal. S. P. Ire* 1611–14, pp.376–7); Fynes Moryson reported the same about juries. Yet although the transformation to which Davies refers was precisely that which Conway as a representative of Catholic Ireland feared, there is an interesting and crucial difference between Conway's objection to the process and what Davies indicates was a matter of everyday practice, a distinction which was to become increasingly marked in the following centuries. Conway attacked the teaching of English on the grounds that it was designed as part of a Protestant conspiracy to inculcate heresy in the native children. Davies's observation pointed to something quite different: he argued that there were some among the native population who wanted to acquire English, or at least to have their children acquire it, on the grounds that it was in their legal, political, and economic self-interest to do so. They could not take advantage of common law (or not without the problems posed by interpretation) unless they had access to English. It was utilitarian for them to have it and use it and therefore they put their children to learning it. The same point was made later in the century by Gratianus Lucius (John Lynch) in *Cambrensis Eversus* (1662), an attack on the work of the twelfth-century calumnist Giraldus:

I have known many persons who had but a slight acquaintance with Irish books; yet so great was the delight they found in reading them that they would hardly allow them out of their hands, were they not forced by the reproofs of their parents to apply their energy to studies that would be more useful to their material advancement (Cahill 1939: 129).

The translator of the *Annals of Clonmacnoise* into English in 1627 (their translation was an innovative and revealing act in itself) criticized parents who 'neglect their books and choose rather to put their children

---

[5] Davies' comments were disingenuous since even where the law was practised it was notoriously corrupt (Canny 2001: 302); Davies availed himself of some 7,500 acres.

to learn Eng[lish] rather than their own native language' (Cunningham 2000: 129). It was a significant development which foreshadowed a later pattern in relation to the central role of Irish parents in the Anglicizing process. And it was a change which was observed, and responded to, in various ways by representatives of the Gaelic order.

It was argued earlier that the learned classes of the native culture had been largely indifferent to the threat posed by the cultural colonialism with which they were faced. This was essentially a form of native cultural confidence, since Gaelic culture had long been assailed by the colonizers verbally, but to little material effect. So to this point the bardic class (with only a few exceptions such as that presented at the close of the previous chapter) appears to have had only a limited sense of the danger to the language and culture and reacted accordingly. But the situation in the early seventeenth century was new and of a different order, and its consequences took many of the Irish literati by surprise. The Flight of the Earls, the confiscation of Gaelic aristocratic land, and the plantation of New English settlers had severe implications for Gaelic culture and those who upheld it, most importantly in the realm of traditional patronage. Once the Gaelic social order had begun to crumble from the top down, the bards (the poets, keepers of law, history, and genealogy—in effect the guardians of the cultural heritage) could no longer rely upon their aristocratic patrons, and the effect was dramatic. The new economic order created a new cultural situation and a Gaelic contemporary of Davies, Aindrias Mac Marcais, recorded the impact of the changes with a lament: 'Gan gáire fá ghníomhradh leinbh, | cosc ar cheol, glas ar Ghaoidheilg (There is no laughter at children's doings, | Music is prohibited, the Irish language is in chains) (Ó Fiaich 1969: 105). Haicéad, an important poet and political priest, rendered a more bitter complaint in 'Faisean Chláir Éibhir' (These fashions on the plain of Éibhear):

> Is cor do leag mé cleas an phlás-tsaoilse:
> mogh in gach teach ag fear an smáilBhéarla
> 's gan scot ag neach le fear den dáimh éigse
> ach 'hob amach 's beir leat do shárGhaelgsa'

> (A trick of this false world has laid me low:
> servants in every home with grimy English
> but no regard for one of the poet class
> save 'Out! And take your precious Gaelic with you!')
> (Ó Tuama and Kinsella 1981: 90–1)

Gaelic literature may have died from the top down, but the language was to die from the bottom up.

One revealing early Irish response to the economic and cultural changes which were taking place was the anonymous satire *Pairlement Chloinne Tomáis* (The Parliament of Clan Thomas), a work in two parts of which the first was composed circa 1608–1615. Often read as an aristocratic satire on the peasantry in general, it has recently and more coherently been reinterpreted as 'an attack upon the economic and social ambitions of the emergent entrepreneurial class, which had exploited the uncertainty of the late sixteenth and early seventeenth centuries to better its lot' (Caball 1993: 47). That class, portrayed as 'churls' in the poem, was constituted precisely by the type of people described by Davies as having a utilitarian attitude towards the English language for their own purposes (Clan Thomas has a predilection for litigation). Though many of the bards would have known English, and it was considered an accomplishment for the Gaelic aristocracy to have it (as many of them did, despite the protestations considered at the end of the last chapter), the appearance of a relatively prosperous group of entrepreneurs, rather than socially traditional figures, willing to use the language, and to take on English habits and values along with it, was clearly profoundly disturbing to the historical defenders of Gaelic culture. Reflected in *Pairlement Chloinne Tomáis* for the first time in terms of its everyday existence, the activity of this group was a clear sign that the old order was in danger of being supplanted by new forces and this, together with the harsh economic realities which were beginning to face the bardic class, accounts for the hostile and satirical tone of the text. It is, as one commentator describes it, a good example of 'the obsessive contempt which [the bardic class] consistently displayed towards those from the lower ranks of Irish society' (Canny 1982: 112).

The political and cultural assault on this new economic and social class was wide-ranging and its basis was an accusation in essence of treachery towards traditional Gaelic culture, not least in their use of the enemy's language.[6] Significantly the clerk of one of the parliaments was called Domhnall an Bhéarla, and as Kiberd has pointed out, at this time the old word for foreigner, 'gaill', was sometimes supplanted by the metonymic 'Béarla' (the English language), as in the line from the contemporary

---

[6] The satire was not simply constructed in terms of the fact that they use English since they also use contemporary Gaelic slang terms, which denotes their lower social status (O'Rahilly 1932: 253).

poem 'Is treise Dia ná fian an Bhéarla' (God is stronger than the English-speaking churls) (Kiberd 1996: 10). In one section of *Pairlement Chloinne Tomáis* Clan Thomas meet with a young English tobacco-seller, Roibín an Tobaca, and they agree to buy from him.[7] But Bernard Ó Bruic asks who is going to speak English to him, a task for for which Tomás volunteers:

Táinig an t-óglaoch gallda ⁊ beannuigheas go ceannsa agas adubhairt: '*God bless you, Thomas, and all your company*'. Do fhreagair Tomás dó go neamhthuaisceartach agas as eadh adubhairt: '*Pleshy for you, pleshy, goodman Robin*'. 'Dar anmuin mo mháthar', ar Bernard Ó Bruic, 'do dhubhshloigis rogha an Bhéarla'. Do thionóslad cách 'na thimpchioll ag machtnughadh uim Bhéarla Thomáis

(The young Englishmen arrived and greeted them politely and said: '*God bless you, Thomas, and all your company*'. Tomás answered him in no uncivilized fashion and said: '*Pleshy for you, pleshy, goodman Robin*'. 'By my mother's soul', said Bernard Ó Bruic, 'you have swallowed the best of English'. Everybody gathered round him marvelling at Tomás's English) (Williams 1981: 40, 97).

The satire is of course on the corrupt and broken English spoken by these social upstarts who, though they had abandoned their own native culture and by implication the historical traditions which went with it, were unable to master the language of their colonial rulers. When Tomás asks the price of the tobacco, '*What the bigg greate* órdlach *for the what so penny for is the la yourselfe for me?*', the fact that Roibín is able to understand at all indicates a significant social and economic development. His ability to answer Tomás demonstrates that he is used to dealing with such macaronic language, a talent acquired in his exploitation of the gradually emerging single Irish market which, as Canny has noted, had been forged precisely by such itinerant traders (Canny 2001: 392). '*Two penny an ench*', Roibín replies,

'Créad é?' ar Diarmuid Dúr. 'Órdlach ar an dá phinginn', ar Tomás. 'Déana tacuigheacht oruinn', ar cách. 'Do-dhéan', ar Tomás ⁊ adubhairt: '*Is ta for meselfe the mony for fart you all my brothers here*'. Adubhairt Roibín: '*I thanke you, honest Thomas, you shall command all my tobaco*'. '*Begog, I thanke you,*' ar Tomás.

('What is it?' asked Dour Diarmuid. 'Two pence an inch', said Tomás. 'Act on our behalf', they all said. 'I will', replied Tomás, and he said: '*Is ta for meselfe the mony for fart you all my brothers here*'. Roibín said: '*I thanke you, honest Thomas, you shall command all my tobaco*'. '*Begog, I thanke you,*' said Tomás.) (Williams 1981: 40, 97)

---

[7] Smoking was of course a practice imported on the back of colonialism; the word 'tobacco' itself was a borrowing from the New World—first into English (1577) and then Irish.

The satire is effective from the bardic point of view since the upstarts are made to look clumsy and foolish even at their own treacherous game. But like much satire this is deeply conservative, concerned with the depiction of historical change simply as deterioration and threat. From the viewpoint of those being satirized, however, the situation was rather different. And this dichotomy between those who wished to conserve Gaelic culture in its traditional form and those who wished to adapt to the changes brought about by the colonial order by adopting the English language was one which would be replayed in the eighteenth, nineteenth, and indeed twentieth centuries. There is one more thing worth noting about the setting of this linguistic exchange: it is a site of economic transaction, an activity with which English was to be primarily associated despite the fact that there is some evidence to suggest that the acquisition of Irish was not entirely uncommon amongst those of the settler community who needed to conduct business with the natives.[8] Traders such as Roibín the tobacco seller were one such group, but depositions by Protestant survivors of the 1641 insurrection make it clear that bilingualism, or at least a working knowledge of Irish, was not extraordinary (Canny 2001: 452–4).[9]

Yet if there were those amongst the different speech communities who picked up the language of the other as a useful tool, there were others who maintained an antagonistic stance. Fynes Moryson, the English colonial adventurer, secretary, and official historian to Lord deputy Mountjoy, gave an account of the language attitudes of some of the Irish in his *Itinerary* (1617).

But the lawe to spreade the English toongue in Ireland was ever interrupted by Rebellions, and much more by ill affected subjectes, so at this time whereof I write, the meere Irish disdayned to learne or speake the English tongue, yea the English Irish and the very Cittizens (excepting those of Dublin where the lord Deputy resides) though they could speake English as well as wee, yet

---

[8] The utilitarian view of language was not confined to the Irish appropriation of English; in 1627 the King instructed the Irish Treasury to give Edward Keating, a colonial bureaucrat, a pay increase on the grounds that 'he is a loyal and efficient servant and knows Irish, which makes him more useful' (*Cal. S. P. Ire* 1625–32: 202).

[9] In *De Rebus in Hibernia Gestis*, Stanihurst asserted of the 'Anglo-Irish' that 'they speak English and Irish because of their daily commerce with their Irish neighbours' (Stanihurst 1584: 145). By the mid seventeenth century English was increasing in prominence as the language of economic activity even though Irish was still found in the Pale (Walsh 1920: 248); it remained, as it long had been, the language of politics and administration. Even the record of the Irish Confederacy was in English.

Commonly speake Irish among themselves, and were hardly induced by our familiar Conversation to speake English with us (Moryson 1903: 213).

He also noted that 'the Cittizens of Watterford and Corcke having wives that could speake English as well as wee, bitterly to chyde them when they speake English with us'.

Moryson's account, in which he had little good to say about the Irish apart from their whiskey, is most interesting for his more general observations on the relationship between language and nationality, a linkage which was brought out clearly as part of the emerging new sense of Irish identity which was being forged in the late sixteenth and early seventeenth centuries. In fact his observations were pre-empted by Spenser's claim that 'the speech being Irish, the heart must needs be Irish'. But Moryson's comments could serve as a summary of one of the central doctrines of cultural nationalism, which was, as noted in the previous chapter, a political, philosophical, and linguistic movement which was to be influential in later European history (not least in Ireland) and which was to be theorized, as opposed to expressed, only towards the end of the eighteenth century by German Romantic thinkers. Moryson asserted that,

> this communion or difference of language, hath alwayes been observed, a spetial motive to unite or allienate the myndes of all nations ... And in generall all nations have thought nothing more powerfull to unite myndes then the Community of language (Moryson 1903: 213).[10]

Once popularized, the postulated relationship between language and nationality formed an important part of both colonial and anti-colonial struggles across the globe, from early modern Ireland to late twentieth-century Africa.

The early seventeenth century saw Gaelic Ireland in disarray; military and political defeat was compounded by the real threat of the type of linguistic, religious, and social changes of which the anonymous and prescient 'Fúbún fúibh, a sluagh Gaoidheal' had warned in the mid

---

[10] In *The Supplication of the Blood of the English Most Lamentably Murdered in Ireland, Cryeng Out of the Yearth for Revenge*, the anonymous author specified the failure to impose a common language at the time of the first conquest as one of the causes of continuing historical difference and violence: 'uniformitie in speeche would both have united them and us in affection'. The text observed that the Irish 'see what force uniformitie of speeche hath to procure love and frindship, to continewe a societie and fellowshipe' (Anon 1598: 65). It may be that this awareness of the role of language in the formation of cultural identity, particularly national identity, arises precisely from colonialism.

sixteenth century. From within this context, however, there was already a Catholic response to the dangers, as revealed in the Jesuit Conway's description of native reaction to the banning of Catholic schools and the introduction of English as the language of instruction. He asserted that these efforts,

> did not have the desired effect, and the natives did not only go to England, but rather preferred to remain in ignorance, than run the risk of their faith and religion by doing so, or went secretly and quietly to many foreign parts, but particularly to Spain, where his Catholic Majesty assisted them, and gave them some Colleges (McDonald 1874: 204).

Conway's reference is to one of the results of the Tridentine reforms, the twenty or so Irish colleges and seminaries founded throughout Europe in the period between 1590 and 1690, of which the most important were the Franciscan colleges at Louvain and Rome (Cahill 1939: 125). They were the key institutions which educated the Catholic (Old English and Gaelic) exiles who were to return as Counter-Reformation missionaries to Ireland.

From the mid sixteenth to the mid seventeenth centuries the Protestant Reformation and the Catholic Counter-Reformation were engaged in struggle across Europe. In Ireland, however, it is important to remember that more concerted attempts to impose Protestantism, as opposed to more ad hoc and somewhat inconsistent efforts, were not really undertaken until after the successful prosecution of the conquest in the early seventeenth century. Indeed it is one of the oddities of Ireland in this period that before the achievement of English military victory, the Catholic Counter-Reformation had already gained momentum. One commentator has argued that the Counter-Reformation began as early as the 1560s (it was certainly the case that conformity was being replaced by recusancy in the late 1570s), and has proposed that the fact that 'the Counter-Reformation *preceded* the Reformation in Ireland may explain why the Reformation so signally failed in Ireland' (Bartlett 1988: 48). After the defeat of the Gaelic chieftains, however, with the attendant social, religious, and political changes which it brought with it, the focus of Irish Catholic resistance turned to continental Europe, as Conway indicated. For the Irish Earls were not alone in fleeing Ireland: scholars and clerics followed them to the intellectual and theological hothouse of Catholic Europe. And what they discovered there was transformative in terms of religious and political beliefs and practices, and hugely significant in the development of Ireland's future.

Their first lessons revealed to them both the doctrinal differences which divided Catholicism and Protestantism and, hard as this may have been for the newly arrived Gaelic refugees, the weakness of Irish Catholicism in the face of Protestant Reform (it was demonstrated that the Gaelic Irish were only weakly Christianized) (Canny 1982: 95). It became clear that Catholic renewal was required and the first mode by which this was attempted was modelled on the practices which Protestants had pioneered some forty years before: the use of the printing press (at Louvain) to produce Catholic catechetical literature for the clergy and the more educated laity in the Irish language.[11] The literature which issued has been classified into three types: fundamental catechetical works for the laity (appropriate for a predominantly oral culture) such as Ó hEodhasa's (O'Hussey) *An Teagasg Críosdaidhe* (The Christian Catechism) 1611; more sophisticated manuals on novel liturgical developments or doctrines in contention between the two faiths for the instruction of the native clergy such as Céitinn's (Keating) *Trí Biorghaoithe an Bháis* (The Three Shafts of Death) 1631; and personal devotional works for those already familiar with Catholic dogma such as Ó Maoil Chonaire's (Conry) *Sgáthán an Chráibhidh* (Mirror of Faith) 1616 (Canny 1982: 95–6). These texts, and others like them, represented an attempt by the Louvain Franciscans to forge a clear strategy of supplying militant Counter-Reformation materials in the vernacular. The point is attested by the preface to Mac Aingil's (Mac Caghwell) *Scáthán Shacramuinte na hAithridhe* (Mirror of the Sacrament of Confession) 1618:

Mar atá leabhar Aifrinn ag an Eaglais Chatoilc, do-conncas d'eiricibh na hÉirionn gné leabhair Aifrinn do bheith aca féin dá ngoirid Leabhar an Chumainn agus nírbh olc an t-ainm sin dhó, dá gcuiridís 'fallsa' leis. Ó Nar chuireadar, ní leasainm dhó Leabhar Iffrinn Eireaceachda do thabhairt air. Do chuirsead an leabhar so agus mórán don Bhíobla a nGaoidhilg agus as lór a neimhchirti sgríobhthar iad.

(As the Catholic Church has a prayer book the heretics of Ireland saw to it that they had their own kind of prayer book called the Common Book and it is not a bad name if you added the word 'false' to it. As this was not done, it is no misnomer to call it the Book of the Hell of Heretics. This book and a lot of the

---

[11]  The Council of Trent (1545–63) had sanctioned vernacular preaching and the publication of pious texts in the vernacular as a central Counter-Reformation strategy (Palmer 2001: 37).

Bible were translated into Irish and they were written in the fullness of error) (Cronin 1996: 61, 86).

Such polemic may usefully be read against Ó Domhnaill's preface to the Protestant New Testament; both were entries in the war of printed books.

These catechetical texts are interesting linguistically in that they embody a shift in style which signals the changing social conditions in Ireland itself. Though they were published in Europe, the texts were designed for an Irish readership; but these were texts unlike any that had previously appeared both in the fact that they were printed and more significantly in their departure from the literary and linguistic norms which had been used under the bardic order. Ó hEodhasa's *An Teagasg Críosdaidhe*, for example, contains an address to the reader which was written in bardic metre and the literary language, but the prose text is clear and direct. The preface to Ó Maoil Chonaire's *Sgáthán an Chráibhidh* declared apologetically that the text did not conform to bardic conventions: 'we have not skill or fluency in Irish, and no more have we been from student days to this near the old books, but far removed from them and from the literary craftsmen from whom we might obtain sufficiency of elegant old sayings, that would not be too obscure'. Despite this, however, he added the rejoinder that,

if we can only, with the help of God, set down these things clearly and intelligently, we consider that there will be more judicious, discreet people who will pray for us because of what we have done, than there will be of those who try to find fault with our best endeavour because of the simplicity of the style in which we have written it, especially for the benefit of simple people, who are not skilled in all the subtleties of Irish (Wall 1943: 102).

Mac Aingil was also self-exculpatory about his Gaelic style: 'nách do mhúnadh Gaoidhilgi sgríobhmaoid, achd do mhúnadh na h-aithríde, agus as lór linn go ttuigfidhear sinn gé nach bíadh ceart na Gaoidhilgi aguinn' (our aim in writing is not to teach Irish but repentance and it is enough for us if this is understood even if our Irish is not correct) (Cronin 1996: 63, 87).

The semi-apologetic tone of these prefaces is comprehensible in the light of the radical departure which they represent from the bardic tradition. For the bards the idea of writing simply for the understanding of the unlearned would have been incoherent; that was not their function. Nor was it their role traditionally to comment on religious

matters, and particularly not to have a hand in the teaching of the faith.
Thus for writers such as Ó hEodhasa and Ó Maoil Chonaire, both from
bardic backgrounds, and Mac Aingil, a gifted poet in his own right, to be
writing avowedly popular manuals in simple style on religious matters
was evidently a change which the bards would neither have appreciated
nor approved. In fact it was a shift which reflected both the decline of
bardic culture and the Counter-Reformation's adaptability in the face of
the social and cultural changes taking place in Ireland. But if these
writers felt it necessary to excuse their style and to some extent their
purpose, they were succeeded by a writer who felt no such compunc-
tion. Teabóid Gallduff's (Theobald Stapleton) *Catechismus seu Doctrina
Christina Latino-Hibernica* (Catechism or Christian Doctrine in Latin and
Irish) (1639) contained a bold attack on the bards and their culture.
Gallduff was of Old English stock (etymologically the name means 'dark
foreigner') and had no bardic lineage nor connection to any great Gaelic
family. Perhaps it was the lack of anxiety of historical influence which
encouraged him to be so forthright:

For that reason, it is right and very fitting for us Irishmen to esteem, love and
honour our own natural native language, Irish, which is so concealed and so
suppressed that it has almost passed out of people's minds; the blame for this
can be put on the poets who are authorities on the language, who have put it
under great darkness and difficulty of words, writing it in contractions
and mysterious words which are obscure and difficult to understand (Ó Cuív
1969*a*: 148).

The Gaelic patrons of the bards were not spared either: 'many of our
nobles are not free [from blame] who bring the native natural tongue
(which is efficient, complete, dignified, cultured and acute in itself) into
contempt and disregard, and who spend their time developing and
learning other foreign tongues'. Stapleton's own method was not to
write 'strictly according to the Gaelic orthography but solely as the
words are commonly spoken' (Ó Cuív 1951: 44). Such assaults on the
poets and their sponsors together effectively amounted to a declaration
that a new mode of writing had appeared (with simplified spelling and
no difficult abbreviations). But the shift was to be more than stylistic,
since the collapse of the Gaelic social order meant that from the
seventeenth century onwards writers started to appear who were not
part of the non-regional professional literary class which had maintained
Early Modern Irish in a stable form. The work of such writers reflected

their spoken regional dialects; the literary language itself became gradually geographically diverse and over a considerable period the distinct forms of Scots Gaelic, Manx, and Modern Irish emerged.

In this regard what is also notable about Gallduff's preface is his confidence in the Irish language as a vernacular language which deserves to be honoured in its own right no matter what its utility, which was of course a significant statement against the historical forces which were operating upon the language. Moreover, Gallduff's Catechism had a grammar appended to it, an example of the privileging of the modern, vernacular languages which was characteristic of Renaissance thought and which in this case demonstrated the extent to which Counter-Reformation ideas had spread to the Irish debates by the mid seventeenth century. Mícheál Ó Cléirigh's (Michael O'Clery) *Foclóir na Sanasán Nua* (New Vocabulary or Glossary) (1643) was another sign of this development, since the compilation of glossaries and dictionaries was an important stage in the formation of many of the modern European nation states.[12] One final distinctive point about Gallduff's text was its use of Roman rather than Gaelic characters. This modernizing typography in fact followed the example of Carsuel's Protestant text *Foirm na nUrrnuidheadh* (1567). The Scots have since used Roman type consistently, whereas in the nineteenth century the use of Gaelic type was reaffirmed in Ireland for political reasons, particularly by the revivalist organizations (Deane 1997: 100–9). At de Valera's insistence the 1937 *Bunreacht na hÉireann/Constitution of Ireland* was also published in Gaelic type.

Given the historical context, military defeat and the destruction of the Gaelic order, it might be imagined that early seventeenth-century Ireland would be bare of learning. But this would be a false impression, since as one cultural historian has commented, 'we are struck by the immense amount of literary and scribal activity that continued despite the unsettled state of the times'. Aware of the imminent possibility of the loss of the national written heritage, 'devoted workers, who included members of the old professional classes and religious orders, set about collecting and recopying old manuscripts and utilising their contents for fresh compilations'; it amounted to 'one of the great rescue operations

---

[12] In England the first English dictionary proper, Cawdry's *Table Alphabeticall*, was published in 1604. In Ireland An tAthair Pádraig Ó Duinnín's (Fr. Patrick Dinneen) *Foclóir Gaedhilge agus Béarla (An Irish–English Dictionary)* (1904) was one of the major achievements of late nineteenth-century linguistic nationalism.

of a country's traditions'(Ó Cuív 1976: 529–30). It was almost as if at precisely the point when it was nearly too late, the Irish literate class perceived what was happening and took action—if not to prevent the historical process, since that was beyond their control, then at least to forestall its potentially catastrophic effects. One of the most significant texts to arise out of this campaign was the history of Ireland from the earliest times to 1616, the *Annála Ríogachta Éireann* (Annals of the Kingdom of Ireland, more usually known as the Annals of the Four Masters) compiled between 1632–6 by Mícheál Ó Cléirigh and his main coadjutants Cúchoigríche Ó Cléirigh , Fearfeasa Ó Maoilchonaire, and Cúchoigríche Ó Duibhgeannáin. The other great text was Céitinn's *Foras Feasa ar Éirinn* (A Basis of Knowledge about Ireland)(1634) which was a systematic attempt to reclaim Irish historiography from the colonists (he specifically attacks the versions of Irish history propagated by among others Cambrensis, Spenser, Camden, Hanmer, and Moryson). From his enormous collection of various types of material, gathered peripatetically, Céitinn constructed a readable history of Ireland to the end of the twelfth century; written in an accessible style, which was to prove both popular and highly influential, it led critics to dub him 'the father of modern Irish prose' (Cahill 1939: 134).

Céitinn's history was significant both for its synthesis of previously disparate material and on the basis of its dispute with Ireland's colonial historians. The argument was an attack on their sources, their methodology and their prejudices:

The refutation of these new foreign writers need not be pursued by us any further, although there are many things they insert in their histories, which it would be possible to confute; because, as to the most part of what they write disparagingly about Ireland, they have no authority for writing it but repeating the tales of false witnesses who were hostile to Ireland, and ignorant of her history (Céitinn 1902: vol.1, 75).

Céitinn reread Irish history from an anti-colonial perspective in two important ways. First, he asserted that the ancient Gaelic moral order was close to Christianity, which served to explain why Christianity had been planted in Ireland without great difficulty. This was in contradiction to the English arguments that the twelfth century conquest had been a Christian act against a pagan culture (Canny 1982: 100). Second, Céitinn produced a euhemeristic reading of the *Lebor Gabála* (The Book of Invasions), a medieval chronicle of the history of Ireland from creation to the twelfth century, which proposed that the explanatory principle behind Irish history was a series of invasions. His account, based on this principle, created a version of Irish history in which the Gaelic Irish and the Anglo-Normans were but two of the peoples who had invaded Ireland and established themselves there. By explaining away their historical differences, and pointing instead to their common faith, Céitinn produced a new vision of Irishness based on 'a multifaceted manifesto for the future of the Catholic people in the kingdom of Ireland' (Cunningham 2000: 226). The corollary of this revolutionary version of history was that the recent colonists, the New English Protestants, were the common foe of both the Gaelic Irish and the Old English.

Céitinn's text dealt with the language question in Ireland in an account of issues such as the origins of the Gaelic language, its historical development from its Biblical beginnings, the source of the names Gaedheal and Feinius, the division of the language into five specialized branches, and its arrival in Ireland itself. Citing Archbishop Creagh (the Catholic Archbishop of Armagh who published a catechism in Irish and a grammar of the language in the sixteenth century which is now lost), he affirmed the antiquity of the language: 'the Gaelic speech has been in common use in Ireland from the coming of Neimhidh, six hundred and thirty years after the Deluge, to this day'. He also used the treatment of Irish as part of his argument that the recent colonial conquest was pagan rather than Christian by stressing the different attitudes to the language of the conquered shown by the victors. The Christian conqueror 'extinguishes not the language which was before him in any country which he brings under control', whereas the pagan seeks 'to bring destruction on the people who are subdued by him and to send new people from himself to inhabit the country which he has taken by force'. He also provided an historical contrast: William the Conqueror,

did not extinguish the language of the Saxons, seeing that he suffered the people who used that language to remain in the country, so that it resulted therefrom that the language has been preserved from that time down among the Saxons. Howbeit, it is a pagan conquest which Hengist, the chief of the Saxons made over the Britons, since he swept them from the soil of Britain, and sent people from himself in their places: and having altogether banished everyone, he banished their language with them (Céitinn 1902: 1, 75).

This can be compared to Stanihurst's declaration that it was a fault of the first English colonists that 'they did not banish the Gaelic from the country at the time when they routed the people who were dwelling in the land before them'. Céitinn argued that what Stanihurst reveals in such a statement is the fact that the Elizabethan conquest and contemporary colonial practices were like those of Hengist in Britain:

it is the same way Stanihurst would like to act by the Irish; for it is not possible to banish the language without banishing the folk whose language it is: and, inasmuch as he had the desire of banishing the language, he has, likewise, the desire of banishing the people whose language it is, and accordingly, he was hostile to the Irish; and so his testimony concerning the Irish ought not to be received (Céitinn 1902: 1, 75).

Céitinn's answer to the accounts of Stanihurst and the other colonial apologists was the first major native response in Irish to the received colonial version of history. Against the dominant story of a Christian, civilizing mission designed to rescue Ireland from paganism, Céitinn turned the story around: the Protestant English colonists were rude conquerors, destroying a proud and ancient Gaelic and Christian (Catholic) nation. Their attitudes towards the Gaelic language said as much.

Céitinn's own attitude to the language is revealed both in the fact that he wrote his revisionist history in Irish, and that he composed it in a form of the language which was not that of the Gaelic bardic elite. Cunningham argues that Céitinn's exile in Counter-Reformation Europe, in which he would have witnessed the vernacular efforts of his co-religionists, would have led him to agree with Gallduff's assertion that 'there is no nation on earth that does not respect, read and write its own language as a matter of honour' (Cunningham 2000: 128). From this she concludes that Céitinn's use of Gaelic was an important part of his redefinition of the Irish people, 'deliberately chosen and skilfully used so that the linguistic medium was a significant part of the message' (Cunningham 2000: 127). There is no doubt that Céitinn's use of the language was a ploy to draw attention to the distinction, both contemporary and historical, between the Catholic Irish and the new English-speaking colonists. Though there would have been those among the Old English, like Stanihurst, who did not have the Gaelic, Céitinn's linguistic choice in an address to the Gaelic Irish and the Old English which stresses their confessional, historical, and political unity, indicated that 'Irish was widely spoken and understood within most Old English areas of Ireland, and at all social levels' (Canny 2001: 415). It would also have served as an implicit rebuke to those who had lost their language and taken on that of the conquerors.

As noted above, Céitinn's work had done much to foster a significant political development which had taken place in the latter part of the sixteenth and the first half of the seventeenth centuries. This was the emergence of an early form of Irish nationalism of which the core element was a national identity whose basic ideological tenets were loyalty to the Catholic faith and to the Irish fatherland. Its importance lay in its inclusiveness: it united the Old English and the native Gaelic interests. From the Gaelic perspective, the concept of *patria* was influential upon the Earl of Tyrone, Hugh O'Neill (an unlikely historical candidate for leadership of the Gaelic Irish in some ways since he was brought up by the Hovenden family in the Pale). Allegiance to *patria* was an important element in the Ulster-led rebellion which became the Nine Years War, and it eventually became clear during the war that the essence of the struggle was for Ireland itself rather than the relatively local issues with which it began. From the Old English point of view, a sense of *patria* developed out of a relatively long-standing distinction, as noted in Chapter two, that had been made between the English born in Ireland and the English born in England. This difference came to a head in the distinct political interpretations as to the best way to reform Ireland; as noted earlier the Old English favoured gradualism and conciliation, while the New English argued for change by the sword, principally through confiscation and plantation of land. With regard to the faith, the spread of the Counter-Reformation among the Old English and, after Kinsale and the Flight of the Earls, among the exiled Gaelic Irish, meant that the religious differences between these two groups were dissolved in the face of a common recognition of the authority of the post-Tridentine church. Both of these factors together created a new sense of identity, forged to a large extent by the efforts of the bardic class, by which the 'sean Ghaill' (old foreigners, or English) were recognized as Irish Catholics like the Gaedhil and included under the new term 'Éireannaigh' (Irishmen); the 'nua Ghaill' (new foreigners, or English), and more generally the 'Sasanaigh', were now the enemy of a united people.[13] Further encouragement to this new sense of national unity was given by the actions of the crown after the accession of James I. The king, worried at the cost of maintaining a large army as an agent of political,

---

[13] The semantic history of 'Ghaill' and 'Sasanach' is significant in this regard; Dinneen records that both could mean Protestant as well as English.

cultural, and religious reform after the apparently decisive victory at Kinsale, opted instead to reduce the army and favour the New English interest, a choice which laid the way open to corruption, abuse, and the increased alienation of the Old English and the surviving members of the Gaelic aristocracy. An example of such practice was the manipulation of the English legal and administrative structures which were extended to the Gaelic areas with the intention of spreading the benefits of local government and justice (Ellis 1998: 357). The aim was frustrated by the Plantation of English and Scottish settlers under a policy which remained central to Crown policy; the settlers had no reason, as they saw it, to share power with their religious and political opponents and acted accordingly. Thus despite periods of stability and even a relaxation of anti-Catholic measures under Charles I, once the political circumstances in England and Scotland reached crisis point between 1637–40, the cumulative bitterness and estrangement felt by Irish Catholics eventually erupted in the Irish Insurrection of 1641 and the Confederate War 1641–53; it was a war where in a sense the nightmares of both the Éireannaigh and the Sasanaigh were realized. It also laid the ground for the more conclusive Williamite war towards the century's end.

In the midst of all this historical change and turmoil, what was the stance of the poetic representatives of the old Gaelic order? Examples have been considered which reveal its complexity: the dismissal of the English-speaking 'churls' in *Pairlement Chloinne Tomáis* alongside the apparent readiness of important members of the bardic class such as Céitinn to reinvent history in order to include the Old English as Catholic Irish. But the generally received opinion of the poets' response to historical change has been that they were a deeply conservative group, holding fast to antiquated traditions and values, and trapped in a medieval mindset which prevented them from reacting to the disaster facing them with the decline of the Gaelic order at the end of the sixteenth and beginning of the seventeenth centuries.[14] Recent reinterpretation of poetic material of this period by Caball, drawing on the work of Bradshaw and Ó Buachalla, has viewed it from a different perspective. Such new readings have treated it as a more dynamic and flexible medium which re-evaluated and re-presented long-standing

---

[14] This view is encapsulated in O'Riordan's *The Gaelic Mind and the Collapse of the Gaelic World*; a critical and opposed account is proposed in Ó Buachalla's review of her work, 'Poetry and Politics in Modern Ireland' (Ó Buachalla 1992).

concepts of ethnic and cultural identity in line with the more general changes taking place within the Gaelic and Old English communities which were noted above (Caball 1998: 12).

Elizabethan bardic poetry was dominated by the continuation of the traditional forms and themes of the genre; politically and culturally confident, it tended to see the Tudor Protestant Reformation forces simply in terms of a rival ethnic identity, though as 'Fúbún fúibh, a shluagh Gaoidheal' demonstrated, there was an early awareness of the potential threat which that rival posed. The poets also began the extension of the boundaries of Irishness to begin to include the Old English settlers, which clearly positioned them at the heart of the developments which were taking place in other historical modes elsewhere. Towards the end of the century, however, the bards were evidently becoming aware not simply of the dangers posed by the Sasanaigh but also of the problematic social changes which were beginning to take place and the consequences for their own roles. Bardic culture had long been attacked by representatives of the state. In 1537, for example, Cowley wrote to Lord Chancellor Cromwell to complain that

Harpers, rymours, Irishe cronyclers, bardes and isshallyn [*aois ealadhan*] commonly goo with praisses to gentilmen inthe Englishe Pale, praysing in rymes, otherwise callid danes, their extorcioners, roberies, and abuses, as valiauntnes, which rejoysith theim in that their evell doinges; and procure a talent of Irishe disposicion and conversacion in theme, which is likewyse convenient to bee expellid (Ó Cuív 1976: 520–1).

But, as is often the case, rhetorical polemic and calls for proscription were largely second order threats, particularly this early in the sixteenth century. The real disruption to the Gaelic order took place later and was economic and legal: the dispossession of the Gaelic lords, together with the Flight of the Earls after Kinsale, the plantations of the new English, especially in Munster in the 1580s and Ulster after 1608, and the prescription of common law after 1605, all seriously undermined the traditional functions of the bards. So much so that the professional role of the bard declined rapidly in the late sixteenth and early seventeenth centuries, a process which was hastened by the bitter disappointment of James's indifference to his Gaelic ancestry, upon which genuine hopes had been placed. One poet, Ó hIfearnáin, later gave some advice to his son, which again highlights the concern of parents for their children's cultural and linguistic options, and the importance of this in changing traditional attitudes:

Ná lean do dhíogha ceirde
Ná cum do ghréas Gaoidheilge,

(Follow not your useless trade,
Fashion not your poem in Irish)
(Ó Fiaich 1969: 105).

Despite this sense of disillusion and often despair, however, Caball sees the dynamic aspects of both professional bardic poetry and the new amateur poetic work as playing a crucial role in the formation of modern Irish nationality based on the type of re-assessment of traditional definitions of Irish identity discussed earlier. Its necessary elements were articulated by the bards as a commitment to a common culture, a shared Counter-Reformation Catholic religion, and a sense of the territorial integrity of Ireland.

What was the attitude of the bardic class to the English language? As noted earlier, it depended on who was using it and for what purposes. Yet though it may have been, per se, an accomplishment for a Gaelic noble, and useful perhaps for the poets, as a widespread instrument of communication it was simply a corollary of English Protestant rule, the linguistic wing of colonialism so to speak. The views of Dáibhí Ó Bruadair, perhaps the greatest of the bardic poets, can be taken as typical of the opinions of the last representatives of a disappearing professional class. In 'Nach ait an nós' (How Queer this Mode) 1643, Ó Bruadair wrote disparagingly of the vogue for English manners and language after the arrival of the Duke of Ormonde as Lord Lieutenant in November 1643:

Nach ait an nós so ag mórchuid d'fhearaibh Éireann,
d'at go nó le mórtus maingléiseach,
giodh tais a dtreoir ar chódaibh gallachléire,
ní chanaid glór acht gósta garbhbhéarla.

(How queer this mode assumed by many men of Erin,
With haughty, upstart ostentation lately swollen,
Though codes of foreign clerks they fondly strive to master,
They utter nothing but a ghost of strident English)
(Ó Bruadair, 1910: 18–19).

The neologism 'garbhbhéarla', rough or crude English, makes the tone of the poem clear: a deep contempt both for the upstarts and for the language which accompanied their non-traditional activities.

Irish was 'commonly and usually spoken' even in Dublin according to a petition to the Dublin Municipal Council in 1657, and was still 'scandalising the inhabitants and magistrates of the city' (Walsh 1920: 248), but Ó Bruadair's attack on the increasing shift towards English by the Irish of a particular class was sharp and recalls that of *Pairlement Chloinne Tomáis*. An anonymous poem of the late seventeenth century, 'Diarmuid Mac Muiredhaigh Cecinti' (Diarmaid Mac Muireadhaigh sang this) added a note of angry lamentation and blame to the recording of the disaster which had befallen the bards, their patrons, and the culture itself:

> Innsigh dhósan gur léur liom
> go bfuilid uaisle Éiriond
> mon-uar ag tréigin a gceirt
> san nGaeidhlig na nuam noirrdheirc
>
> Níor thréighte dhóibh í ile
> air bhéurla chríoch gcoigríchthe
> teangaidh aerdha bhlasda bhinn
> bhéurla do bheannaidh na tailginn....
>
> Ní hí an teanga do chuaidh ó chion
> acht an dream dár dhual a dídion
> (mon-uar) dár bhéigin a ndán
> sa nduar do thréigin go tiomlán
>
> (Tell him that I know well that Ireland's nobles,
> alas! give up their right to the melodious
> Irish
>
> It should never be laid aside for the speech
> of foreign lands, the merry, tasteful, sweet
> tongue, the language the shavelings blessed . . .
>
> It is not the language which has come into
> disesteem but those who should defend it, they
> who have been, alas! obliged to abandon their
> poems and verses all)
> (Walsh 1918: 90–1, 93–4).

Another revealing indication of the bardic attitude to English is rendered in a prose section of Ó Bruadair's epithalamium 'Iomdha scéim ar chur na cluana' (Many Pretty Settings) (*c.* 1660–63). In it the poetic persona makes an observation on the town of Cromadh and the general weakness of the ale there, save that kept by the minister who has his own special brew. He continues:

Gidheadh ní hionmhain liomsa an bhiotáille sin, atá d'olcus fhéadaim mo theanga do chuibhrioghadh dochum an ghaillbhéarla do labhairt go líomhtha gurab dom leith clí fhágbhaim teaghlach an tsagairt sin gach uair ghabhaim ina ghoire.

(However, I do not fancy that beer, such is the difficulty which I experience in endeavouring to fetter my tongue for fluent speech in the language of the foreigner, so that I always leave the manse on my left hand every time I go near it)
(Ó Bruadair 1910: 112–13).

Ó Bruadair knew English, as he knew Latin, but what is demonstrated here is the feeling of unease which the poet has with regard to this alien language; he even forgoes the pleasure of a drink to avoid having to speak it. It is a scene which was replayed later in *A Portrait of the Artist as a Young Man*, as noted earlier, in the episode in which Stephen Dedalus frets in the shadow of the colonial tongue.

The most pathetic record of Ó Bruadair's stance towards English was given in 'Cathréim an Dara Séamuis' (The Triumph of James the Second), written in October 1687 during a period of great and religious optimism for the Gaelic Catholic population. It celebrated the accession of James II to the throne of England and the victory over Protestantism which this heralded, though the celebration was of course somewhat premature:

> Atáid bhar bhfirchliar sámh gan dímhiadh
> d'áis an chaoimhniadh chomhachtaigh
> is cléirche Chailbhín béas nach anaoibh
> gan pléidh a bpeataoi ar phópaireacht
> atáid ar bínnse Dálaigh Rísigh
> sdá n-áileadh saoi do Nóglachaibh
> re héisteacht agartha an té nach labhrann
> béarla breaganta beoiltirim

> (Your true clergy now live in peace, undishonoured,
>     By the grace of this powerful, kindly knight,
> And the clerics of Calvin—a change not unpleasant—
>     Harangue not their pets upon popery;
> On the bench now are seated the Dalys and Rices,
>     And a sage of Nagles is urging them
> To listen to the man who can't speak
>     The lip-dry and simpering English tongue)
> (Ó Bruadair 1917: 88–9).

Here we have the reverse of the situation described by Davies at the beginning of the century: then it was Irish people urging their children to learn English in order to be able to represent themselves legally, now the Catholic nobles elevated to the judiciary (Daly was Justice of the Common Pleas, Rice was Baron of the Exchequer, Nagles the Attorney General) are encouraged to be attentive to those who cannot speak English, that 'lip-dry and simpering tongue' which Ó Bruadair elsewhere called 'gliogarnach gall', foreign prattling.

Ó Bruadair's work brings us towards the end of the period under consideration in this chapter. It was a period in which the future of Ireland itself was at stake in military terms, beginning with the aftermath of the defeat of the Gaelic forces and punctuated by the major war in the mid-century; it was also the preface to the most decisive period of warfare in Irish history before the twentieth century. But it was not just history itself which was fought over in this century, it was also the writing of history, its possession, the right to record it, and the need for the legitimacy which it conferred. It is no coincidence that one of the most important pieces of recent drama which questions the writing of history, its purposes, its effects, its validity, and its truth-status, was set in this period. Brian Friel's *Making History* was first performed in the late 1980s, another period characterized by the questioning and challenging of Irish historiography.[15] The text takes as its central theme the life of Hugh O'Neill, Earl of Tyrone, rebel, defeated chieftain, exile. Throughout the play O'Neill is aware not simply of the momentous historical and political significance of his rebellion against the Crown, but also of the importance of how the events are, and can be, narrated by the historian. The historian in the play is the Archbishop of Armagh, Primate of All Ireland, Peter Lombard, with whom O'Neill keeps up an insistent dialogue on the nature of historiography itself (in reality Lombard was the author of *De Regno Hiberniae Sanctorum Insula Commentarius*, written in 1600 and published in Louvain in 1632). Challenged for example on the veracity of his history, Lombard replies to O'Neill:

If you're asking me will my story be as accurate as possible—of course it will. But are truth and falsity the proper criteria? I don't know. Maybe when the time comes my first responsibility will be to tell the best possible narrative. Isn't that what history is, a kind of story-telling? (Friel 1989: 8).

[15] For an account of the debates around Irish revisionism see *The Making of Modern Irish History: Revisionism and the Revisionist Controversy*, Boyce and O'Day 1996.

As an afterthought he adds: 'maybe when the time comes, imagination will be as important as information'. Lombard also expresses scepticism about a history being comprehensive or exhaustive and rejects the idea that history itself 'contains within it one "true" interpretation just waiting to be mined', believing instead that it holds several possible narratives which are determined by the needs, demands and expectations of audiences (Friel 1989: 15–16). People think, Lombard declares, 'they just want to know the "facts"; they think they believe in some sort of empirical truth, but what they really want is a story' (Friel 1989: 66).

The play is structured by the device of anachronism, and it is an address to Friel's own contemporary moment as much as to the past in its questioning of what it means to talk of historical truth, in its highlighting the narrativity of history, and in its presentation of the difficulty of writing for (in both senses of the word) an audience. Such questions were not of course explicitly addressed in this self-reflexive way in the seventeenth century, though there is little doubt that the historians were aware of their audiences. But it is interesting to look at a number of texts which have been considered in the present and previous chapters, and indeed the texts which will be explored in the chapters to come, from this perspective. For the histories and accounts of language and languages are also part of the process by which larger histories are forged and history itself is made. The Anglo-Irish and New English accounts of the Irish language were key to this practice, as was Céitinn's response to them. And before and just after the Williamite War the battle over the language was rejoined in Lynch's *Cambrensis Eversus*, (1662) and Sir Richard Cox's *Hibernia Anglicana* (1689–90). Lynch's argument was a 'vindication of the national character and constitutional independence of Ireland, against the outrageous calumny and opprobrious traduction of all unprincipled adversary writers' (O'Flanagan 1795: iii). Defending Irish against the charge that it was a language of rebellion, he made the comparison with Welsh, and asked why language difference should be considered a sign of treachery in Ireland if not in Wales. And if it is not a language of revolt, Lynch demanded, why then must it be abolished? He also praised, in a manner which was to become a reflex in the eighteenth and nineteenth centuries, the enduring qualities of Gaelic:

The Irish language is certainly not more adapted for the contrivance of conspiracy than any other, nor less distinguished for its ornamental elegance:

for it is so copious, that if it does not equal, it comes very near the Spanish in gravity, the Italian in courtesy, the French in conciliating love, or the German in impressing terror. By the thunder of its eloquence the sacred orator often deters the wicked from their vices and attracts them, by its blandishments, to virtue. It is numbered as one of the original languages of Europe (O'Flanagan 1795: 43).

Sir Richard Cox, the Lord Chancellor, saw it differently. In his address to the reader he described Céitinn's *Foras Feasa ar Éirinn* as 'an ill-digested Heap of very silly Fictions' and picked on one element in the native histories of Gaelic to act as a cipher for their general corruption. Céitinn had cited Archbishop Creagh's claim that Gaelic had been in use in Ireland from 'six hundred and thirty years after the Deluge, to this day'. This was in a sense a claim for the antiquity and thus purity of Irish (features which were to figure prominently in eighteenth century debates in particular), and Cox refuted it with a triumphant flourish:

As for the Irish language, how much soever some of the Bards do brag, That it is a Pure and Original one; yet it is so far from that, that it is the most compound Language in the World, (the English only excepted). It borrows from the Spanish *com estato*, ie how do you do &c. from the Saxon the Words *Rath* and *Doon ie* Hill and many more: From the Danish many Words; from the Welsh almost half their Language ... From Latin they derive all their Numeral Words, *unus bene, duo dwo, tres three, quator cahir* ... All things that were not in use with them formerly are mere English Words, as *cotah, dublete, hatta, papere, botishy, breesty,* and abundance more. *Holinshed* makes too satirical an Observation, That there is no Irish Word for *Knave* (Cox 1689: 1, iii).

The last point is in fact made by Stanihurst, whose work was collected by Holinshed, from whom a number of the Gaelicized English examples also derive. Cox's point presumably referred to the fact that Irish culture was so uncivilized that it had no requirement for the term knave since it did not recognize the lack of virtue that such a term designates—such cognizance only having arrived with the colonists. What Cox's text did was to challenge the history articulated by the native writers with the aim of legitimizing colonial rule; what Lynch aimed to achieve was of course precisely the opposite. They are both marked by the time of their production, cancelling each other out in a bitter rhetorical process of assertion and denial; it was a struggle which was also to take place on other fields at the end of the seventeenth century, and its legacy will be considered in the next chapter.

# CHAPTER FOUR

# Education, antiquity, and the beginnings of linguistic nationalism, 1690–1789

'Gather up the fragments' (John vi, 12)
(epigram to Bishop Nicolson's *Irish Historical Library*, 1724).

The Williamite wars which culminated in the Treaty of Limerick in 1691 were to leave a legacy of bitterness, anxiety, and disruption which was to dominate Irish life for the next two and a half centuries or more. Religious antagonism was a structuring principle of the seventeenth century in Ireland, and after the atrocities committed on both sides of the mid-century civil war, the victorious Protestant forces began to act against their Catholic enemies. Catholic clergy were rounded up in the 1650s, the 1670s, and, after the historical pause afforded by the accession of James II, in 1697 (Barnard 1993: 268). In 1675 'Proposals for the more Effectual Subjugation of the Irish to the Crown of England' were intended to ensure that 'the Popish hierarchy and regular clergy should be extirpated under severe penalties; the secular clergy should be allowed only in remote parts where English is not spoken, and then only until Protestant divines skilled in Irish might be had' (*Analecta Hibernica* 1930: 74). The Protestant proselytizing principle was re-invoked and the Proposals ordered that the Bible, liturgy, catechism, and thirty-nine articles of the Church of England should be printed 'in the Irish Tongue in a Roman Character as those bookes are now printed in the Welsh language'. They also stipulated that teachers should be sought to learn and teach Irish, 'it being impracticable to destroy the Mother-Tongue of any People by the Severest Methods of Conquest' (*Analecta Hibernica* 1930: 74).

These proposals were effectively a blueprint for the set of laws which followed upon the Williamite victory, the Penal Code, whose aim was to erect and consolidate a legal, political, and civil system designed to privilege the rights and welfare of the Protestant Ascendancy over those of the Catholic majority.[1] The changes which the Penal Code brought about were a corollary of the shift which had seen the amount of land owned by Catholics fall from about sixty per cent in 1630 to twelve per cent in 1700. But it is important to be clear about the use of the term 'Protestant' in the phrase 'Protestant Ascendancy'; it did not simply equate with non-Catholic, since there were divisions within Protestantism which were at times as bitter as those between Protestantism and Catholicism, particularly in the period 1690–1720 and then towards the end of the eighteenth century. Dissenters from the established Church such as the Presbyterians were also subjected to the Penal Laws, though not to the same degree as Catholics; the 'Protestant' in 'Protestant Ascendancy' referred in essence to those who followed the doctrines of the Established Church (Bartlett 1988: 51).

One of the earliest of the Penal Laws was the 'Act to Restrain Foreign Education'(1695). As noted in the previous chapter, Catholics had long been sending their children to Europe for education according to the faith and this was a source of concern for English authorities, not least because of its perceived political dangers. Those subject to such instruction, it was proclaimed,

have in process of time engaged themselves in foreign interests, and been prevailed upon to forget the natural duty and allegiance due from them the Kings and Queens of this realm, and the affection which they owe to the established religion and laws of this their native country, and returning so evilly disposed into this kingdom, have been in all times past the movers and promoters of many dangerous seditions, and oftentimes of open rebellion (*Stat. Ire* 1786: 7 W 3. c.4).

The remedy was the complete prohibition of Catholic education abroad, and the penalty for failure to comply was the stripping away of all legal rights and the forfeiture of goods and land. Also, because toleration of Catholic schooling in Ireland was considered 'one great reason of many of the natives of this kingdom continuing ignorant of the principles of true religion, and strangers to the scriptures, and of their neglecting to

---

[1]  The term 'Protestant Ascendancy' was coined later in the debate on the Catholic relief bill in 1782 and was popularized in the early 1790s. For an examination of the shifting uses of the term and concept see W. J. McCormack, 1985: 61–96.

conform themselves to the laws and statutes of this realm, and of not using the English habit and language' (*Stat. Ire* 1786: 7 W 3. c.4), no Catholic was permitted to teach children on pain of a fine of twenty pounds or three months in prison for each offence.

Education and religion were to be key issues in the eighteenth century, though they were openly contested chiefly in its first and last quarters. For Catholics the choice was clear: either accept the law as it stood, send their children to Catholic Europe (a practice not only prohibited but expensive), or use the alternative system which sprang up beyond the legal constrictions imposed by the ruling authorities. Most Catholics who elected for any education for their children at all opted for the last option and sent their children to the hedge schools. These were schools which were conducted by local teachers, paid by subscription, who usually taught basic literacy and numeracy through the medium of English. Occasionally the hedge schools taught Greek and Latin and even literacy in Irish, but the system of education which the schools sustained—though highly impressive in its survival and in the standards it maintained in the light of the forces arrayed against it—does not sustain some of the more exaggerated claims made for its achievement by cultural nationalists (Dowling 1968: 55–61).[2] With regard to the  Catholic Church's stance towards the question of education and the Irish language in this period, it is revealing that it used English rather than Irish as its normal medium in speech and writing. As Ó Cuív notes, it is fair to say that 'despite the fact that many individual churchmen were well disposed towards Irish, the Catholic church made little positive contribution towards maintaining the language' (Ó Cuív 1986: 380). Towards the latter part of the century, Bishop O'Brien, writing from Brussels, appealed to the Sacred Congregation of Propaganda in Rome for support for his Irish–English dictionary. He did so on the basis that 'the preservation of the Irish language among the clergy and Catholic population of Ireland is essentially connected with the preservation of the true Faith'. Experience, he notes,

has taught us that it is only those ignorant of Irish or those who become fluent in English who abandon the Catholic religion and embrace that of Protestants. No Irishman whether from the country or anywhere else who spoke only Irish

---

[2] Cahill claimed in 1940 that as a result of the hedge school system intellectual achievement 'was higher among the native Irish than amongst the colonial class with all their rich endowments and State subsidies' and that it was 'far higher than the educational standard which prevails in Ireland today' (Cahill 1940a: 17).

or Latin and was utterly ignorant of English has ever been known to attend a Protestant sermon or communion service (Jones 1952: 32–3).

But this linkage of the Catholic faith and the Irish language was well ahead of its time; the connection was not upheld by the institutional Church until the late nineteenth century. Symptomatically, Rome sent O'Brien only a small contribution towards the cost of the dictionary (which was published in 1768). More tellingly, when Maynooth was opened as the intellectual centre of Catholic education in 1795 its language of instruction was English.[3]

For Protestantism there was an important contradiction which had to be addressed, and it was one which stretched back to the Elizabethan period: how to resolve the conflict between the need to proselytize in the Irish language and the need to Anglicize and eradicate Catholicism. In 1709 and 1710 the Lower House of Convocation, representing the unelevated clerical members of the Established Church, resolved that 'a competent number of ministers duly qualified to instruct the natives of the Kingdom and perform the office of religion for them in their own language' should be found and maintained. The resolution was rejected by the higher body of the Bishops as 'destructive of the English interests, contrary to the law and inconsistent with the authority of synods and convocations' (Cahill 1940b: 597). In Dublin, however, the idea had already found some favour and Archbishop King encouraged the appointment of the Gaelic genealogist Cathal Ó Luinín (Charles Lynegar) to the post of lecturer in Irish to the divinity students at Trinity in 1708. In 1711 the Provost and Fellows of Trinity composed a testimonial for Ó Luinín and confirmed that he had

taught many of the Students in the said College the Irish language, who have made a considerable Progress therein. And we are humbly of Opinion, That if the said Work were promoted and encouraged, it might prove a Means, by God's Blessing, to convert the Irish Natives, and bring them over to the Establish'd Church (Risk 1966: 18).

The post was not a success financially, however, and like many of the other Gaelic scholars of the day Ó Luinín was plagued by poverty; he ended up in prison for debt.

---

[3] At a time when the government was wooing moderate Catholic opinion and the French Revolution had forced the closure of a number of the continental colleges, the Catholic Church accepted state support for its principal Irish seminary. O'Rahilly sees this as the culmination of a century and a half of official church neglect of the Irish language (O'Rahilly 1932: 12).

There were conflicting positions within the Church of Ireland on the language issue and this is reflected in the argument between the Reverend John Richardson and the Reverend E. Nicholson in the early eighteenth century. In *A Proposal for the Conversion of the Popish Natives of Ireland* (1711) Richardson proposed 'to send missionaries among the natives, to instruct them in their own Language', to print Protestant texts and to institute Charity Schools 'for the *Instruction of the Irish Children, gratis*, in the *English Tongue*, and the *Established Religion . . .* the Benefit of which Schools may be extended to the Children of *Poor Protestants*' (Richardson 1711: lxxvii). Arguing against anticipated objections that teaching the Irish in Irish would be detrimental to English interests, that it would keep up a language difference and therefore a difference in religion, and that it would encourage the use of the Gaelic language, Richardson made a robust defence. Teaching through the medium of the native language is, he maintained, the only way to convert the Irish and therefore,

we are indispensably bound to make this Use of the Language, out of Charity to their Souls, and in Obedience to our Saviour's express Command . . . it being evident, that Difference of Language doth not keep up Difference of Religion; and that it is not the *Irish* Language, but the *Popish* Religion that is repugnant to the *English* Interest (Richardson 1711: 109–10).

Citing Scotland, in which of course a form of Gaelic was spoken in certain areas, Richardson argued that language diversity itself is not the problem in Ireland: Irish, he said, 'hath not any Marks of the Beast upon it'. To clinch the argument for Protestant instruction in Gaelic, he asserted the political dangers of neglecting it and with an eye to the financial implications which always haunted English colonial policy, he pointedly noted that the entire cost of his extensive plan would amount to no more than 'The Yearly Charge of Four Regiments, or the Expense of one Year's War in Ireland'.[4]

Richardson followed up his *Proposal* with *A Short History of the Attempts that Have Been Made to Convert the Popish Natives of Ireland, to the Established Religion* (1712). In it he pointed out the counter-productive nature of the

---

[4] Richardson warned that '*Ireland* is a Nursery to supply some neighbouring Popish Kingdoms with Men, when they have Occasion for them; by which Means the Crown of *Great Britain* and *Ireland*, loses a great Number of Native Subjects (who might be very useful in War and Peace, at Home and Abroad)' (Richardson 1711: 147). The reference is to the Wild Geese, the Irish soldiers evacuated to France under the terms of the Treaty of Limerick and the recruits to the Irish brigades in continental armies in the eighteenth century.

attempt 'to Convert the *Irish*, by attempting to abolish their Language, or by any severe and disagreeable Methods'.[5] Such policy, he argued, was ideologically naïve since it sought to persuade the Irish by 'enraging and exasperating them; and of gaining their Hearts and Affections, (without which they can never be truly converted) by taking away that which is very dear and valuable to them' (Richardson 1712: 12). The end result was that it 'made few or no sincere Converts, and only provoked them . . . to rebel on the first Opportunity, and to apostasize . . . to that Superstition and Idolatry from which they had not been inwardly converted' (Richardson 1712: 13).

What appears in one light to have been an enlightened attitude to the education of the Catholic population, including the idea of integrated schooling (though Richardson was deeply anti-Catholic), was met with outright hostility by Nicholson, whose views came to be accepted by the Church itself. Nicholson's stance was coloured by his experiences in the west of Ireland during the Williamite wars, which led him to conclude that 'vagabonds, sturdy beggars, thieves, robbers, highwaymen, rapparees or tories, houghers, murderers and rebels do all spring from want of honest education and employment to live by' (Barnard 1993: 262). Apart from the interesting historical insight into the etymological origin of the political term 'Tory' (from the Irish 'tóraidhe' meaning robber, or highwayman, and, in its earliest definition, one of the dispossessed Irish who became outlaws in the seventeenth century) Nicholson's conclusion signals his agreement with Richardson as to the need for, and effectuality of, education as a civilizing colonial process.[6] The source of their disagreement was the medium in which such education should be conducted. Nicholson attacked Richardson's plan for teaching in Gaelic on the grounds that the situation in Ireland was more difficult than in other colonial situations precisely because the native Irish were not without faith; his point was that they had too much faith. Native language education, he argued, 'tho' such a method be the only way among infidels, yet among our Irish Papists it can have no effect; for in the 1st place their priests have effectual bars by their

[5] In *The Querist* (1750) Bishop Berkeley asked 'whether there be any instance of a people being converted in a Christian sense, otherwise than by preaching to them and instructing them in their own language' (Berkeley 1837: 374).
[6] Ó Ciosáin points out that the literal meaning of 'tóraidhe' meant 'pursued', which signifies a physical state rather than a social category such as 'thief'. By the early eighteenth century in Britain it had come to mean Jacobite (Ó Ciosáin 1997: 179).

excommunications and influence over their blind zealots to hinder them hearing us at all' (Nicholson *c.*1715: 27). Other reasons for his objection to Richardson's scheme included the fact that it would maintain a distinction between the English and the Irish linguistically, that it was unnecessary given the spread of English, and that the money would be better spent elsewhere in the education of Irish children directly in English and Protestantism. If that were done the outcome would quickly prove to be satisfactory: 'the old ones will soon die, and if the young ones be rightly educated, popery and Irish barbarism will soon be ended' (Nicholson 1715: 28).

Henry Newman, Secretary to the Society for the Propagation of the Gospel, drafted a letter (*c.*1715) to the Archbishop of Canterbury about the problem caused by the language question. Noting that all agreed that education 'will be the most effectual means to bring [Catholics] over [rather] than the compulsory and penal laws', Newman argued that opinions on the different methods were held tenaciously and divisively and sought the Archbishop's help in resolving the issue. His own preference was 'to put in clergymen who will propagate the charity schools, read the service and preach in Irish'; to further the design he assured the Archbishop that 'there lie ready several hundred Common Prayer Books and Catechisms in the Irish Language in Quires at His Grace's Command, to be given gratis as he shall direct' (*Analecta Hibernica* 1931: 73). But this comment reveals the difficulty of Protestant proselytizing in the eighteenth century. For although Richardson gained the financial support of the Society for Promoting Christian Knowledge for the printing of six thousand copies of the Book of Common Prayer and Lewis's Protestant Catechism (translated by Richardson), together with three thousand copies of Richardson's *Short History*, the texts largely remained in quire. In 1717 four thousand volumes rotted in the SPCK warehouse in London and Richardson admitted that he had sold only five copies of his work (Barnard 1993: 256). The reality of the situation after the initial frenzy of the early eighteenth century was that the Church of Ireland lost interest in proselytizing in the native language as surely as the Catholic Church remained indifferent to it. Instead the Established Church adopted the policy so vehemently espoused by Nicholson, that of Protestant education in the English language, and between the 1720s and the end of the century there is little mention made in Church records of the language issue. The official position of the state itself was given in the *Royal Charter for Erecting English Protestant*

*Schools in the Kingdom of Ireland* (1733). The aim was 'to teach the Children of the Popish and other poor Natives of our said Kingdom, the English Tongue, and to teach them to read, especially the Holy Scriptures, and other good and pious Books, and to instruct them in the Principles of the Protestant Religion' (Corcoran 1916: 108).

In Ulster the situation was different since there were Irish-speaking Protestant clergy in some areas where the Scottish settlers were themselves Gaelic-speakers. The religion of these planters was predominantly Presbyterian and the hostility of the Established Church made it unlikely that they would follow state doctrines with regard to the language. This may explain the resolution of the General Synod of Ulster, the governing body of the Irish Presbyterian Church, to use Gaelic in their attempts to convert Catholics. The 1710 proposal was reaffirmed by the Synod of 1716 and bolstered by the intention to institute corresponding societies in Ulster and Dublin 'for encouraging this Christian design of the conversion of the Irish', to set up a charity school in Dundalk 'for teaching to read Irish', and to print 'the Catechism in Irish with a little short Irish Grammar' (published in 1718) (Fitzsimons 1949: 256). Teaching in Irish was maintained by the Presbyterians at Dundalk over the next century or so by ministers such as Patrick Simpson, Robert Drummond, Colin Lindsay, Andrew Bryson, and William Neilson (whose *Introduction to the Irish Language* was published in 1808) (Blaney 1996: 14). However, despite this tradition, and the involvement of Presbyterians in the flourishing interest in Irish in late eighteenth-century Belfast, there is no further reference to any official Presbyterian Irish language policy in the records of the General Synod of Ulster until 1833. It appears that the Presbyterians, at least implicitly, agreed with both Catholics and their fellow Protestants on the relative futures of the English and Irish languages.

The early eighteenth century saw the start of serious antiquarian interest in Irish language and culture. The most important text was Edward Lhuyd's *Archaeolgia Britannica* (1707), and in the Gaelic preface to the 'Focloir Gaoidheilge-Shagsonach no Bearladoir Scot-Sagsamhuil Irish-English Dictionary' (whose importance was recognized by its translation in Bishop Nicolson's *Irish Historical Library*) he defended its significance.[7] The utility of this first dictionary, he argued, lay in the help

---

[7] Lhuyd's contribution to the development of the linguistics of the Celtic languages was highly significant; see Kidd 1999: 196–7.

it could give in understanding the historical origins of Britain, the better comprehension of the names of persons and places in the British Isles, the aid it might provide in comparative philology (to use the term anachronistically) and its assistance in antiquarian research. He also made the claim that it would be helpful to the clergy and others who 'have any Office or Place of Trust over the common People' (Nicolson 1724: 214). Answering the argument that 'it were better to teach all manner of Persons in the three Kingdoms to speak *English*', Lhuyd agreed that it would be 'of universal advantage in order to promote Trade and Commerce' but asked how it could be accomplished since 'we have been now for several hundred Years, subject to and conversant with the *English* and *Scots* in the Lowlands of *Scotland*; and yet how many thousands are there in each Kingdom that do not yet speak *English*?' (Nicolson 1724: 214–15).

Writing in the mid nineteenth century, John Windele calculated that by the 1730s, around two thirds of the Irish population spoke Gaelic as their everyday language (1,340,000 from a total of just over two million) (Ó Cuív 1986: 383). Yet even by the beginning of the eighteenth century, patterns which had begun in the previous two centuries were starting to become more markedly evident. The spread of English as a written and spoken language, which had been an official state policy for centuries, was underway; though at first somewhat slow and piecemeal, the forces gathered against Irish meant that its gradual decline had commenced. Over the next one hundred and fifty years, the Irish people's abandonment of their native language, under various forms of historical pressure, was to be almost complete. Yet rather than proscription by State edict, the most effective agent for progressive Anglicization was the utility of the English language in the changing economic, social, and cultural conditions faced by the Gaelic-speaking population. Sir William Petty, political economist, subscriber to Bacon's doctrine of 'useful knowledge', and shrewd colonial observer, stressed the importance of Anglicization for the Irish themselves in his *Political Anatomy of Ireland* (written in 1672 but published in 1691). His remedy for the recent disturbances in the colony was the appointment of English priests and the influence of English women since 'when the Language of the Children shall be *English*, and the whole Economy of the Family *English*, *viz*. Diet, Apparel, *&c*. the Transmutation will be very easy and quick' (Petty 1691: 31). He also advised the Irish 'to decline their Language' on the grounds that it, continues a sensible distinction, being not now necessary; which makes those who do not understand it, suspect, that what is spoken in it, is to their prejudice. It is their Interest to deal with the *English*, for Leases, for Time, and upon clear Conditions, which being perform'd they are absolute Freemen, rather than to stand always liable to the humour and caprice of their Landlords, and to have everything taken away from them which he pleases to fancy (Petty 1691: 101).

Petty's comments are evidently those of the abstract economist who pays no attention to the political situation in which contracts and exchanges take place; his apparent belief that English landlords cheated the Irish simply because the Irish could not understand the language is probably disingenuous. There is, however, an element of truth within it. After all, why bother acting illegally if you could work the system to your advantage simply by dint of the fact that your tenants could not understand the terms upon which they paid rent and held land.

The argument that self-interest was proper motivation for the Irish to drop their language in favour of English was also made by Richardson, ironically in his proposal for the teaching of Protestantism to the native population through the medium of their own language since,

to make this Use of the [Irish] Language at present, is the most effectual Way to diminish the Use of it hereafter: For, if we prevail with them to conform to our Church, their Prejudices being thereby in a great Measure removed, they will more readily fall in with our Customs and Language; and being qualified equally with our selves for any Office or Employment, their Interest will soon induce them to speak *English* (Richardson 1711: 110).

This was the first deployment of an argument which was to be propagated repeatedly by proselytizing societies both in this and following centuries; whereas later Irish cultural nationalists argued for the use of Irish in order to preserve it, here the proposal is to employ Gaelic in order eventually to destroy it. On the other hand, Nicolson, his opponent in the language debate, argued precisely that Gaelic should not be used for conversion because English was already superseding it, and again the reason given was that it was in the perceived self-interest of those who learned it:

there is hardly a boy of 16 years old in Ireland but can understand and speak English. Their parents encourage them to it for their own trading and dealing with their English landlords. Most of the old people will not learn it, or do scorn to speak it, and those are so stiff in popery and riveted by the superstition of their language and customs that they would never be converted by speaking Irish never so much to them (Nicholson 1715: 27).

His conclusion was that 'English is now so universally spoken by all the young Irish here that we may hope in the next generation Irish will be quite forgotten'. He was supported by Samuel Madden's comment in 1738 that 'as the old affectation of speaking only *Irish* is quite laid aside there is now scarce one in twenty who does not understand and speak English well'. Such conclusions were undoubtedly wrong (Stokes, for example, in an important survey at the end of the century, calculated that there were eight hundred thousand monoglot Gaelic speakers and that half the population spoke the language by preference) (Ó Cuív 1986: 383) but they certainly pointed to the direction in which the linguistic tide was flowing. Indeed the response of Gaelic poets indicates as much. The Ulster poet Peadar Ó Doirnín's 'O Ghaoidhilge Mhilis' (Oh Sweet Gaelic) praised the language as 'sweet, soft and copious, swift, strong, sonorous and irresistible as the waves of the sea'. It continued: ''S d'andeoin a ngliocais táir cinnte i státa. 'S go luan an Brátha béir mo mhuirnin féin' (In spite of their craftiness you, my own dear native tongue, still hold your place in the land, and shall do 'till the last day) (Cahill 1940*b*: 594). But the Armagh poet Art MacCubhthaigh commented on the actuality of decline:

> Tá mo chroí-se réabtha ina míle céad cuid
> 's gan balsam féin ann a d'fhóirfeadh dom phian,
> nuair a chluinim an Ghaeilge uilig á tréigbheáil,
> is caismirt Bhéarla i mbeol gach aoin

> My heart is torn in a hundred thousand pieces,
> And no remedy will soothe my pain,
> When I hear Irish being abandoned
> And the din of English in everyone's mouth
> (Ó Fiaich 1969: 107).

For the Munster poet Seán Ó Tuama, only the promise of the achievement of the Jacobite fantasy heralded the restoration of the lost Gaelic order, the primacy of the Catholic faith, and the banishment of the linguistic usurpers:

> Brisfid is réabfaid is déanfaid ruaig
> ar bhruithinisc bhaoth an Bhéarla dhuairc,
> cuirfid na Gaeidhil 'na n-ionadaibh féin,
> sin mise lem ré's an éigse suas

They will defeat and plunder and expel
The vain rabble of surly English-speakers,
They will put the Irish into their due positions,
That means myself, for my lifetime, and poetry on top
(Ó Fiaich 1969: 107).

Such sentiments were prompted by a conservative desire for restoration rather than any revolutionary impulse (Cullen 1969: 24), and they were articulated best by perhaps the last of the great Irish poets to benefit from the education and privileges of the old Gaelic order, Aodhagán Ó Rathaille (Egan O'Rahilly). After the Williamite wars the confiscation of the estate of Sir Nicholas Browne, upon whose lands Ó Rathaille's family were sub-tenants, signalled the collapse of the old order; around 1703 Ó Rathaille lost his family home and left Sliabh Luachra, the place of his childhood, for an impoverished livelihood in Corca Duibhne in Kerry. In Ó Rathaille's poetry occasional bursts of Jacobite optimism are spliced with an overwhelming bitterness and sense of defeat, both of which are evident in the attitude towards the English language. In 'Tarngaireacht dhuinn fhírinne' (The prophecy of Donn Firinne) for example the poet attacks the denial of the Jacobite succession and looks forward to the time when the rightful possessors are restored to the monarchy:

Is truaillighthe, claonmhar, 's is tréason don druing uilc,
Cruadhmhionna bréige fá shéala 's fá scríbhinn,
'Ga mbualadh le béalaibh ar gcléire is ar saoithe,
'S nár dhual do chloinn tSéamuis coróin tsaor na dtrí ríoghachta.

Stadfaidh an tóirneach le fóirneart na gréine,
Is scaipfidh an ceo so de phórshleachtaibh Éibhir;
An tImpre beidh deorach is Flóndras fá dhaorsmacht,
'S an 'bricléir' go modhmharach i seomra ríogh Séamus

Beidh Éire go súgach 's a dúnta go haerach
Is Gaedhilg 'gá scrúdadh n-a múraibh ag éigsibh;
Béarla na mbúr ndubh go cúthail fá néaltaibh,
Is Séamus n-a chúirt ghil ag tabhairt chonganta do Ghaedhealaibh.

It is foul and evil, it is treason in that wicked race,
To brandish audacious perjuries, sealed, and in writing,
Before the faces of our clergy and our nobles,
That the children of James have no hereditary title to the noble crown of the three Kingdoms.

The thunder will be silenced by the strength of the sunlight,

And this sorrow will depart from the true descendants of Eibhear:
The Emperor will shed tears, and Flanders will be in dire bondage.
While the 'Bricklayer' will be in pride in the halls of King James.

Erin will be joyful, and her strongholds will be merry;
And the learned will cultivate Gaelic in their schools;
The language of the black boors will be humbled and put beneath a cloud,
And James in his bright court will lend his aid to the Gaels.
(Ó Rathaille 1911: 166–7).

The pain and anger felt by Ó Rathaille at the loss not simply of land and possessions but of status and place within a fast-disappearing Gaelic cultural order is demonstrated by a prose piece, 'Seanchuimhne ar Aodhagán Ua Rathaille' (A Reminiscence of Egan O'Rahilly), in the section entitled 'Air faghail Sagsanach éigin crochda as crann a gcoill Chill Abharne' (On finding some Protestant [or Englishman] hanging from a tree in the wood of Killarney) (Ó Rathaille 1911: 262). In this story an English minister orders Irish carpenters to cut down a bough of a tree (probably the tree in the cloister at Muckross Abbey) for furniture but none of the Irishmen will carry out the task and so the minister's son attempts it. The son is trapped between two branches of the tree by the neck and is strangled. While the 'siapach Sasanaigh' (base Englishman, or Protestant) is dangling, the minister 'squeals like a pig in a bag' and then 'Aodhagán Ua Rathaille ó Shliabh Luachra na laochradh' (Egan O'Rahilly from Sliabh Luachra of the heroes) chanted to him:

> 'Is maith do thoradh a chrainn,
> Rath do thoraidh ar gach aon chraoibh,
> Mo chreach! Gan crainn Inse Fáil
> Lán det thoradh gach aon lá.'

The poem continues:

'What is the poor wild Irish devil saying?' ar an ministir.
'He is lamenting your darling son,' ar gaige bhí láimh leis.
'Here is two pence for you to buy tobacco,' ar an méithbhroc ministreach.
'Thank'ee, a mhinistir an Mhic Mhallachtan' (*i.e.*, an diabhal), ar Aodhagán, agus do chan an laoidh:-

> 'Hurú, a mhinistir a thug do dhá phinginn dam
>    I dtaobh do leinbh a chaoineadh!
> Oidheadh an leinbh sin ar an gcuid eile aca
>    Siar go hearball timcheall'.

Despite the wag's translation of his words, what in fact Ua Rathaille says to the minister is:

> 'Good is thy fruit, O tree,
> May every branch bear such good fruit,
> Alas! that the trees of Innisfail
> Are not full of thy fruit each day.'

And to the minister's charity he responds:

'Thank'ee, Minister of the Son of Malediction' (*i.e.,* the devil), replied Egan, and he spoke this lay:-

> 'Huroo! O minister, who didst give me thy two pence
> For chanting a lament for thy child;
> May the fate of this child attend the rest of them
> All, even to the last.'

(Ó Rathaille 1911: 264–5).

The contempt and hatred for the rapacious English planter, a follower of Cromwell who had despoiled the local church and now wanted the beautiful tree, is compounded by Ó Rathaille's clever portrayal of the minister as linguistically inferior. It is Ó Rathaille, the Irishman skilled in both the English language and Gaelic poetic composition, who is able to mock and ridicule the stupid Englishman. Here the representation of the poor, ignorant Irish, lacking the tongue of their masters and thus unable to make themselves understood, is turned on its head; Irish is in this context a native weapon against the colonizer. The representation is repeated in Friel's *Translations* (1981), in which the colonial English are depicted as unlettered and bare of learning in contrast to the clever and able Irish. But these are unusual examples and the desperate plight of Gaelic Ireland from Ó Rathaille's point of view is more accurately described in the bitter threnody 'An Milleadh d'imthigh ar Mhór-Shleachtaibh na hÉireann' (The Ruin that Befell the Great Families of Erin) (*c.*1720):

> Tír gan eaglais chneasta ná cléirigh!
> Tír le mioscais, noch d'itheadar faolchoin!
> Tír do cuireadh go tubaisteach, traochta
> Fá smacht namhad is amhas is méirleach!
>
> Tír gan tartha gan tairbhe i nÉirinn!
> Tír gan turadh gan buinne gan réiltean!
> Tír do nochtadh gan fothain gan géaga!
> Tír do briseadh le fuirinn an Bhéarla!

> A land without meek church or clergy!
> A land which wolves have spitefully devoured!
> A land placed in misfortune and subjection
> Beneath the tyranny of enemies and mercenaries and robbers!
>
> A land without produce or thing of any worth of any kind!
> A land without dry weather, without a stream, without a star!
> A land stripped naked, without shelter or boughs!
> A land broken by the English-prating band!
> (Ó Rathaille 1911: 6–7).

One of Ó Rathaille's contemporaries, Aodh Buidhe Mac Cruitín (Hugh MacCurtin), also observed the progress of the English-prating band, and the means by which it was gained:

> Féach na flatha ba fairsing in Éirinn uair
> . . . . .
> gur éirigh Galla agus ceannaithe caola an chnuais
> le tréimhse eatortha ag teagasc a mbéas don tsluagh;
> do réir mar mheallaid a mbailte dob aolta snuadh
> tá Béarla i bhfaisean go tairise is Gaeilge fuar.

(Consider the rulers who once were generous in Ireland . . . until foreigners and the cunning avaricious merchants came between them, teaching their own customs to the people; according as they seduce our fairest towns English becomes fashionable and Irish decays)
(Ó Cuív 1986: 397).

The work of MacCruitín provides an insight into the historical and linguistic forces which were in opposition in the early eighteenth century. His *Brief Discourse in Vindication of the Antiquity of Ireland* (1717) for example is a direct response to Cox's *Hibernia Anglicana* (1689–90) and attempts a detailed defence of Irish history in English from a native point of view. It is significant because MacCruitín was a member of one of the hereditary bardic families and thus was trained in Gaelic scholarship; he was therefore able to read Irish medieval manuscripts, sources to which Cox had no access. In terms reminiscent of Céitinn's denunciation of the Anglo-Irish Chroniclers, MacCruitín described Cox and other such apologists for English rule as 'ignorant in the true Antiquities and Histories of Ireland' and full of 'Malice and Hatred towards the Antient Inhabitants [of Ireland] and their Posterity' (MacCruitín 1717: ix). He was allegedly paid back in kind; it is said that for the offence caused to Cox by the *Vindication*, MacCruitín was jailed for a year.[8] One point of interest concerning the *Vindication* is the fact that it is written in English. Why, it might be asked, would a member of the bardic profession (and a highly respected one as is clear from the list of subscribers to the book) write a defence in English, rather than Irish, particularly given his statement in the preface to the *Vindication* that 'I confess my self not sufficient to write correctly in the English language' (MacCruitín 1717: ix)? Why did he not write in Gaelic? The answer, which indicates the developing relations between the English and Irish languages as media of public discourse, lies in the audience which MacCruitín wished to address. Céitinn's defence of Irish history and antiquity in the previous century was written in Gaelic and intended for the native learned readership. MacCruitín's work was directed towards the Protestant Ascendancy and those in Ireland literate in English. It was an attempt to contest English histories of Ireland on and in the terms of the colonizer (literally and metaphorically) and so it was a complex task; but by that point in history there was already little choice. MacCruitín's *Elements of the Irish Language*, published in Louvain in 1728 and supposedly written during his year in jail, was the first printed grammar of Irish in the English language; the preface to *The English-Irish Dictionary. An Focloir Bearla Gaoidheilge*, published in Paris in 1732 with Conchobhar Ó Beaglaoich (Conor O'Begly), was also in English.

English was slowly but gradually winning the war of the languages. As noted above, in 1799 Whitley Stokes calculated that of a population of more than four and a half million, 'at least eight hundred thousand of our countrymen speak Irish only, and there are at least twice as many who speak it in preference' (Stokes 1799: 45). But the fact was that English had become the hegemonic language of prestige, power, and economic exchange. The process by which this change occurred was neither simple nor rapid, however, and there were various complexities which hindered it. First was the growing rhetorical antagonism to English, a force which developed as the last representatives of the old Gaelic order realized that the language and culture which they had for so long ignored or treated with curiosity and indifference, was now the means by which colonial power was being consolidated. One example of such an attitude is the poem by Donncha Caoch Ó Mathúna, composed as an encomium

---

[8] In 1859 Sir John Gilbert claimed that Cox 'availed himself of his position to imprison illegally for a year in Newgate Hugh MacCurtin, an Irish historiographer of the County Clare' (Gilbert 1859: vol. 3, 313); there is no contemporary evidence to support his contention.

to the Irish language in order to defend himself against those who had heard him speak English at a Cork market and thereby presumed he was an Englishman (Breatnach 1961: 147). But there are a number of significant features to this specific example; the occasion of the poem was the poet's speaking English, at a site of economic barter, in a large Irish city, and his reaction to being identified as an Englishman tells us much about the contemporary situation. Annoyed at being taken for an Englishman, he writes in praise of the Irish language; but by implication what the poet points to is the fact that it was not unusual for an Irish person to be speaking English at market in a city, and that the mistake involved was simply that the hearer assumed that English-speakers must thereby be English. Precisely this linkage of language and national identity had been formulated in the early seventeenth century and it was to become a major factor in later debates.

The second complication with regard to the spread of the English language in Ireland in the eighteenth century was that the ways in which it spread and took root, and the effects on the language as it did so, were not greeted with universal acclaim even by the Anglo-Irish themselves. One early example of a reaction against a variety of English in the seventeenth century involved a Scottish schoolmaster, Fullerton, who attempted to take over the teaching of English to a group of Irish children. Bourke, charged with the care of the children, appealed to the law to ban Fullerton from interfering, because 'by reason of the pronunciacion of the Scottish or English [he] cannot breake children to reduce them from the Irish to the perfect touch of the English speach, which is very difficult and consistes most of their first tutorshipp and educacion' (*Analecta Hibernica* 1931: 21). But one of the most important commentators on English in Ireland was Swift, whose sensitivity to the importance of language and historiography in the construction of tradition is made clear in his appeal to standardize the English language in England itself, the *Proposal for Correcting, Improving and Ascertaining the English Language* (1712). In Ireland Swift saw various serious linguistic problems, one being the variety of English used by the Planters (many of whom were of course, like Fullerton, of Scottish origin) which he satirized in 'A Dialogue in Hibernian Style' (*c.*1735).

A:   What kind of man is your neighbour Squire Doll?
B:   Why a meer buddogh. He sometimes coshers with me. And once a month
     I take a Pipe with him, and we strole it about for an hour together.

A:   Well, I'd give a Cow in Connaugh to see you together. I hear he keeps good horses.

B:   None but garrauns, and I have seen him often riding on a Sougawn. In short he is no better than a Spawleen; a perfect Monaghen. When I was there last, we had nothing but a Maddor to drink out of, and the Devil a Night-gown but a Caddow. Will you go see him when you come into our Parts?

A:   Not *without* you go with me:

B:   Will you lend me your snuff-box, *till* I take a pinch of Snuff?

A:   Do you make good Cheese and Butter?

B:   Yes when we can get milk; But our Cows will never keep a drop of milk without a Puckaun.

(Swift 1973: 278).

Swift's view was that language was central to the political health of the nation (in the *Proposal* he equates it in importance with the reform of the civil and religious constitution and the national debt); he was implacably opposed to novelty or innovation, seeing them as signs of degeneracy and a falling-off from the standards of a golden age.[9] Taken together with his opposition to the newly emergent bourgeoisie and his own complex Anglo-Irish identity, it is unsurprising that his stance towards the language of the settlers in Ireland was harsh.

In fact Swift argued in 'On barbarous denominations in Ireland' (*c.* 1740) that his own attitudes towards the variety of English used by the Irish were simply a reflection of the general opinion towards it. Though it was true that there was variation within Britain itself (England and Scotland were united in 1707) and that in London 'the trading people have an affected manner of pronouncing', as did many at court, and that 'there is an odd provincial cant in most counties of England, sometimes not very pleasing to the ear', and that 'the Scotch cadence, as well as expression, are offensive enough', yet there was something unique about the English used by the Irish English.

None of these defects derive contempt to the speaker; whereas, what we call the Irish Brogue is no sooner discovered, than it makes the deliverer, in the last degree, ridiculous and despised; and, from such a mouth, an Englishman expects nothing but bulls, blunders, and follies. Neither does it avail whether the censure be reasonable or not, since the fact is always so (Swift 1973: 281).

The Irish 'brogue' provokes prejudice and thus the very form of the speech supersedes the content: it does not matter what the Irish person

[9] For a discussion of Swift's politics of language see Crowley 1996: 59–67.

says since as soon as they open their mouth their language is damned as nonsense.[10] And, as a good linguistic conservative, the question of whether this is right or wrong is not important for Swift since it is a matter not of rational justice, but of preserving what just is. The significant thing was that 'what is yet worse, it is too well known that the bad consequence of this opinion affects those among us who are not the least liable to such reproaches, further than the misfortune of being born in Ireland, although of English parents, and whose education hath been chiefly in that kingdom'(Swift 1973: 281). Swift's concern in the *Proposal* with regard to the English language was that if history is not recorded 'in Words more durable than Brass, and such as Posterity may read a thousand years hence' then it could not be guaranteed that 'Memory shall be preserved above an Hundred Years, further than by imperfect Tradition' (Crowley 1991: 29–30). His worry in 'On barbarous denominations in Ireland' was more mundane: that he might sound just like the rest of the ignorant Irish.

Swift was embarrassed by the possibilities which 'the brogue' presented for the identification of the barbarous and stupid Irish, and it was used throughout the century in just this way in depictions of the Stage Irishman.[11] There were, however, counter-representations of this figure and one playwright who deployed this type was Swift's godson Thomas Sheridan, in plays such as *The Brave Irishman* (1754). Despite the fact that Captain O'Blunder is equipped with the usual brogue and bulls, the point of the play is more concerned with English misrepresentations of the Irish than stupidity or malice on the part of the Irish. Like Swift, and no doubt under his influence, Sheridan was sensitive to the political significance of language. He argued that 'nothing can be a greater national concern than the care of our language' and noted that the distinct nations of the newly created Britain 'spoke in tongues different from the English, and were far from being united with them in inclinations, and were of course pursuing different interests'. Thus 'to accomplish an entire union with these people, was of the utmost importance to them, to which nothing could have more effectively contributed, than the universality of one common language' (Sheridan 1756: 213–14).

---

[10] 'Brogue' is recorded in the *OED* as a coinage in the *London Gazette* in 1705, but Braidwood points out that it is used in the Ulster–Scots Protestant George Farquhar's *The Twin Rivals* in 1702 (Braidwood 1975: 5).

[11] Leerssen gives an important reading of the significance of the Stage Irishman in 'The Fictional Irishman in English Literature' (Leerssen 1996: 77–150).

Sheridan undertook the creation of this 'band of national union' (as Noah Webster described his own aim in the United States a few years later) in a series of textbooks designed to forge a standard pronunciation of the English language. Of particular interest were the lengthy sections in these texts dedicated to the elimination of 'the brogue'. *A General Dictionary of the English Language* (1780), for example, contained the 'Rules to be observed by the Natives of Ireland in order to attain a just Pronunciation of English'. Samuel Johnson's response to the *Dictionary* was somewhat blunt: 'what entitles Sheridan to fix the pronunciation of English? He has, in the first place, the disadvantage of being an Irishman . . . ' (Croghan 1990: 25). But perhaps the perceived difficulty was in fact an advantage since it is often outsiders who know the rules best; mid and late eighteenth-century London was staffed by a number of influential elocution masters who hailed from Ireland and Scotland.

But there was another response to 'the brogue' which marked both an emerging attitude to the English language among the native Irish and a new confidence among the Anglo-Irish Ascendancy. John Keogh's *A Vindication of the Antiquities of Ireland* (1748), one of a number of texts published by members of the tentatively confident Catholic middle class in the mid eighteenth century, castigated the 'national prejudice' of the English 'which occasions them to cast such Calumnies and Aspersions on the Irish, without any manner of Foundation'; 'prejudice', he noted 'cannot speak well of any one' (Keogh 1748: 74). With regard to language, he observed that

> The Irish are reflected on by the English, because they have a kind of Tone, or Accent, in their Discourse, (which they are pleased to call a Brogue). I think this ought to be no Disgrace to them, but rather an Honour, because they distinguish themselves by retaining the Tone of their Country Language; which shows, that they have a Knowledge of it (Keogh 1748: 75).

In point of fact, he argued, the Irish have more right to criticize the English in this respect since 'there is hardly a Shire in England, but has a different Tone in pronouncing the English Tongue; so that oftentimes one Shire cannot understand another' (Keogh 1748: 75–6). In London particularly 'they refine and mince the English tongue to that degree, that it is scarcely intelligible'.[12] As to the charge against the Irish, which

---

[12] 'Mincing' was in effect a class-laden accusation since it referred to the act of speaking with affected elegance or pronunciation; 'to mince' was first used in this sense in 1549. The sense of effeminacy also dates from this period, though the camp associations appear later.

was in effect little more than that they sound as though they are Irish (which is to say not English), Keogh responded:

You may as well reflect upon the French, Dutch, Germans, Danes, Spaniards, Swedes, &c. because they retain the Tone of their respective Languages by which you may readily distinguish them. Now most other Nations escape the censure of the English, but the unfortunate Irish, who must have Calumnies heaped on them (Keogh 1748: 76).

Keogh described this specific anti-Irish prejudice as simply the result of 'Ignorance and Stupidity', but its origins lie in the history of the political and social relations between England and Ireland. Language, as a sign of national difference, was a focus of significant contention; as usual, language debates were part of larger arguments.

At the end of the century there was another important contribution to the 'brogue' debate in Maria Edgeworth's *Essay on Irish Bulls*, published in 1802, two years after *Castle Rackrent* (often rather patronizingly described as 'the first regional novel', as though the metropolis or the Home Counties were not regions). Reviewing the literary representation of Irish characters, Edgeworth observed that

Much of the comic effect of Irish bulls, or of such speeches as are mistaken for bulls, has depended upon the tone, or brogue, as it is called, with which they are uttered. The first Irish blunders that we hear are made or repeated in this peculiar tone, and afterward, from the power of association, whenever we hear the tone we expect the blunder (Edgeworth 1802: 191–2).

Her point was that although an Irish accent is a 'great and shameful defect, it does not render the English language absolutely unintelligible' (Edgeworth 1802: 200).

There are but few variations of the brogue, such as the long and the short, the Thady brogue and the Paddy brogue, which differ much in tone, but little in phraseology; but in England, almost all of our fifty-two counties have peculiar vulgarisms, dialects, and brogues, unintelligible to their neighbours...Indeed the language peculiar to the metropolis, or the *cockney* dialect, is proverbially ridiculous (Edgeworth 1802: 200–1).

Like Keogh, Edgeworth made a comparison with England which was favourable to the Irish case: linguistic variation in Ireland did not produce the sort of miscomprehension which was common in England. But her claim about the English language used in Ireland was more radical in its implications since she continued to assert that 'the Irish, in general, speak *better English* than is commonly spoken by the natives of England' (Edgeworth 1802: 199). She restricted this claim to the 'lower classes' in both countries, and particularly in Ireland to the more isolated regions. In those counties, however, she declared that 'amongst those who speak English we find fewer vulgarisms than amongst the same rank of persons in England'. In fact their English was a pure relic of the highpoint of English cultural achievement:

The English which they speak is chiefly such as has been traditional in their families since the time of the early settlers in the island. During the reign of Elizabeth and the reign of Shakespeare, numbers of English migrated to Ireland; and whoever attends to the phraseology of the lower Irish, may, at this day, hear many of the phrases and expressions used by Shakespeare. Their vocabulary has been preserved in its near pristine purity since that time, because they have not had intercourse with those counties in England which have made for themselves a jargon unlike to any language under heaven (Edgeworth 1802: 199–200).

The claim that an earlier form of the English language had been preserved in Ireland had been made before; Stanihurst asserted that 'the dregs of the old ancient Chaucer English' were maintained in Wexford as well as Fingal in the sixteenth century (Stanihurst 1577: 4). Yet this was a highly significant vindication of the Irish use of English, for it proposed Ireland as the location where the glorious language of the golden age could still be found, where the wells of English (a phrase Johnson borrowed in the preface to his dictionary from Spenser) remained undefiled.[13]

This is a remarkable defence of the English language in Ireland and denotes an assertion of Anglo-Irish cultural confidence at a time when political confidence was more problematic. Though Irish was still the language of the great majority of the inhabitants of Ireland at the end of the century, English was the medium of economic and social potential. In a dispute over the compulsory status of the teaching of Irish at a Catholic seminary in France in 1764, one advocate in its favour argued that 'the Irish people are attached to their native language and wish to preserve it. It is true that the language of commerce and public business is English [but] Irish is necessary for the instruction of the poor Irish Catholics' (Walsh 1973: 4). Irish was becoming recognizably the

---

[13] For a discussion of archaic features in forms of Hiberno-Irish, see Bliss 1979 and Braidwood 1964.

language of the poor, English was the language used by the powerful, the aspirant, and those, as William Petty had predicted in 1691, who simply wanted to protect their own interests (bilingualism was necessary for anti-tithe and rent agitators from the 1760s on). The process was hastened by the promise of material advancement, occasionally in immediate terms, as Arthur Young noted in his *A Tour in Ireland* (1780): 'Lord Shannon's bounties to labourers amount to 50l a year. He gives it to them by way of encouragement; but only to such as can speak English, and do something more than fill a cart' (Young 1780: vol.2, 50).

It was of course not just the Irish 'brogue' which was attacked in the eighteenth century since many impugned the native language too; Nicholson described it as 'that barbarous language (so intimately fraught with cursing and swearing and all vile profaneness)' (Nicholson 1715: 27). Typically it was Swift who launched the harshest rhetorical on-slaught: in an advertisement in a Dublin newspaper of Irish lands for rent or sale, he discovered 'near a hundred words together, which I defy any creature in human shape, except an Irishman of the savage kind, to pronounce'. How, he asked, could a gentleman reproduce 'such odious sounds from the mouth, the throat and the nose … without dislocating every muscle that is used in speaking'? His counsel was to eradicate the language, since nothing 'hath more contributed to prevent the Irish from being tamed, than this encouragement of their language, which might easily be abolished, and become a dead one in half an age, with little expence, and less trouble' (Swift 1973: 81). Whether this anti-Irish diatribe wholly reflects Swift's views is, however, debatable since he has been credited with the translation of the Irish 'Pléaráca na Ruarcach' (The Description of an Irish Feast), probably with the help of Anthony Raymond (Cronin 1996: 125).

The form of Gaelic in a different sense was also a concern to the Protestant Bishop of Down and Connor, Francis Hutchinson, in his *Tegasg Kreesdee. A Kristian Katekism* (usually catalogued as *The Church Catechism in Irish*) (1722). He pointed to the difficulty of Gaelic characters ('awkward, and of an ill Figure'), the fact that there are fewer letters than in English, and the problem caused by the obscure relations between Gaelic orthography and Irish pronunciation (though for an English-speaker this is an odd charge to raise). His example was: '*ionfhoghomtha* to *be learned*, which is spoken only *inomota*; fourteen letters, and seven of them Quiescents' (Hutchinson 1722: n.p.). For Hutchinson the source of these problems was sinister: the less intelligible the language was, 'the better is answer'd the Ends of those who were Masters of it...the Popish Priests kept the Laity in Subjection to 'em, by means of their Ignorance and the Obscurity of their Language') (Hutchinson 1722: n.p.). Bishop Gallagher, one of the few Catholics to appear in print in Irish in the eighteenth century, concurred, at least in regard to the problems caused by Gaelic script and orthography. His *Sixteen Sermons in an Easy and Familiar Style on Useful and Necessary Subjects* (1736) (which achieved fourteen editions by 1820) was printed in Roman type, with simplified spelling which attempted to approximate more 'to the present manner of speaking, than to the true and ancient orthography' (Gallagher 1736: iv). Such revision was to become an important ideological issue for nineteenth- and twentieth-century language revivalists.[14]

In his proposal to convert the Catholic Irish, Richardson described Gaelic as 'not the Language of the Court, but of a poor, ignorant and depressed people, from whom we can have no Expectations' (Richardson 1711: 119). Yet though the Gaelic-speaking population may have been oppressed by the state, and though they were mostly poor, they cannot be said to have been wholly ignorant or unproductive. Despite the fact that there was little Irish literature printed in the period, it was, paradoxically, a time of enormous scribal activity; there are four thousand Irish manuscripts extant from the eighteenth and nineteenth centuries compared with around a hundred from the sixteenth, and two hundred and fifty from the seventeenth centuries (Ó Cuív 1986: 391). Chief amongst the poets was Ó Rathaille, some of whose work was discussed earlier, but the hereditary and professional poets of the bardic order were displaced in the eighteenth century by non-professionals whose main employment was as farmers, teachers, priests, and innkeepers. Though it became to a great extent the poetry of the dispossessed, and though it no longer conformed to the thousand-year-old conventions of syllabic metrics, using instead accentual verse, it was a rich and fertile popular tradition in its own right. Indeed one commentator has argued that eighteenth-century Gaelic Ireland was a place and time of 'extraordinary cultural growth rather than of decay' (Ó Tuama 1995: 132). According to this view, though economically impoverished, the native culture gained from the loosening of the traditional

---

[14] Ó Cuív (1969*b*) offers a history of the character of Irish; the political significance of 'the Irish character in print' is assessed by Deane 1998: 100–9.

authoritative restrictions in political, moral, and social affairs, which in turn issued in the development of new literary and cultural modes.

Gaelic scholarship did of course suffer from the effects of the Penal Code in the early eighteenth century. Thady Roddy, friend of Roderic O'Flaherty, the author of the influential history of Ireland *Ogygia, seu Rerum Hibernicarum Chronologia* (1685), bemoaned in 1700 the fact that his collection of books in Irish, on topics ranging from genealogy to mathematics, was becoming redundant. Although within the past twenty years there had been a limited group of native readers who could read and understand them, now, he declared, there were few remaining

absolutely perfect in all them books, by reason that they lost the estates they had to uphold their publique teaching, and that the nobility of the Irish line, who would encourage and support their posterity, lost all their estates too, so that the antiquaryes posterity were forced to follow husbandry, etc., to get their bread, for want of patrons to support them (Breatnach 1961: 129).

Despite the damage which was caused by the destruction of the patronage system, however, the Gaelic tradition survived, though in different forms. And the recognition of the significance of Gaelic material for the discovery and preservation of Irish history grew throughout the period. Lhuyd, who purchased most of O'Flaherty's library (Edmund Burke later arranged in turn for Lhuyd's library to be deposited at Trinity), defended his work on the Irish language in the *Archaeologia* on the basis that 'the Old and Ancient Languages are the Keys that open the Way to the Knowledge of Antiquity' (Nicolson 1724: 192). Native writers were also aware of the need for antiquarian-type research, not least in the group of writers gathered in the dámh-scoil headed by Seán Ó Neachtain in Dublin in the first few decades of the century. Tadhg Ó Neachtain, son of the principal, complained that 'now there are none of the nobles of the Gaelic race who do not repudiate their language, selling their names and the grandeur of (their ancestor) Gaoidheal Glas' (Breatnach 1961: 131). Notwithstanding this impediment, these scholars produced important work, including the first English translation of Céitinn's *Foras Feasa ar Éirinn*, poetry (including Jacobite verse) and texts on geography, grammar, and lexicography.

One of the most important of these scholars was Aodh Buidhe MacCruitín, whose work was mentioned earlier. He was a contributor to a debate about the Irish language which was to run for a century or

more and which was concerned with its unique characteristics in contrast to those of other languages. In a sense this was an Irish version of
the literary arguments in late sixteenth-century England which centred
on the relative merits of the classical languages versus the English
vernacular. But it was also very much an eighteenth-century debate,
one in which, as in this example from an English text, particular
languages were ascribed distinct characteristics which coincide with
the national character:

The Italian is pleasant, but without sinews, like a still fleeting water; the French
delicate, but even nice as a woman scarce daring to open her lips for fear of
spoiling her countenance; the Spanish is majestical, but runs too much on the *o*,
and is therefore very gutteral and not very pleasant; the Dutch manlike, but
withal very harsh, as one ready at every word to pick a quarrel (Peyton 1771: 29).

In this case, needless to say, all are found wanting compared to English,
which takes the good qualities from all of them and leaves 'the dregs to
themselves'. In the Irish versions of this exercise in the linguistic
construction of national identity, the characteristics of Gaelic were
either praised or deprecated depending on the point of view of the
commentator. Petty argued that Irish, since it had not been the language
of a flourishing empire (compared with Greece, Rome, and presumably
England) 'hath but few words' of its own and had borrowed mostly
from its conquerors (Petty 1691: 106). Ó Beaglaoich and MacCruitín
(Begly and MacCurtin) contradicted him by stating that 'of all the living
and dead languages none is more copious and elegant in the expression,
nor is any more harmonious and musical in the Pronunciation than the
IRISH' (Begly and MacCurtin 1732: i). Later in the century, as antiquarian confidence increased, the claims were repeated. Colonel Vallancey
declared Irish 'masculine and nervous; harmonious in its articulation;
copious in its phraseology; and replete with those abstract and technical
terms, which no civilised people can want'; 'free from anomalies,
sterility and heteroclite redundancies . . . it is rich and melodious; it is
precise and copious' (Vallancey 1773: i–ii). And in an important assertion which again reflects the developing assurance of both a cultural and
political class, the Gaelic language was proclaimed to be in some
ways superior to English. A proposal for an Irish language society in
Dublin in 1752 noted that 'the mother tongue of this nation, has been
long neglected and discouraged by the introduction of strange languages
not so full or expressive' (Ó Cuív 1986: 415). More significantly,

in her innovative and important collection *Reliques of Irish Poetry* (1789) Charlotte Brooke drew attention to the difficulty of translating between the lexical variety of Irish and a more restricted vocabulary in English:

I am aware that in the following poems there will sometimes be found a sameness, and repetition of thought, appearing but too plainly in the English version, though scarcely perceivable in the original Irish, so great is the variety as well as the beauty peculiar to that language (Brooke 1789: v–vi).

The difficulty arose from the inability of translation to do justice to the qualities and potential embodied in Gaelic:

It is really astonishing of what various and comprehensive powers this neglected language is possessed. In the pathetic, it breathes the most beautiful and affecting simplicity; and in the bolder species of composition, it is distinguished by a force of expression, a sublime dignity, and rapid energy, which it is scarcely possible for any translation fully to convey; as it sometimes fills the mind with ideas altogether new, and which, perhaps, no modern language is entirely prepared to express (Brooke 1789: v–vi).

The problem was particularly acute with English, since 'one compound epithet must often be translated by two lines of English verse, and, on such occasions, much of the beauty is necessarily lost'. It is significant that although Brooke's avowed intention was to introduce the 'British muse' to her 'elder sister in this isle', it is clear from her remarks that the languages in which these muses are articulated inhabit distinct cultural ranks and needed, as part of a larger cultural and political project, to be reconciled (Brooke 1789: viii).

Copiousness was one defining criterion of Gaelic, others were its age and purity; all three were used in implicit appeals for recognition of the authenticity of Irish identity. In his *Vindication of the Antiquity of Ireland* (1717) MacCruitín attacked Cox's accusation that 'Irish is a Mixture of other Languages' by asserting that anyone who reads the proper historical authorities will 'find sufficient reasons to believe that the Scythian language (and consequently the Irish which is no other but the same) is one of the Antientest in the World' (MacCruitín 1717: xiii). A little later in the century Charles O'Conor, an Irish Catholic, was a crucial and highly successful figure in the promotion of the knowledge of Gaelic culture and civilization among the Anglo-Irish literati. Though not a language revivalist, O'Conor defended the antiquarian significance of Irish in grand terms as a 'Language near as old as the Deluge' and 'the *most original* and UNMIXT Language yet remaining in any part of *Europe*. Thus he argued, 'Our Language is the most original Dialect of the Language of Japhet, and that from which the *Grecians* and *Latins* borrowed more than from any other in the world; it ought, one should think, to engage the attention, or rather care, of this learned Age' (O'Conor 1753: 51). The purity of the language was an important issue politically since it was deemed to reflect on the nation, especially if the language could be shown to have Biblical origins.[15] If the language, and by corollary the culture, could be seen to have retained its integrity, then despite the vicissitudes of political history the essence of Irish identity could also be argued to have survived. This is in effect an early example of a standard reflex of cultural nationalism, though it is one which is based on a misunderstanding of linguistic and cultural contact and exchange, a mistake which informs attempts such as the late nineteenth-century Irish attempts to avoid 'béarlachas' (Anglicisms), or twentieth-century efforts in England to disallow 'Americanisms', or the Académie Française's regulations to outlaw foreign expressions in French. In Ireland the claim for linguistic purity was essentially a denial of the multi-cultural aspects of its history to which the lexicon itself bore witness. Irish derived words from (to cite a few illustrative examples) Latin: 'leabhar' (liber, book), 'eaglais' (ecclesia, church), 'scríobh' (scribo, to write), 'Domhnach' (Dominus, Sunday), 'mallacht' (maledictio, curse) 'cistin' (culina, kitchen); from Old Norse: 'margadh' (markaðr, market), 'beoir' (bjórr, beer) fuinneog (vindauga, window); and from the Norman-French: 'dinnéar (diner, dinner), 'garsún' (garson, boy), 'seomra' (chaumbre, room) 'áirse' (arche, arch), and contae (cuntee, county). Later borrowing from English was unsurprisingly heavy, as the language developed to meet the changes of history, but the process was not unilateral: Irish gave English a few, but not many, items such as 'gob' (as well as 'gobshite'), 'cack', 'shebeen', 'galore', 'whiskey', 'slogan', and 'shanty' as well as 'Tory'. But the claims for linguistic and cultural purity are instructive generally: they usually appear, as in eighteenth-century Ireland, when other issues are at stake. It is this perhaps which explains Daniel Thomas' rejection in his *Observations* (1787) of proposals to eradicate Irish on the grounds of its merits compared to those of the English language:

---

[15] See Kidd 1999: chapter two, for an account of the Mosaic foundations of early modern European identity and the role of claims for the antiquity of vernacular languages.

What, shall a language confessedly derived from one of the first tongues which subsisted among polished nations, be abolished, merely to make room for another compounded of all the barbarous dialects which imperfectly communicated the thoughts of savages to each other? (Thomas 1787: 23).[16]

Assertions of the great old age of the language were also indirect claims about the status of the Irish nation. Of course this is not to say that Gaelic is not in fact a language of considerable antiquity, but that such statements need to be placed in their historical and ideological context in order to comprehend their significance. In *Focalóir Gaoidhilge-Sax-Bhéarla, Or, An Irish-English Dictionary* (1768), Archbishop O'Brien proclaimed Irish to be 'the most ancient and best preserved Dialect of the old Celtic tongue of the Gauls and the Celtiberians' and 'the primitive Celtic' itself 'the first universal language of all Europe' (O'Brien 1768: i–ii), claims which were characteristically bold in an era just prior to the first great discoveries of systematic comparative philology. There were other declarations, however, which were clearly marked by the context of their production. Swift had offered a satire upon the use of etymology as historical evidence in his 'Discourse to Prove the Antiquity of the English Tongue' in which he seeks to 'make manifest to all impartial readers, that our language, as we now speak it, was originally the same with those of the Jews, the Greeks and the Romans' (Swift 1973: 232). His examples include the Latin 'turpis', nasty or filthy, which is clearly a syncopated English word with one letter removed in order 'to prevent the jarring of three consonants together' (turd piss); the name of the philosopher Aristotle, which derived from the fact that 'when the lads were come, he would *arise to tell* them what he thought proper'; and the Hebraic name Isaac, which 'is nothing else but *Eyes ake*; because the Talmudists report that he had a pain in the eyes'. But the ridicule did not prevent General Charles Vallancey, a tireless worker among the Anglo-Irish for Gaelic research, from producing writings which were highly speculative and often extraordinary.[17] Basing his work on earlier Irish

[16] Such a claim contrasts with Moryson's defence of the hybridity of English in the early seventeenth century: 'they are confuted, who traduce the English tounge to be like a beggars patched Cloke, which they should rather compayre to a Posey of sweetest flowers' (Moryson 1617: 437). Stanihurst on the other hand praised the pristine English spoken in Ireland against the fire-new English of England (see Chapter two, note 10).

[17] Vallancey, raised in England of Huguenot parentage, was a military engineer who became Engineer in Ordinary in Ireland; his brief was the colonial fortification of Ireland (his work included reviews of Charles Fort in Kinsale and the Cork harbour defences, and the building of Queen's Bridge—now Mellows Bridge—in Dublin). His cartographic endeavours led him to antiquarianism.

accounts which were modelled on the Biblical story and the dominant Scytho-Celtic paradigm of linguistic history, Vallancey argued in his *Essay on the Antiquity of the Irish Language* that the Irish

received the Use of *Letters* directly from the *Phoenecians*, and the Concurrence of them all in affirming that several Colonies from *Africa* settled in Ireland, induced the Author of the following Essay, who had made the ancient and modern Language of *Ireland* his peculiar study for some years past; to compare the *Phoenecian Dialect* or *bearla feni* of the Irish with the *Punic* or Language of the *Carthaginians* (Vallancey 1772: vii).

Despite being sensitive to 'the ridiculous light most Etymologists are held in', Vallancey's confidence in the historical longevity of Irish led him to a comparative study of 'the old Iberno-Celtic, and the dialects spoken on the vast continent of North America':

| **Algonkin** | | **Irish** |
|---|---|---|
| *bi laoua* | it is charming | *bi luaig'* ( *g* not pron.) |
| *kak ina* | every thing | *cac' eini* |
| *kak eli* | all | *cac' uile* |
| *na biush malatat* | it is not worth bartering | *na bi fiu she malarta* |
| *ta koucim* | come hither | *tar c'uigim* |
| *ma unia* | assist me | *me uait'nig'e* (pro. *uani*) |
| (Vallancey 1773: iv). | | |

Vallancey had little Irish and less comparative philology, but the significance of his work was not its accuracy but the energetic endeavour with which it was undertaken, and the contribution it made to the stimulation of interest in Gaelic language and civilization more generally (his linguistic theories appear to have convinced Charles O'Conor, for example) (Sheehan 1953: 233).

In fact Vallancey's interest was an instance of a more general and important movement which began in earnest in the eighteenth century and which grew into one of the most significant and determining forces in nineteenth- and twentieth-century Irish history: Irish cultural nationalism, in which the Irish language had a central role. As noted in Chapter three, Moryson had commented on the role of language in the formation of national identity in the early seventeenth century, and in Ó Beaglaoich and MacCruitín's *English-Irish Dictionary. An Focloir Bearla Gaoidheilge* (1732) 'language' was simply defined as 'teangadh tíre' (tongue of the country). Vallancey reiterated the claim in his simple assertion that 'a nation and a language are both of an age' (Vallancey 1773: xiv). He also argued that in cases such as that of the Irish,

> the language itself, is a species of historical inscription, more ancient and more authentic also, as far as it goes, than any precarious hearsay of old foreign writers, strangers in general, to the natural, as well as civil history of the remote countries they describe (Vallancey 1773: i).

Some early eighteenth-century Irish commentators acknowledged this point and it led them to express their concern that the Irish language had been neglected by the Irish themselves to the considerable detriment of their national history and identity. Ó Beaglaoich and MacCruitín complained that the fact that the Irish

> can so strangely neglect cultivating and improving a language of some Thousands of Years standing may seem surprising to all learned foreigners, and I believe will do so to the Irish themselves, when they recover out of their Error, and take a little time to consider how much they deviate, in this particular, from the Practice and Policy of their Ancestors, and how inexcusable they are for neglecting so sacred a Depository of the Heroic Achievements of their Country (Begly and MacCurtin 1732: i–ii).

Ó Beaglaoich and MacCruitín specifically criticized the Irish gentry, while in *An Teagasg Críosduidhe / The Catechism or Christian Doctrine* (1742) Donlevy asserted that it would be a discredit to the nation 'to let such a Language go to wrack, and to give no Encouragement, not even the Necessaries of life, to some of the Few, who still remain, and are capable to rescue those *venerable Monuments of Antiquity* from the profound obscurity, they are buried in' (Donlevy 1742: 507). Others saw the issue as not so much one of self-neglect by the Irish but as more of a determined attack by hostile forces on the language and therefore the nation. An unlikely source of such sentiment was the Protestant proselytizer Richardson in his proposal to use Gaelic for the conversion of the Irish Catholics in 1712: 'Difference of Language being generally a Sign of Difference of nation, [an] Attempt against a Language, will look like a Design against the Nation that speaks it' (Richardson 1711: 111). The theme was take up late in the century in Daniel Thomas's *Observations* in a scarcely coded warning to the Bishop of Cloyne as to the dangers of attempting to abolish Irish:

> Be so good to consider, what is the distinctive mark of natives of different countries? What but language. Any design therefore to destroy the vernacular

tongue, is an attempt to annihilate the nation, and let your Lordship well weigh, whether the mouths which you now wish to close, may not soon open with harsh thunder in your ears (Thomas 1787: 28).

Perhaps the clearest statement of the relationship between language and national identity, and one which was to become familiar both in its tone and content in the following centuries, came in Donlevy's appeal in favour of Gaelic in the mid century. It is no wonder, he argued, that Irish,

a *Language* of neither Court, nor City, nor Bar, nor Business, ever since the Beginning of *King James* the *First's* reign, should have suffered vast Alterations and Corruptions; and be now on the Brink of utter Decay, as it really is, to the great Dishonour and Shame of the *Natives*, who shall pass everywhere for *Irish-Men*. Although *Irish-Men* without *Irish* is an incongruity, and a great Bull (Donlevy 1742: 506–7).

There are a number of important points made by these writers: that Irish is not the language of power; that it is now corrupt and in danger; that the neglect of the language is both the fault of the Irish themselves and the result of colonial hostility to it; that Gaelic is the sine qua non of Irish identity. This last claim, that '*Irish-Men* without *Irish* is an incongruity, and a great Bull', was to become central in later debates since the clear supposition is that Irishness is simply not possible (in the present or future) without the Irish language. In its absence people may pass as Irish, but they will not in essence be Irish. This was a belief which was to be asserted often and was to prove highly contentious; in the twentieth century some argued that it damaged the cause of the language.

# CHAPTER FIVE

# Culture, politics, and the language question, 1789–1876

'Wherever a separate language is found, there a separate nation exists'

Fichte, *Addresses to the German People*, 1808.

Charlotte Brooke's *Reliques of Irish Poetry* (1789), a collection of Gaelic poetry and translations, had the dual aesthetic and political intention of encouraging 'a cordial union between two countries that seem formed by nature to be joined by every bond of interest, and of amity' (Brooke 1789: viii). Mutual recognition of the Irish and British poetical traditions, she proposed, could have an important historical role in bringing Britain 'to cultivate a nearer acquaintance with her neighbouring isle'. Tacitly pointing to the historical tensions which existed between the patriot politicians in Ireland and the British parliament, Brooke stressed the need for Britain to recognize the legitimacy of Anglo-Irish identity. The eirenic muses were to 'conciliate for us her esteem, that the portion of her blood which flows in our veins is rather ennobled than disgraced by the mingling tides that descended from our heroic ancestors' (Brooke 1789: viii). The unifying function of the Irish language in particular within Ireland was promoted in the United Irishmen's newspaper *The Northern Star* in 1795. Patrick Lynch's Irish classes at the Belfast Academy were advertised as 'particularly interesting to all those who wish for the improvement and Union of this neglected and divided kingdom'. By learning Irish students could 'more easily and effectively communicate our sentiments and instructions to our Countrymen; and thus mutually improve and conciliate each other's affections' (Ó Snodaigh 1995: 63).

Communication and cultural contact are also the purpose of inter-lingual dictionaries and phrasebooks, and a good example is Muiris Ó Gormáin's 'English-Irish Phrasebook' (dated around 1770). The guide covers a whole range of social activities, including '*To thank and shew a kindness/carrthanacht do thaisbeanadh*', '*A discourse between two/Comradh eidir dís*', and '*To breakfast/na cíallanna bhriseadh*'. One section gives advice on translation pertinent to a more corporeal version of cordial union than that envisaged by Brooke:

> *the bed is narrow* / *ta an leaba cumhann*
> *the bed is wide enough* / *ta an leaba farsainn go leór*
> *you pull the clothes* / *ta tu tarraing anéadaigh*
> *you have got my pillow* / *bhfuair tu mo philiúr* (sic)
> *lay your head on the bolster* / *leag do cheann air a philiúr*
> *give me the chamber pot* / *tóir a pota seómra dhamh*
> *where is the chamber pot* / *ca bhfuil a pota*
> *there is no such thing* / *niel a léit ann*
> *I cannot sleep* / *cha dtig liom colladh*
> (McCaughey 1968: 205).

Ó Gormáin worked as a scribe for Charles O'Conor, who collaborated with the Chevalier O'Gorman (no relation) in the latter's projected history of Clare; O'Gorman employed Ó Gormáin to copy Irish manuscripts. O'Gorman introduced O'Conor, through the offices of Vallancey, to Colonel Burton (later Baron Conygham), a member of the Anglo-Irish Ascendancy who was interested in the preservation of Irish manuscripts and records and who became one of the founders of the Royal Irish Academy. Another academician, J. C. Walker, member of the first elected council and the committee of antiquities, was also a friend of O'Conor; Walker's *Historical Memoirs of the Irish Bards* (1786) was an important text in the awakening of Anglo-Irish interest in the Gaelic tradition. O'Conor helped Brooke with the *Reliques*; Brooke worked with Patrick Lynch in editing *Bolg an tSolair* (published in Belfast in 1795). Lynch's guide to self-instruction in Irish in *Bolg an tSolair* borrowed heavily from Ó Gormáin's phrasebook ... (Sheehan 1953).[1] All of which is intended to illustrate that in the late eighteenth century in Ireland, members of the two worlds of the Catholic Gaelic tradition and that of the Protestant Ascendancy were meeting and collaborating on the fertile ground of Irish antiquarianism. It was in many ways an awkward coalition and certainly one which was historically ironic,

---

[1] Lynch and Brooke collaborated on *Bolg an tSolair* (1795) which contained Lynch's Irish grammar, vocabulary, and familiar dialogues.

a fact not lost on some of the Gaelic contributors to it. In 1781 O'Gorman wrote to O'Conor, telling him Conygham had indicated that he hoped Oxford University would send its collection of Irish manuscripts to Trinity College Dublin. His wry comment was: 'in short, I found the Col. still animated with the most warm zeal for the antiquities of his Country. It must indeed be very pleasing to us old Irish to see such a Spirit at present diffused among our very late oppressors' (Sheehan 1953: 227).

One impetus for the great growth of interest in Irish antiquarianism was the more general 'Celtic Revival' in Britain, prompted initially at least by two literary events: the publication of Gray's 'The Bard' (1757) and MacPherson's fraudulent *Fragments of Ancient Poetry Collected in the Highlands of Scotland and translated from the Gaelic or Erse Language* (1760). Gray's poem was based on an inaccurate account of a massacre of Welsh poets by Edward I; MacPherson's versions of the Ossianic epic claimed that the Scottish literary tradition was older than the Irish (including the assertion that the ancient Fenian cycle was of Scottish origin) (Cronin 1996: 98). The work of both writers contributed to a widespread stirring of nationalist sentiment in Ireland, but in a form which was historically novel (as O'Gorman's comment indicates). For the concern with native historical and cultural traditions in the late eighteenth century was not led, as might be expected, by the gradually emergent Catholic middle class, but by members of the Protestant Ascendancy. And it was part of a larger political agenda for the ruling class in Ireland, since although it had been furnished with its own parliament since 1692, it was involved in an ongoing struggle against the supremacy of the Westminster parliament (especially after the Declaratory Act of 1720). The Octennial Act of 1762, the granting of Free Trade in 1779, and the legislative independence of the Irish parliament after 1782 all bore witness to the growing political alienation of the Ascendancy from their British counterparts and to a sense of their own distinctive cultural identity. Their 'discovery' of Gaelic literature was part of that process.[2]

[2]  Kidd makes the curious claim that 'eighteenth-century Protestant Gaelicism was not only of marginal political importance, it was also short-lived'. This seems a serious underestimation of the political significance of cultural activities which focused on the distinction between the British and the Anglo-Irish, particularly before 1798. The claim appears to be undermined by the assertion that far from being extinct, Protestant Gaelicism flourished anew between 1830 and 1848, and again from the 1890s and was 'influential in the formation of modern Irish nationalism' (Kidd 1999: 176–7). One of the aims of this and the previous chapter is to

If the political success of the Patriot party, under Grattan's famous slogan, 'Ireland is now a nation!... She is no longer a wretched colony', marks one aspect of this historical movement, then the foundation of The Royal Irish Academy signifies its cultural consolidation. The academy was founded in 1785 and granted its royal charter in 1786, and its membership was principally composed of politicians, members of the judiciary, the clergy, the gentry, and academics. The preface to volume one of the academy's Transactions (1787) put forward its intellectual self-justification and its agenda for the future of Ireland:

> Whatever therefore tends, by the cultivation of useful arts and sciences, to improve and facilitate its manufactures; whatever tends, by the elegance of polite literature, to civilise the manners and refine the taste of its people; whatever tends to awaken a spirit of literary ambition, by keeping alive the memory of its antient repuation for learning, cannot but prove of the greatest national advantage. To a wish to promote in these important respects the advancement of knowledge in this kingdom, the Royal Irish Academy for Science, Polite Literature and Antiquities, owes its establishment (Breatnach 1956: 89–90).

Though the academy's focus was intended to be science, polite literature, and antiquities, in practice the concerns of its members ranged across the field of what would today be described as Irish studies. With regard to language work, it is important to note that the academy led the way in not seeking to study Gaelic as a living language, despite the fact that around half of the population spoke the tongue, but as the medium of the nation's historical records.[3] Though this may appear a peculiar stance in one sense, it is understandable in its historical context. The fact was that the study of the nation's achievements in the past could be a cause of historical pride and cultural identification in the present, but it could also be an activity with potentially dangerous political implications, especially after the failed rebellion of the United Irishmen in 1798. It was for this reason that several of the societies formed to foster Irish antiquarianism held firmly to a neutral line on political questions; the Gaelic Society of Dublin (founded in 1807) ordained in its principles

---

demonstrate that the linguistic component of modern Irish nationalism began to develop at least as far back as the eighteenth century, and that Anglo-Irish antiquarian interest was an important stage in that process. For a helpful analysis of this period see 'The Development of an Irish Self-Image in the Eighteenth Century' (Leerssen 1996: 294–376).

[3] For a summary of the information on the extent to which Irish was spoken from the beginning of the nineteenth century, see Ó Cuív 1951: 77–94.

that 'no religious or political Debates whatever shall be permitted, such being foreign to the Object and Principles of the Society' (Gaelic Society 1808: xvii). Societies such as the Iberno-Celtic Society (1818), the Ulster Gaelic Society (1828), the Irish Archaeological Society (1840), the Celtic Society (1845), and the Ossianic Society (1853) either had such a rule or simply ignored political issues (Cronin 1996: 132).

It is perhaps this tension between culture and politics which explains the apparently odd positions of many of the leading political figures of the late eighteenth and early nineteenth centuries on the language question.[4] Henry Flood, patriot leader and staunch opponent of political rights for Catholics, left his estate and wealth in his will (1795) to Trinity College in order that,

they do institute 'as a perpetual establishment, *a professor of and for the native Irish or Erse language*', and that they do appoint, if he shall then be living, Colonel Charles Vallancey to be the first professor thereof ... seeing that by his eminent and successful labours in the study and recovery of that language, he well deserves to be so appointed; [and] to *the purchase of all printed books and manuscripts in the said native Irish or Erse language*, wheresoever to be obtained (Barron 1835a: V, 159).

His cousin, evidently preferring domestic to national priorities, mounted a successful legal challenge to the bequest on behalf of the family. Among the leaders of the United Irishmen, Theobald Wolfe Tone was unconcerned with the language, while others such as Lord Edward Fitzgerald, Thomas Russell, Dr William Drennan, and Robert Emmet seem to have made some, albeit minimal, efforts to learn Irish (Ó Fiaich 1969: 108). One of their political enemies, the most famous of the protestant patriots, opponent of the Acts of Union (1800), and supporter of Catholic Emancipation, Henry Grattan, also had a clear view of what the future relations between Gaelic and English should be. In a letter to the Secretary to the Board of Education in 1812, Grattan, sitting as a Whig MP at Westminster, argued that the curriculum of the Board's Parish Schools in Ireland should be a standardized 'study of the English tongue, reading, writing and arithmetic' along with horticulture, agriculture, and 'treatises on the care and knowledge of trees'. Christianity, he argued, should be taught, but not denominationally, since the 'one great

---

[4] The conflict between cultural and political nationalism is a constant theme from the end of the eighteenth century to the present. Once the genie of cultural nationalism had escaped, one of political nationalism's recurrent tasks was to find ways of mastering its enormous potential.

object of national education should be to unite the inhabitants of this island'; for this reason too English rather than Irish should be the medium of instruction (Grattan 1812: 336). Indeed, as he saw acutely, the two subjects of study were closely linked, at least in terms of their potential political effects:

I should be very sorry that the Irish language should be forgotten; but glad that the English language should be generally understood; to obtain that end in Ireland, it is necessary that the schools formed on a national plan of education, which teach the English language, should not attempt to teach the Protestant religion, because the Catholics who would resort to learn the one, will keep aloof if we attempt to make them proselytes to the other (Grattan 1812: 336).

If the issues of language teaching and denominational religious instruction were confused, Grattan concluded, the effect would be the neglect of 'one great means of uniting our people' and the further sundering of the Irish: 'we should continue to add to the imaginary *political* division, supposed to exist in a difference of religion, a real political division formed on the diversity of language'(Grattan 1812: 336).

One major Irish political figure who was of necessity keenly aware of the real cultural and political divisions of early nineteenth-century Ireland was Daniel O'Connell, the century's most successful Catholic political nationalist leader. His position on the language question was perhaps the most apparently peculiar of all. O'Connell had impressive credentials as a potential proponent of cultural as well as political nationalism. His aunt, Eibhlín Dubh Ní Chonaill, was the author of the famous *Caoineadh Airt Uí Laoghaire* (The Keen for Art O'Leary), while O'Connell himself was a native Irish speaker. Despite this, however, O'Connell achieved fame solely in the political rather than the cultural arena as leader of the movement for Catholic Emancipation and later the campaign for the Repeal of the Union. Indeed his attitude to Gaelic signalled a division which was to separate political from cultural nationalism throughout the nineteenth century until its last decades. His personal stance appears to have been pragmatic in practice. For example, in 1832 he defended Jeremiah O'Connor, who had been imprisoned for making an anti-tithe speech in Gaelic. O'Connell forced the policeman testifying against O'Connor to use the Irish language, but this is likely simply to have been a tactic in order to embarrass the legal and political authorities. His clearest statement on the issue was given in a report on his attitudes in 1833:

Someone asked him whether the use of the Irish language was diminishing among our peasantry. 'Yes,' he answered, 'and I am sufficiently utilitarian not to regret its gradual abandonment. A diversity of languages is no benefit; it was first imposed on mankind as a curse, at the building of Babel. It would be of vast advantage to mankind if all the inhabitants spoke the same language' (Daunt 1848: 14).

Reflecting on the consequences of this view he continued:

'Therefore, although the Irish language is connected with many recollections that twine around the hearts of Irishmen, yet the superior utility of the English tongue, as the medium of modern communication, is so great, that I can witness without a sigh the gradual disuse of the Irish' (Daunt 1848: 14–15).

When a manuscript Irish-English dictionary by his uncle, Peter O'Connell, was presented to him, he rejected it. The Gaelic scholar Eugene O'Curry recorded that 'Mr O'Connell had no taste for matters of this kind, and he suddenly dismissed his namesake, telling him that his uncle was an old fool to have spent so much of his life on so useless a work' (Cronin 1996: 116). Despite notable exceptions such as the contradictory figure of the Clare M. P. William Smith O'Brien, such a derogatory attitude was not unusual among political nationalists since they tended to see the language question as a side issue, if not an actual hindrance to the cause.

   This is a remarkable point on which to reflect given that what was being dismissed by nationalist politicians was the everyday language of a great many among their core constituency. It may be instructive, when attempting to comprehend the strangeness of the situation, to imagine a scene at one of O'Connell's 'monster meetings': thousands amongst the multitude gathered to hear him would have listened to him speak of their political rights to self-determination in a language which they understood but poorly. And the Dublin and London journalists (and the government's spies) would have had prime positions at the front in order to record his message in the English language and to pass it on in the same medium.[5] It might properly be asked of such a situation: who precisely was the audience here and who was excluded? With O'Connell in particular the key to his attitude lies not in his response to Irish as a vehicle of the Irish past, which he acknowledges, but in his view of

---

[5] O'Connell made two speeches in Irish at local meetings; at the Tralee meeting 'the reporters from the London papers were ludicrously puzzled, sitting poised and understanding not a word' (Reynolds 1954: 171).

English as simply politically useful as a 'medium of modern communication'. O'Connell subscribed to the political philosophy of utilitarianism and in his view the English language, at the dawn of the age of mass communications, meant access to specific, useful forms of modernity. It signified inclusion within a larger world in which the crucial political, social, and economic decisions were made. In a sense O'Connell's position was the logical conclusion of the advice given by the colonialist Sir William Petty to the Gaelic Irish in 1691, as noted earlier. To recognize the political utility of the choice of English was O'Connell's achievement; his failure to acknowledge the cultural consequences of the choice was either a notable oversight or a calculated decision.

If the political wing of Irish nationalism paid scant attention to the language, then the cultural nationalist wing was of course far more concerned with it. Indeed to a great extent the language issue was the defining question for cultural nationalists. James Hardiman's *Irish Minstrelsy, or Bardic Remains of Ireland* (1831), for example, was an important anthology of Irish poetry ranging from the ancient to the contemporary. In it he asserted that from the reign of Henry VIII, 'the English rulers were bent upon the total annihilation of our national language' (Hardiman 1831: 1, xxix). Bent on the destruction of the Irish, 'the revilers of the people have not spared even their speech' and under the Penal Code,

The inquisitors of the Irish parliament denounced [Gaelic] as the dialect of that phantom of political frenzy, popery. According to a favourite model of native reasoning, it was resolved to reduce the poor Catholics to a state of mental darkness, in order to convert them into enlightened protestants. A thick cloud of ignorance soon overspread the land; and the language of millions ceased to be a medium of written communication... (Hardiman 1831: 1, xxxii–iii).

Such sentiments outraged Sir Samuel Ferguson who expressed his antagonism to Hardiman in a series of articles for the *Dublin University Magazine* in 1834. Accusing Hardiman of political treachery by way of literary translation, Ferguson's own attempts at the translation of Irish poetry attempted to convey in the English language the 'savage sincerity' (Ferguson 1834: 154) of the original texts. Ferguson's work was later influential at the beginning of the Gaelic Revival, particularly for Yeats, but the antagonism between Hardiman's espousal of the centrality of the Irish language to a conception of Irish nationality and Ferguson's belief that such nationality could be expressed in English, was a forerunner of later divisive debates.

The outstanding figure in the cultural nationalist movement, at least before the end of the century, was Thomas Davis, a literary friend of Ferguson and a Protestant middle-class supporter of O'Connell who eventually came to disagree with him over Repeal. Davis was the lead figure amongst the Young Irelanders, a group of radical nationalists gathered around the influential journal *The Nation*. He was influenced by the tenets of European cultural nationalism, a movement which had its philosophical basis in German romanticism and which, among other central beliefs, fixed upon language as the key to understanding human history.[6] Though it appeared in various European locations, some of which, such as Poland, Hungary, and Italy, were to emerge as nations under the influence of the political movements which it inspired, its base was Germany (or the lands which were later to become Germany). Philosophers working in the post-Kantian tradition of German romantic thought argued for the centrality of language to our sense of the past. Schlegel described language in general as 'the storehouse of tradition where it lives on from nation to nation' and took it to be 'the clue of material and spiritual connexion which joins century to century—the common memory of the human race' (Schlegel 1847: 407).[7] By corollary it was but a short step to arguing that what was true of language in general must also be true of particular languages: since language itself was the record of humanity, then specific languages were the witnesses to the histories of their users, or in other words of nations. If Kant, as is often asserted, universalized reason, then his followers nationalized language.

The argument for the irreducible link between language and nationality which was made in such texts was the theorized form of a connection which was first made in English by the colonizers in Ireland in the Renaissance period, as noted in Chapters two and three. In his *On the Diversity of Human Language Structure and its Influence on the Mental Development of Mankind* (1836) Von Humboldt, an influential linguist and philosopher in this tradition, defined a nation as 'a body of men who form language in a particular way', a stipulation which constituted a significant part of his determination of what became in effect one of the

---

[6] For a discussion of the philosophical basis of cultural nationalism in Europe and its influence on Irish cultural nationalism see Crowley 1996: 123–31.

[7] The romantic connection between language and tradition was to prove durable. In his historical account of the vicissitudes of the Irish Language, Corkery blithely asserted in 1954 that 'to say tradition is to say language' (Corkery 1954: 14).

modern definitions of nationality. From the national uniformity, which 'distinguishes each particular turn of thought from those that resemble it in another people', 'the *character* of that language arises':

> Every language receives a specific individuality through that of the nation, and has on the latter a uniformly determining reverse effect. The *national character* is indeed sustained, strengthened, and even to some extent engendered by community of habit and action; but in fact it rests on a likeness of *natural disposition*, which is normally explained by community of *descent* (Humboldt 1836: 152).

The crucial shift here is the basis of the definition of 'nation' from its etymological origins (Latin *nasci*, to be born) to the modern *OED* sense of 'a distinct race or people, characterized by common descent, language or history, usually organized as a separate political state and occupying a definite territory'. In this regard Fichte's *Addresses to the German Nation* (1808) is an illustrative text of cultural nationalism; its premature optimism, in that there was no German nation as such to address, was typical of the movement's confidence that history was on its side. In its later version, the language–nationality relation was held to have the specific political implications which are to be found in the *OED* definition. That is to say, the argument which developed was that a distinctive use of a language entailed a group identity, or nationality, and that the very existence of such a group implied the right to political independence of its users. As Fichte summed the point up: 'it is beyond doubt that, wherever a separate language is found, there a separate nation exists, which has the right to take charge of its independent affairs and to govern itself' (Fichte 1968: 49). In nineteenth-century Europe and beyond, if sovereignty was the key to the dignity of the nation, then it was language which dignified a particular group with the status of nationhood in the first place.

German romanticism was influential upon the group of Irish cultural nationalists led by Thomas Davis (who visited Germany in 1839–40). In particular the emergent definition of the nation as a linguistic and cultural entity entitled to political independence supplied such nationalists with a justification which the political nationalists did not have. After all, did not the Irish have a language of their own, a culture of their own, a history of their own, and thus a nation of their own? And, the argument followed, should they not also then have their own national territory? It was little wonder that in Ireland, as across Europe, nationalists influenced by such thinking fought with rifles in their hands and dictionaries in their pockets; rifles to gain independence, dictionaries as the means to justify it.

*The Nation*, the journal of the Young Irelanders which was edited by Davis, made the link between the Irish and their cultural nationalist counterparts elsewhere and made the bold assertion that 'we are battling for Ireland; if we conquer, 'twill be for mankind' (*The Nation* 1842–5: I, 377). Like other 'provincials fighting for nationality' in Poland, Italy, and Hungary, language was the key issue since,

> to impose another language on a people is to send their history adrift among the accidents of translation—'tis to tear their identity from all places—'tis to substitute arbitrary signs for picturesque and suggestive names—'tis to cut off the entail of feelings and separate the people from their forefathers by a deep gulf (Davis 1914: 97–8).

This was an argument which led Davis to assert that 'nothing can make us believe that it is natural or honourable for the Irish to speak the speech of the alien, the invader, the Sassenagh tyrant, and to abandon the language of our kings and heroes' (Davis 1914: 101). And in his articulation of the clear link between the survival of the Gaelic language and the future of the Irish nation, Davis supplied a central tenet of belief for later Irish cultural nationalists: 'a people without a language of its own is only half a nation. A nation should guard its language more than its territories—' 'tis a surer barrier, and more important frontier, than fortress or river' (Davis 1914: 98). O'Connell saw Gaelic as a barrier to communication in the modern medium of English; it was precisely for this reason that cultural nationalists inspired by Davis argued for its retention.

Davis's arguments were pivotal in that they stretched back to eighteenth-century debates and acted as an inspiration of the Gaelic revivalism of the late nineteenth century. The link back to the previous century was the incorrect idea, a category mistake in the view of Donlevy, that a person could somehow be Irish without speaking the Gaelic language. Prompted by Davis, an anonymous writer in *The Nation* asked the questions which were to dominate a significant part of late nineteenth- and early twentieth-century debates in Ireland: 'Do Irishmen wish to see their language again revived?' and coupled it with the demand 'Will they be Irishmen again? or will they not?' (Anon 1843*b*: 35, 555). The significant word in the second question is 'again' since it implies a return to a lost state, a presupposition of a former authentic state of true or full

Irishness. And that was an idea which was to prove both influential and significantly controversial later.

In the late nineteenth century Davis's arguments had become so commonplace that they were effectively truisms for cultural nationalists; one Gaelic League pamphlet was simply called *Ireland's Defence—Her Language* (Kavanagh 1902). Yet Davis's writings were also prophetic in a more controversial manner, for in defending Irish linguistic independence he falls into a mode of argument which was to be popularized in the late nineteenth century both in Ireland and, to worse effect, beyond its borders. Davis proposed that,

The language which grows up with a people, is conformed to their organs, descriptive of their climate, constitution and manners, mingled inseparably with their history and their soil, fitted beyond any other language to express their prevalent thoughts in the most natural and efficient way (Davis 1914: 97).

The rhetoric here bears analysis: that a language is descriptive of the material and historical context in which it has been and is used is uncontroversial. That it is more efficient than any other in expressing the thoughts of its speakers is a question for the philosopher of language and mind. In what sense languages are natural is perhaps a more complex question. But the real issue of contention here is the idea that for its speakers, a language is 'conformed to their organs', since this raises the idea that languages are not simply socially and historically linked to groups of speakers, but in some sense biologically connected to them, in which case the possibility follows that for particular groups, a given language will be unnatural, or non-organic, or biologically alien. It is an idea which may have derived from von Humboldt's definition of national character as resting 'on a likeness of natural disposition' (Humboldt 1836: 152). The elision of the social with the natural is the key ideological reflex and Davis continued this line of argument with the question:

And is it befitting the fiery, delicate-organed Celt to abandon his beautiful tongue, docile and spirited as an Arab, 'sweet as music, strong as the wave'—is it befitting in him to abandon this wild liquid speech for the mongrel of a hundred breeds called English, which, powerful though it be, creaks and bangs about the Celt who tries to use it? (Davis 1914: 98).

Here the biologically distinct Celt is cast as having a proper language which is under threat from an impure, foreign tongue, also described by Davis as 'a medley of Teutonic dialects'. The discourse of purity (pristine Gaelic, motley English) links back to the eighteenth-century debates about the status of Irish as a language of antiquity and national continuity, as well as, ironically, the Renaissance colonial debates about 'degeneration'. But it also pre-empts later arguments about race, breeding, and 'mongrelism' which were viciously inflected.

The cultural writings of Davis mark an important development in the language debates in the nineteenth century, but their immediate impact among political activists was limited. After the death of Davis in 1845 and the abortive rising inspired by the Young Irelanders in 1848, the previous division between the political and cultural wings of Irish nationalism was reinstated. Among the revolutionary Fenians, for example, despite John Devoy's assertion in 1926 that 'the intention to restore the language was as strong . . . as that of establishing an Irish republic' (Ó Fiaich 1969: 110), there is little evidence of any serious interest in the language issue as compared to the development of physical force republicanism. The notable exception to this was Jeremiah O'Donovan Rossa, founder of the cultural and political Phoenix Society in 1856 which was later incorporated within the Fenian movement. O'Donovan Rossa went against the prevailing drift towards English as the language of economics by making Irish the language of his grocer's shop, and its advertising, in Skibbereen; he is more famous, however, for his imprisonment (1865–71), his organization of the 'skirmishing fund' in America, and his direction of the first nationalist bombing campaign in Britain in 1881–5.

The coupling of language and nationalist politics in the work of some of the Young Irelanders developed as an important issue again towards the end of the nineteenth century, but even in the mid century there were signs of an emerging pattern. Canon Ulick Bourke's *College Irish Grammar* (1856) was a significant attempt to provide the means for education in Irish in schools and it rendered a model of the intertwining of the triple net of language, nationality, and religion which was to become highly influential.[8] Echoing Davis's stress on the purity of Gaelic, Bourke asked: 'should it not be our pride and our boast to have such a language, while other countries rejoice in their jargon—in their compound of languages?' (Bourke 1856: 5). Extolling the role of the Christian Brothers and their educational mission, and citing his mentor John MacHale, the Catholic Archbishop of Tuam (the first

---

[8] The most famous exponent of this motif is Stephen Dedalus. Challenged by his nationalist friend Davin to 'try to be one of us', Stephen replies that in Ireland the soul is caught by nets which hold it back: 'You talk to me of nationality, language, religion. I shall try to fly by those nets' (Joyce, 1992: 220).

member of the Irish hierarchy to espouse the language cause), Bourke argued that the Irish language should be fostered even for its own sake.[9] But if not, then it should be guarded 'for our own sake': 'We know the language of a nation is the exponent of the nation's antiquity—the index of their refinement—the mouthpiece of their history—the echo of a nation's greatness and fame; shall we, then, let our language die?' (Bourke 1856: 7). Included in Bourke's grammar is 'The Celtic Tongue', a pretty dreadful piece by another Catholic priest, Father Mullin. Stanza three depicted the history and present plight of the language:

> And now tis sadly shrinking from the land that gave it birth
> Like the ebbing tide from shore, or the spring-time from the earth;
> O'er the island dimly fading, as a circle o'er the wave—
> Still receding, as its people lisp the language of the slave.
> And with it, too, seems fading as a sunset into night,
> All the scattered rays of Freedom, that lingered in its light!
> For, ah, though long with filial love it clung to Motherland,
> And Irishmen were Irish still, in *tongue*, and heart, and hand!
> Before the Saxon tongue, alas! Proscribed it soon became;
> And we are Irishmen today, but Irishmen in name!
> The Saxon claims our rights and tongue alike doth hold in thrall,
> Somewhere among the Connaught wilds, and hills of Donegal,
> And the shores of Munster, like the broad Atlantic past,
> The olden language lingers yet—an echo of the Past! (Bourke 1856: 303).

The last line of the poem articulated a stance which was to typify one wing of early twentieth-century cultural nationalism: it exhorted the Irish 'to show what Erin ought to be, by pointing to the Past!'

Religion and education were key grounds upon which language debates were conducted in the early to mid nineteenth century, which signalled a return to the preoccupations which had dominated the early eighteenth century. In the later period, however, the conditions of the contest had changed since Protestant proselytizing was challenged by the tardy but sustained campaign by the Catholic Church to impose post-Tridentine standards on the laity. Ó Cuív argues that during this period the Catholic clergy's concern was 'to guide and support the people in the practice of the catholic faith, and they certainly did not set out to wean them from the Irish language'. Yet he also adds that despite the goodwill

---

[9]  MacHale wrote poetry in Irish and translated the *Pentateuch* (1861), the *Iliad* (1844–71), and Moore's *Irish Melodies* (1871); he was a supporter of the Tithe War and O'Connell's Repeal Movement.

of a number of individual churchmen towards Irish, the Catholic Church did little to support the language, not even 'using it rather than English as far as possible as their normal means of communication, both spoken and written' (Ó Cuív 1986: 380). After 1782, when Catholic colleges became legal, English was the language of Catholic higher education (Maynooth is the best example after its foundation in 1795). In a sense the Church was simply conforming to a wider social process. But it did play an active part in that process: Catholic secondary schools were not under the control of the government until 1878 and they also used English as their medium (Wall 1969: 85). A retrospective and harsher assessment of the impact of the Catholic Church's attitude was provided by Donnchadh Ruadh in *An Claidheamh Soluis* in 1899: 'for my own part I believe that the priests are more to blame for the decay of Irish than any other class of the population . . . The priests are to blame as a body for their attitudes towards English . . . I would not have the people look expectant to their Parish priests to take the initiative in the language movement' (Ruadh 1899: 454–5).

The stance of the church certainly led to apparently illogical situations, as Conor McSweeny pointed out in 1843:

I have seen an Irish bishop, with mitre on head and crozier in hand, delivering an elaborate English discourse to an Irish congregation, while a priest stood in the pulpit interpreting it sentence by sentence. This prelate was the son of an Irish peasant, born and reared in one of the most Irish districts in Ireland. Many of his audience might have been, and probably were his playmates in childhood and boyhood, and must have heard him speak the language of his father and mother; but he had never learned it, and was now too distinguished a dignitary of the church, to remember anything of the language of the vulgar herd he had left below him (McSweeny 1843: vii, 55).

There were, as noted earlier, exceptions to the rule: Archbishop John MacHale was a native speaker and life-long advocate of the Irish language, and the Christian Brothers took it as part of their mission to promote Irish in their schools.[10] But even MacHale, an important member of the Catholic hierarchy, offered careful but nonetheless stringent criticism of Catholic policy in his *Irish Translation of the Holy Bible* (1861):

The want of a complete Catholic version of the Canonical Scriptures, in our own native language, has long been felt and deplored in Ireland. Though this

---

[10]  Other members of the hierarchy who tried to resist Anglicization were Bishop Cornelius Egan of Kerry and Bishop Murphy of Cork (Ó Loinsigh 1975: 8).

want is to be obviously ascribed to the religious persecutions to which so many of our privations can be traced, it must be confessed that it could even now have been supplied by vigorous exertions... it is to be regretted that our language, has not yet been made the vehicle, of conveying the entire wisdom of the inspired writings, to the people (MacHale 1861: v).

As Cronin argues, however, this lack of concern with the language has to be viewed in historical context, since for all of the differing branches of religious belief the main concern in the nineteenth century was 'control of the educational system. Questions of language and culture were of secondary importance' (Cronin 1996: 106). Thus although in 1799 in his *Projects for Re-Establishing the Internal Peace and Tranquility of Ireland*, Whitley Stokes had argued that 'it is easier to alter the religion of a people than their language' (Stokes 1799: 45), in practice the opposite proved true. What in fact happened was that the Tudor policies of religious and linguistic domination were half-realized in the nineteenth century: Catholicism continued as the dominant form of religious belief for the majority, but the Gaelic language was rapidly displaced by English as the language of not only power but (for the first time) of everyday activity for the majority of the population. The victory of Catholicism and the diminuition of Gaelic were not, however, un-opposed and ironically it was the Protestant churches which again turned to the Irish language as the key to gaining religious influence in the early nineteenth century, as they had early in the previous century.

Sectarian antagonism had become a powerful force by the end of the eighteenth century and during the early part of the nineteenth century, and was particularly focused around agrarian protest, Penal Code reform, the foundation of the Orange Order in 1795, the real and imaginary atrocities of the 1798 rebellion, and the repercussions of the Acts of Union. It had been fostered not least by the British government's determination to prevent political alliances between different religious groupings. Protestant proselytizing therefore needs to be considered with three aspects in mind. First, there was the general concern amongst the British and Irish political élites about the behaviour of the lower classes, particularly with regard to the influence of popular literature.[11] Second, there existed political and religious anxiety about

---

[11] Many of the Irish proselytizing societies were extensions of Tract Societies (such as the Association for Discountenancing Vice) which were based on British models. Ó Ciosáin 1997: chapter eight gives an account of the development and influence of this phenomenon.

the possibility of Catholic emancipation and, given the size of the respective populations, consequent political domination. And third was the theological impetus behind what has been called the Second Reformation, that is, the renewal of the fundamental Protestant principle of vernacularism. As Stokes put it:

For the diffusion of religious knowledge, it is necessary, that it should be conveyed in the language the people understand . . . One of the fundamental principles of the Reformation was, that every person should address his Maker, and read His word, in his native tongue; yet this was neglected in Ireland, with a view of making the English language universal (Stokes 1799: 45).

Stokes's own contribution to this process was to devise a system of phonetic spelling which he used in the publication of parts of the New Testament and the Book of Proverbs between 1799 and 1815.[12] The Protestant belief in the necessity of the diffusion of the Word to the unconverted was evinced by a linkage of Biblical and contemporary example. Irish peasants, Taylor argued, had to be furnished with the same 'advantage which was given to the Capadocians, and the Phrygians of old, and the Indian of the present day' (Taylor 1817: 14). Dewar made the same point about the pertinence of colonial missionary work: 'I may say, that while Christian Missionaries are sent forth to the Islands of the South Sea, to India, and Africa, the moral and religious instruction of a people so closely linked to us, in civil and political interest as the Irish should not be entirely neglected' (Dewar 1812: 146). If the subjects of Empire abroad merited the trouble of missionary activity in order to spread the Word and save their pagan souls, then surely the natives of what was by then part of the United Kingdom itself were deserving of no less. Such sentiments inspired the formation of Protestant proselytizing societies such as the Hibernian Bible Society, the London Hibernian Society, the Baptist Society and, the most important, The Irish Society for Promoting the Education of the Native Irish Through the Medium of Their Own Language (1818). In addition between 1810 and 1813 the British and Foreign Bible Society printed five thousand copies of the New Testament in Irish and in 1817 an edition of the complete Bible. Prompted by a pamphlet written by a Baptist minister, Christopher Anderson, the London Hibernian Society described the aims of its prominent sister organization:

---

[12] The first attempt to simplify Irish spelling and to attempt to make it more phonetic was Bishop Hutchinson's *Tegasg Kreesdee. A Kristian Katekism* (1722); see chapter four, page 86.

The Irish Society teaches all its Scholars primarily to read the Irish Language. It seeks out the Irish-speaking people as the sole objects of its care; and teaches English only in the way of translation from the Irish. Its Scholars are principally Adults, though it instructs some Children... It employs the unoccupied time of the Inspectors, in visiting the houses of the Irish peasantry, reading to them the Scriptures and exciting a thirst for instruction in the Irish Language exclusively; and distributes the Holy Scriptures in Irish, together with Irish Prayer Books, where acceptable (Blayney 1996: 83–4).

That last phrase 'where acceptable' is telling since it indicates that such proselytizing was not always welcomed by its intended recipients, and again this must be viewed in the context of the active sectarianism of the day. In a criticism of the stance of the Established Church (prior to the institution of the Irish Society), Daniel Dewar, the Principal of Aberdeen University, wrote in his *Observations on the Character, Customs and Superstitions of the Irish* (1812):

The reformation, it is well known, has made very little progress in [Ireland]; the mass of the people remain in connection with the church of Rome. Of these, as has already been observed, there are a million and a half, who understand no tongue but the Irish. Now the established church has made no provision whatever for this population; there is not one of its ministers that preaches in this language (Dewar 1812: 95).

Such Gaelic speakers were predominantly Catholic, but, he added, are they not forced 'to remain in the bosom of the Roman church? Their priests give them that instruction in the venerable tongue of their fathers, which the protestant teachers have always denied them. And yet, these teachers complain of the increase of papists, and of the gross ignorance of the people' (Dewar 1812: 95–6).

Protestant proselytizing was marked by anti-Catholic sectarianism. In his *Reasons for Giving Moral Instruction of the Native Irish Through the Medium of their Vernacular Language* (1817), J. S. Taylor argued that 'morality will not be less moral—nor religion less pure, nor its civilising spirit less corrective of impetuous passions, and erratic sensibilities, *because introduced through the medium of the Irish language*' (Taylor 1817: 11). This may have been abstractly true, but of course the interpretation of what were 'impetuous passions' and 'erratic sensibilities' was politically loaded in this historical context. Taylor continued to specify the corrupt influence of Catholicism which had reduced the Irish 'almost to a state of *satisfied* servitude... a kind of habitual slavery'. The answer to 'this infatuating influence, under which reason must be *silent* or rebellious' was nothing less than 'The Gospel, conveyed through the medium of the Irish language' (Taylor 1817: 12). Once this had been achieved, the convert would become aware of 'the odious deformity of that gothic super-structure whose gloomy and fantastic battlements have so long thrown their shadow over his country, chilling its moral bloom, and causing its virtues to perish untimely' (Taylor 1817: 14).

As well as ordaining religious truth, the dissemination of the Word in Irish was also to have the effect of establishing a new historical and social order of unity and reconciliation. In his restrospective *A Brief Sketch of the Various Attempts which have been made to Diffuse a Knowledge of the Holy Scriptures through the Medium of the Irish Language* (1818), Anderson commented on the objection made by fellow Protestants opposed to his method, that 'Irish is calculated to revive recollections of past transac-tions, which it were better forgotten, as the tendency of these recollec-tions is to disunite the people' (Anderson 1818: 77–8). This is clearly a reference to the transmission of a specific type of native historical knowledge through Gaelic both textually and in the oral tradition. In his answer to the point, Anderson argued that Scriptural teaching in Irish 'is most calculated to heal every irritable feeling, and to allay every animosity which such recollections [the Irish native] may unhappily still cherish'. Such knowledge of the past, he asserted, is the 'poison of disaffection and disunion' to which Biblical knowledge in the native language is the only possible antidote. 'Can it be imagined', he asked,

that principles of obedience to the constituted authorities will be weakened in the minds of an Irishman, by perusing such passages as these?—'Render unto Caesar the things which are Caesar's'. 'Let every soul be subject to the higher powers; for there is no power but of God: the powers that be are ordained of God. Whosoever, therefore, resisteth the power, resisteth the ordinance of God'... 'Submit yourselves therefore to every ordinance of man for the Lord's sake: whether it be to the King, as supreme, or unto governors'... 'Honour the King'... (Anderson 1818: 80–1).

Such truths, he noted, whether expressed in English or Irish, 'are equally well calculated to infuse the most exalted and firmly grounded senti-ments of loyalty to the ruling powers, and of mutual affectionate sentiment of man towards man'. The use of the Biblical text to sup-port specific political arrangements was of course nothing new and perhaps indicates little save the status of the Bible and the potential of interpretation, but it was a rhetorical strategy which was (and is) still powerful and often used. Not many, however, have pushed it to the rather optimistic limit offered by Anderson. Citing Dewar, Anderson tells the story of a Gaelic speaker who had been given a New Testament in Irish. After reading it he is reported to have exclaimed: 'If I believe this, it is impossible for me to remain a rebel' (Anderson 1818: 82). The political message was not, however, always presented quite so directly. The first Secretary to the Irish Society was Henry Joseph Monck Mason, whose *History of the Origin and Progress of the Irish Society* (1844) praised the Irish language for its superiority over 'the English or any compound tongue'.

Having its roots within itself, the meaning of all those terms that express justification, regeneration, repentance, charity, etc. etc. is at once obvious, without the interference of any learned expositor; an advantage which, in a country and religion where a reference to human authority and teaching is an evil of great prevalence, counterbalances any fastidious imagination respecting the barbarism of the tongue (Mason 1844: 14).

Irish, according to this argument at least, is structurally anti-Papist; the historical semantics of the language had the potential to preclude the baneful interference of Catholic priests.

The religious debates had an important impact and became the occasion of considerable rancour and animosity, particularly with regard to the language issue:

on the one hand, the understanding of English is the characteristic of Protestantism; on the other, the Irish tongue is the mark of Catholicism. This man hates his neighbour because he speaks no Irish; and his neighbour treats him with contempt because he is not acquainted with English. By the principle of association, the Protestant confounds Irish with disloyalty and rebellion, and the Catholic considers English as allied to Protestantism and damnable error (Dewar 1812: 99–100).[13]

Mason asserted that 'the two inveterate prejudices in the Irish peasant's mind, are that against the Saxon language, and that against the creed of the Protestant'. But he saw a simple remedy to the problem: 'by employing the Scriptures in the much loved native tongue, you neutralise the second prejudice with the first' (Mason 1829: 5). In fact, as noted earlier,

---

[13] Ó Ciosáin is surely correct to argue for sensitivity to the complexity of cultural practice in this period, particularly with regard to language (Ó Ciosáin 1997: 203). But there are points, especially at times of sectarian tension, when attitudes and beliefs were both crudely expressed and acted upon.

what happened in practice was that although Protestantism was wholly unsuccessful in making a serious impact on the belief patterns of the majority of the native population, the English language did come to displace Irish as the language of the majority. And one part of this process, though not the most important part, was that instruction in Irish, by striking historical irony, came to be associated with Protestantism and so was strongly opposed by the Catholic Church and resented by many Catholics. A hedge-school master, Amhlaoibh Ó Suilleabháin, recorded his plight in 1827 as his skills became redundant. New schools were being built, he complained, which taught only English, while 'nobody is taking any interest in the fine subtle Irish language, apart from mean swaddlers who try to lure the Irish to join their new cursed religion' (De Bhaldraithe 1979: 23). Another school-teacher, Peadar Ó Dálaigh, advertised both his own talents and his religious affiliation in a catchy if sardonic quatrain:

> In teaching the young our old Mother Tongue
> At least I may venture to mention
> I'm better than some who greedily thumb
> The Bible-Society Pension
> (Breatnach 1961: 137).

McSweeny pointed out that,

An Irish prayer-book is a thing which the poor Irish peasant has never seen. Not only has he not been taught the language which he speaks, but his clergy have never encouraged, and have sometimes forbidden him to learn it. This objection arose chiefly, I believe, from the impudent intermeddling of Bible Societies with the religion of the people. By their patronage of the Irish language, they had desecrated it in the eyes of the Irish themselves (McSweeny 1843: vii, 55).

The damage inflicted by the association of Protestant proselytizing and the Irish language in the eyes of the Catholic Church is demonstrated most notably, however, in the scandal of the Presbyterian Home Mission in the 1840s. In 1833 the Presbyterian Missionary Society reported to the Synod of Ulster and argued for the reaffirmation of its eighteenth-century principle of teaching the Irish in their native language, a recommendation accepted by the Synod. The practical result was the setting up of the Home Mission in 1833–4, dedicated to preaching in the vernacular and to the institution of Irish Schools, principally in Ulster. The reported success of the schools, in a series of reports made to the Synod between 1834–42, was astounding, so remarkable in fact that it was scrutinized by the Catholic clergy (the Catholic Church was of course opposed to such schools and there were reports that the sacraments were refused to any Catholics who were involved with them). What sealed the fate of the project, however, and perhaps influenced significantly the ability of the Catholic Church to argue against the practice of teaching in Irish, was the allegation that the success of the Presbyterian Home Mission was in reality a huge fraud committed by teachers who pocketed the money but carried out no instruction.[14] The resultant scandal led effectively to the end of Protestant proselytizing in Gaelic. A further consequence was that the threat to the hegemony of the Catholic Church which preaching in Gaelic had entailed, meant that the native language as a medium for religious instruction was considered at least by some of the Catholic hierarchy with suspicion. This only added to the Church's practical prejudice against the language which had been in place since at least the end of the eighteenth century. And so Irish, often cast as the 'natural' language of the Catholic majority, was by the mid nineteenth century tainted by its associations with Protestantism. As a result influential scholars and commentators on the language blamed both faiths for the decline of the language. John O'Donovan, Gaelic adviser to the Ordnance Survey, reported in his survey letters from Cavan/Leitrim that Protestant proselytizers 'have created in the minds of the peasantry a hatred for everything written in that language, and . . . the society who encourage them could not have adopted a more successful plan to induce them to learn English and hate their own language' (Ó Snodaigh 1995: 58). The letters from Down record a conversation with a priest who commented disparagingly that his colleagues were able to speak Irish 'but as they were all dandies from Maynooth they would not wish anyone to know they understood a word of it' despite the fact that 'they probably never heard a word of English from their grandmothers' (Ó Snodaigh 1995: 59). The Scottish Presbyterian Robert MacAdam, co-founder of the Ulster Gaelic Society and founder editor of the *Ulster Journal of Archaeology* (1853–62), cited among other causes of the plight of Irish,

---

[14] Blayney gives an account of the scandal which is sympathetic to the Presbyterians but ultimately noncommittal as to the truth of the allegations (Blaney 1996: 110–18).

the attitude of the Catholic Church, neglecting to teach Catechism and to give sermons in the language . . . and the efforts of the Protestant Church to beguile the poor Catholics from their faith, the only result being that it had done more harm to the language than foreign persecution for 300 years (Ó Néill 1966: 63)

Education was the other ground upon which the language issue was debated, and despite Grattan's appeal for a non-sectarian education system, provision in the early part of the century was dominated by religion. The hedge school system, largely restricted to the Catholic population, though this was not exclusively true of the Presbyterian north, continued in the period and it is claimed that around 400,000 children (some 70 per cent of the total) were offered elementary education by this means in the 1820s, with the number of schools reaching some 7,600 by 1824 (Dowling 1968: 42). Catholic day schools, tied to Catholic parishes, taught a further 35,000 pupils. Provision was also rendered by the Protestant Charter schools and Erasmus Smith schools which had been established in the early eighteenth century (11,000 students), and by the schools tied to the Protestant proselytizing societies of the late eighteenth and early nineteenth centuries (around 120,000 pupils) (Ó Ciosáin 1997: 40). Ulster was a particular focus for educational activity and Cuideacht Gaoidheilge Uladh (the Ulster Gaelic Society), founded in 1828, included in its aims that of maintaining 'teachers of the Irish language where it most prevails' (Ó hAilín 1969: 91); Belfast was for a long period an important centre of Gaelic language activity. All denominations agreed, though usually for different reasons, that education was crucial for the prosperity of Ireland. Taylor, for example, saw the need to learn from the colonial past and argued that schooling was central to the development of imperial unity:

I perceive that the British people, advised by the examples of the past, counsel better for the future interests of Ireland; they now perceive it as a *mental* authority which must mould the heart of Ireland in conformation to British sentiment, and the interests of a united empire; and they have discovered that the great instrument of this must be EDUCATION (Taylor 1817: 8).

But even if there was general agreement about the need for education, there was less unity with regard to the medium in which the teaching and learning was to take place. Many argued that Irish must be the vehicle of instruction simply as a consequence of the large numbers of Irish speakers. As noted earlier, Stokes asserted at the end of the eighteenth century that more than eight hundred thousand people were monoglot in Gaelic, while twice that number spoke the language by choice. And Dewar claimed in 1812 that 'there are about two millions of people in Ireland who are incapable of understanding a continued discourse in English' (Dewar 1812: 88). Others pointed to the difficulties which diglossia presented. Neilson declared that 'in travelling, in the common occurrences of agriculture or rural traffic, a knowledge of Irish is absolutely necessary' (Neilson 1808: ix), while the scriptural translator Thaddeus Connellan observed that,

It is obvious, that when tribes of men are intermixed who speak different languages, a great deal of the advantages which man should afford his neighbour, must be diminished or lost. The magistrate cannot address his subjects, the pastor his flock, but by the imperfect medium of an interpreter. Lawyers, Divines, Physicians, Merchants, Manufacturers, and Farmers, all feel more or less this inconvenience when they have to do with those, with whom they have no common language (Connellan 1814: ix).

The problem from the point of view of the powerful was evident, but the difficulty was more complex since it did not only affect those in authority when dealing with their subjects. As Petty had argued at the end of the seventeenth century, the language difficulty was even more of a problem for the disempowered when they had to deal with the authorities.[15] For Irish speakers there was a paradox: the Irish language was their own but they needed the English language since without it they had no access to official authorities, forms of power, or even indeed the commercial market. For the Gaelic speaker, Anderson notes,

Irish is to them the language of social intercourse, of family communion; every feeling connected with moral duty is closely interwoven with that language … Can the same be said of English? It is to him the language of barter, or worldly occupations; taken up solely at the market, laid aside when he returns home, a very confined vocabulary (Anderson 1818: 54).

'The English', Coneys asserts, 'is the language of his commerce—the Irish the language of his heart' (Coneys 1842: 73). But for a poor and suffering population the choice which was on offer was no choice at all. The argument which was made about the necessity of

---

[15]　Ó Ciosáin asserts that 'a large proportion of the population regularly participated' in the judicial system in the early nineteenth century; he cites research which demonstrates that a quarter of all families in Mayo in 1839 were involved in litigation and that 70 per cent of the cases were brought by the peasantry (Ó Ciosáin 1997: 29–30).

communicative competence in Irish for those in authority also applied to the English language and Irish speakers. And the Irish were too smart not to heed Petty's lesson, with Irish parents in particular taking it to heart. The English language may well have been 'a necessary sin/the perfect language to sell pigs in' (Hartnett 1978: 84), but it was a necessary sin.

Given this it might be thought strange that the Protestant proselytizers cited earlier argued so strongly for the teaching of Irish. But in fact what they argued for usually was instruction in Gaelic as a preliminary step to an ulterior motive, a method which their eighteenth-century antecedents had also adopted. Dewar proposed that,

The cultivation of either the Irish or the Gaelic is the most effectual, as well as the most expeditious plan that can be adopted for their extinction. Make any people intelligent and rational and they will gradually lose their prejudices; many of them will acquire a taste for general knowledge, and they will seek for it in the general tongue of the empire (Dewar 1812: 97).

He adds that 'all their interest must incline them to this measure' and, most importantly, 'they will find it important to have some English *book-learning* themselves, and to be at some pains to impart it to their children'. The idea of the cultural force of enlightened self-interest was also embraced by Owen Connellan who declared that 'the more the Irish is studied, by the peasantry of Ireland (it being their vernacular language) the better are their minds prepared and their taste formed to learn and understand the English' (Connellan 1834: 61). Thaddeus Connellan put the point simply: 'with respect to the extension of the English language, it appears likely to be promoted at present by the cultivation of the Irish' (Connellan 1814: ix).

Irish was already under pressure in the early nineteenth century from the economic and political forces which had steadily eroded its status over a prolonged period and from the indifference, at best, shown by the Catholic Church; an indifference given an edge by the association of Gaelic language instruction with Protestant proselytization. There were, however, two other major factors in the decline of Irish in the nineteenth century. The first was the Famine of 1845–8 and its effects on the population and economy of rural Ireland, though it is necessary to be careful not to see the event as an isolated historical incident with disproportionate consequences. For what the Famine did in reality was to hasten processes of rural depopulation by the horror of death by starvation (up to a million died in the disaster), and by the migration to the towns and cities, and massive emigration from Ireland, in search of work and relief. Emigration, which had occurred on a large scale after the end of the Napoleonic wars, accounted for a loss of some five million people between 1846 and 1901. And the impact was greatest on the poorest rural areas in which the largest numbers of Irish speakers were concentrated, a factor which acted as a major force in counteracting the growth in the number of Irish speakers (simply by dint of the expansion of the population in general) in the early part of the century. But migration and emigration to English-speaking places do not explain fully the effect of the Famine on the use of Irish. The sheer psychological and cultural impact of the experience of mass starvation is one factor which must be counted as part of any explanation. The sense of helplessness, loss, panic, and uncertainty, perhaps combined with a determination to avoid such a disaster at all costs in the future, no doubt helped to undermine even the most traditional communities. This, combined with the other factors of brutal economic reality and lack of cultural support from the Catholic Church, makes the pace of the decline of the language after the Famine perhaps more comprehensible, though as De Fréine has argued the question is still in need of greater research.[16]

There was one other determinant in this process, again an educational development, and this was the introduction in 1831 of the National Schools. This significant step was a response by the government to demands, articulated to a great extent by the Catholic Church, for a system of state-funded education which would avoid the problems of sectarian education and regulate the haphazard existing provision. The Board of Commissioners for National Education consisted of three members of the Church of Ireland and two each from the Catholic and Presbyterian Churches. There were three important points to note about the National Schools: first, they were established in Ireland some forty years before the 1870 Elementary Education Bill provided similar measures for England and Wales. Second, and crucially, they taught in

---

[16] De Fréine's *The Great Silence* (1965) is the first serious attempt to ascertain why the Irish people gave up the Irish language but it calls for more work. De Fréine postulates the thesis that the loss of the language is explicable by 'collective behaviour' (a mixture of panic, hysteria, and utopianism), an attempt to escape the limitations of intolerable reality created by unprecedented social and cultural change (De Fréine 1977). Lee argues that economic reasons explain the acquisition of English but not the loss of Irish (Lee 1989: 662–3).

English and discouraged the use of Irish.[17] Third, they were highly successful in their educational mission: numbers increased from 107,000 in 1833 to more than half a million by the end of the century, and whatever their ideological intent, they certainly had a large impact on literacy per se in Ireland.[18] For Irish parents the choice was evidently clear: of the various possibilities on offer (Protestant proselytizing schools, hedge schools, largely unregulated parish schools), choosing the state-funded school which taught English, the medium of commerce, authority and, of course, emigration, must have been a relatively straightforward option. It is a choice which Brian Friel's play *Translations* dramatizes. Maire, a pupil at a hedge school in 1833, who is seeking to emigrate (she is the eldest of eleven children), refers to O'Connell's view of English and Irish in an argument with the hedge schoolmaster:

I'm talking about the Liberator, Master, as you well know. And what he said was this: 'The old language is a barrier to modern progress.' He said that last month. And he's right. I don't want Greek. I don't want Latin. I want English (Friel 1981: 25).

She has Irish; she wants and needs English. And Irish parents agreed with her; as the saying went, Irish people loved their language, but they loved their children more. Even Archbishop MacHale's father, a monoglot Irish speaker, hung a bata scóir (tally-stick) around his son's neck every time he spoke Irish; each notch on the bata earning the child a punishment from his father. It was a practice which went on throughout the nineteenth century. In 1853 Sir William Wilde (Oscar's father) reported the actions of a schoolteacher in Gaelic-speaking Connemara on hearing an eight-year-old boy speak Irish to his sister:

The man called the child to him, said nothing, but drawing forth from its dress a little stick, commonly called a screeen or tally, which was suspended by a string round the neck, put an additional notch in it with his penknife. Upon our enquiring into the cause of this proceeding, we were told that it was done to prevent the child speaking Irish; for every time he attempted to do so a new nick

---

[17] Akenson comments that in the national schools system there was no ban on Irish: 'the commissioners were not hostile to the Irish language so much as unaware of it. There was no rule against its use' (Akenson 1975: 381). But this is contradicted by the official policy of the Board of Commissioners in 1884 which is discussed later in the chapter.

[18] Ó Buachalla notes that such widespread educational provision was unusual by contemporary European standards and that 'no country had been the recipient of such educational generosity at the hands of colonial masters' (Ó Buachalla 1981: 18).

was put in his tally, and when these amounted to a certain number, summary punishment was inflicted on him by the schoolmaster (Greene 1972: 10).

P. J. Keenan, a Commissioner of Education whose preferred policy was bilingualism, reported in 1856 on a visit to a National School:

The master adopts a novel mode of procedure to propagate the 'new language'. He makes it a cause of punishment to speak Irish in the school, and he has instituted a sort of police among the parents to see that in their intercourse with one another the children speak nothing but English at home. The parents are so eager for the English, they exhibit no reluctance to inform the master of every detected breach of the school law; and, by this coercive process, the poor children in the course of time become pretty fluent in speaking very incorrect English (Keenan 1857–8: xxi).

The official policy of the Board of Commissioners was set out in a memo in 1884 and declared that 'the anxiety of the promoters of the National System was to encourage the cultivation of the English language and to make English the language of the schools' (Ó Loinsigh 1975: 10). But the methods by which it was carried out were not a result of British colonial policy, nor even endorsed by the Catholic Church (though the representatives of both must have sanctioned it); it was a 'system of policing and flogging [which] was planned and carried out by the parents and schoolmasters working in co-operation' (Greene 1972: 11).[19] And they did so because Irish parents wanted something desperately, as Keenan made clear in his comments on island schools: 'it is natural to inquire how this strong passion for education could have possessed a people who are themselves utterly illiterate ... Their passion may be traced to one predominant desire—the desire to speak English'. And their motivation was clear: escape from poverty. When strangers visited their home the islanders saw that 'prosperity has its peculiar tongue as well as its fine coat'; when merchants dealt with them in 'the yellow gold, they count it out in English'; when they used the law they found that 'the solemn words of judgment have to come second to them, through the offices of an interpreter'; and the schoolmaster and landlord of course speak English. Thus for Irish speakers in even the remotest islands,

---

[19] No doubt part of the problem was simply the poor training and standards of teachers. In 1833 the period of training was three months, extended in 1843 to five months; in 1883 only forty per cent of teachers paid by the state had completed their training (Ó Huallacháin, 1994: 25).

Whilst they may love the cadences, and mellowness, and homeliness of the language which their fathers gave them, they yet see that obscurity and poverty distinguish their lot from the English-speaking people; and accordingly, no matter what the sacrifice to their feelings, they long for the acquisition of the 'new tongue', with all its prizes and social privileges. The keystone of fortune is the power of speaking English, and to possess this power there is a burning longing in their breasts that never varies, never moderates...The knowledge which they thirst for in the school is, therefore, confined to a speaking use of the English Language (Keenan 1857–8: xx).

Archbishop MacHale described the National Schools as 'the graves of the National Language' (Bourke 1856: 6) and in 1899 Douglas Hyde denounced 'the Anglicised products of the "National Schools"... amongst whom there exists little or no trace of traditional Irish feelings, or indeed seldom of any feelings save those prompted by (when they read it) a weekly newspaper' (Hyde 1899: xxi). But such negative attitudes bore little relation to the wishes of parents or the active practical choice made by the vast majority of Irish speakers in the nineteenth century for all of the various reasons set out above. It is a stark fact that Irish speakers made their difficult choice and stuck to it.

There were observers who found native Irish speakers (rather than revivalists) who seemed proud of their language. Dewar, for example, comments on his dealings with 'low and uneducated' Irish people in London in 1812:

When I spoke to them in their own language, their national enthusiasm was kindled, and for a while they seemed to forget that they were in the land of strangers. And though doomed to ignorance, penury, and toil, at home as well as abroad, yet, so fond are they of their country, and of everything connected with it, that he who will talk to them in the tongue of their fathers, which they regard as sacred, and who seems not displeased with their customs, will be considered as their countryman and friend (Dewar 1812: 34).

And in the mid century that well-known idealized figure, the Irish-speaking peasant, began to appear as the repository of authentic Irishness. McSweeny describes the character thus in 1843:

The poor Irish peasant has not been idle. In despite of tyranny, in despite of a still more dangerous influence, the neglect and discouragement of his own clergy, the only protectors who remained to him, and in spite of the necessity of learning for civil purposes a foreign jargon, he has preserved his own language triumphant all throughout. I am proud of being that peasant's countryman (McSweeny 1843: vii, 55).

In the influential *Poets and Poetry of Munster* (1860), George Sigerson, under the pseudonym 'Erionnach' (Irishman), produced a poem by Ó Lionáin in praise of Irish of which the first stanza is:

> Níor chanadh a n-dréachtaibh nuail,
> Teanga is uaisle mar thuile luais;
> Caint is glé-ghlaine ag teacht mar sreabh
> Ná fuil saomh leamh, ná faon amh
>
> Never was heard a strain so sweet,
> A language so noble—a flood rolling fleet,
> A speech so pure bright, so warm and chaste,
> Like a nourishing stream from a mother's breast
> (Sigerson 1860: VIII–IX).

In his introduction Sigerson described Ó Lionáin as appreciating the aesthetic effects of the loss of Irish after 'hearing the inflexible, unendearing language of the "porker" Saxons jarring upon the ear of his country' (Sigerson 1860: viii). He adds that 'in every rural district where the Irish is spoken, curious gems of quaint humour, flashing wit, and a keen knowledge of men and morals adorn that golden casket—a Celtic peasant's heart' (Sigerson 1860: xxiii).

Such myths, though they were to become both popular and influential, belie the reality which was depicted earlier of Irish speakers seeking out the English language with passion and urgency.[20] It can be hardly surprising that they did so. What is more striking, however, is the fact that the massive shift that took place to English brought with it a new attitude to the language which had been left behind. Some might bemoan the loss, some might be angry about it, some might deny it, some might attempt to stop it. But others felt differently towards the language; for reasons which are varied and complex many felt ashamed of Gaelic. Davis noted in 1843 that 'the middle classes think it a sign of vulgarity to speak Irish' (Davis 1914: 105), while his friend and fellow cultural nationalist Sir Samuel Ferguson, observed that 'all things Celtic are regarded by our educated classes as of questionable *ton*' (Ó Snodaigh 1995: 78). Robert MacAdam, in his 'Six hundred Gaelic proverbs collected in Ulster' (1858) commented acutely on the 1851 census, the first to include a question about the use of Irish.

---

[20] Matthew Arnold was the first to make potent cultural and ideological use of the Celtic-Saxon opposition in *On the Study of Celtic Literature* (1867).

The return recorded over a million and a half Irish speakers but MacAdam argued that fear and shame may have distorted the figures:

This large number by no means indicates with accuracy the entire number of persons who understand it, or who have learnt it in their infancy. It is well known that in various districts where the two languages co-exist, but where the English now largely predominates, numbers of individuals returned themselves as ignorant of the Irish language, either from a sort of false shame, or from a secret dread that the government, in making this inquiry (for the first time) had some concealed motive, which could not be for their good (MacAdam 1858: 172).

Bourke contrasted the situation of Irish speakers with that of speakers of Welsh and Scottish Gaelic who took pride in their language 'because they are taught in their elementary schools and encouraged by the nobility and gentry, instead of being ashamed of their mother tongue' (Bourke 1856: 5). And shame, contrary to the claims of Coneys and Sigerson, was the most commonly recorded sentiment of the Irish peasantry towards their language. Keenan reports the example of a Tory islander:

a man who expressed himself in English pretty well, told me that he had been in a boat with a part of fellow-islanders at Moville, in Inishowen, and, to use his own expression, when speaking of his own companions, who spoke Irish only, he said he 'was ashamed of them; they stood like dummies; the cattle go on as well as them' (Keenan 1857–8: xxi).

There were undoubtedly many causes of such sentiments, whether it was the attitude of the socially aspirant, or the feeling of children whose parents had abandoned the language and forced another on them, or the anger and hurt of those who lived in poverty and connected Irish to that; whatever the cause, shame was a major feeling associated with Gaelic. As one of the contributors to the congress held in Dublin in 1882 by the first major revivalist organization, the Society for the Preservation of the Irish Language, put it: 'there is a need to remove the prejudices of the unenlightened *shoneen* who is said to be ashamed to speak his mother's tongue' (Society for the Preservation of the Irish Language 1884: 60). The Society's report for 1882 reiterated the point:

The chief obstacle is caused by the indifference, or apathy of the people generally as to the necessity of preserving the National Language...Our success can be deemed but partial until the parents heartily desire that their children should be familiar with their native tongue, and cherish and promote its cultivation, by regarding it as an essential part of their children's education (Society for the Preservation of the Irish Language 1884: 1).

The story of the struggle to achieve that and other related aims is the subject of the next chapter.

# CHAPTER SIX

# *Language and revolution, 1876–1922*

> 'We must be prepared to turn from a purely political nationalism
> with the land question as its lever, to a partly intellectual and
> historical nationalism ... with the language question as its lever'
>
> W. B. Yeats, letter to *The Leader*, 1900.

If some regarded the Celtic peasant as the repository of Irishness
(including an unflinching attachment to the Gaelic language), others
saw the same type as the embodiment of the problems faced by
language preservers and revivalists. Flaherty argued in 'Practical hints
towards preventing the decay of Irish in Irish-speaking districts' that
'the greatest danger which threatens the language, and one from which it
is certain to suffer, is the prejudice entertained against it by the illiterate
Irish-speaking peasant, whose phraseology it is'. They think, he continued, that

it is the synonym of poverty and misery, and that many of the evils from which
they suffer are traceable to its continued use; that, if they could dispose with it
altogether, they would elevate themselves socially, and be much more respectable members of society (Flaherty 1884: 13–14).

Whether rural agricultural labourers harboured such dreams of social
respectability (as opposed to material subsistence) is open to doubt.
What is clear, however, is that they viewed the English language as a way
to improve their immediate material lot, not least in that it opened up
the possibilities offered by migration and emigration.[1] Yet the privileging of English over Irish as the language of everyday life was not
confined to the poorest of the Irish population, since it was a view

---

[1] The view of English as necessary for material improvement was prevalent but it is
important to put it in context. Hindley's comment that 'the Irish people adopted English
and had their children taught it not because they liked it but because it opened boundless
opportunities to them' (Hindley 1990: 39) is simply wrong; the opportunities were hardly
'boundless'.

shared even by some of the most prominent cultural nationalists of the mid nineteenth century. Eugene O'Curry and his brother-in-law John O'Donovan worked on the topographical section of the Ordnance Survey; O'Donovan also published *A Grammar of the Irish Language* (1845), while O'Curry's major work was his *Lectures on the Manuscript Materials of Ancient Irish History* (1861). Both were native Irish speakers who spoke to each other, and brought their children up, in English. O'Donovan referred to spoken Irish as 'local jargons'; O'Curry argued that the remnants of ancient Irish learning needed to be collected before the death of the language made the task impossible (Greene 1972: 13).

Cultural nationalists later in the century castigated such sentiments and attributed their origins to various causes. English colonialism (the conflation of 'English' with 'British' was widespread) was one clearly identifiable historical source of the problems facing Irish language enthusiasts. The anonymous 'Bearla na bfeinne, The language of my land', published in *The Irish American* and reprinted in Nolan's *Irish Grammar Rules in Prose and Verse* (1877), exhorted:

> When prayer should be given, at morning and even',
> Use you the language of my land:
> It is better by far than the Sassenach's jar,
> Who hates the sweet language of my land (Nolan 1877: 28).

Colonial contempt manifested itself in various ways; the *Morning Post* described Gaelic as 'Kitchen Kaffir' and the *Daily Mail*'s estimation was that it was 'a barbarous language' (Ó Snodaigh 1995: 86). And in the early twentieth century the public use of the language was proscribed; Patrick Pearse lost a case in which he defended a labourer who did not have his name on his cart (the name was in Gaelic and therefore did not count) (Edwards 1977: 79–81). Yet though colonialism was often held responsible for the parlous state of the Irish language, the blame was not solely attributed to Ireland's rulers. In fact the period saw a growth of critical self-examination as part, as Frank O'Connor later put it, 'of a whole national awakening when a small, defeated and embittered country began to seek the cause of its defeat in itself rather than in its external enemy' (Pierce 2000: 500). For example, 'Bearla na bfeinne' begins: 'To neglect is a crime, in the Celt of our time, | To learn the language of my land'. If neglect is a sign of contemporary wrong-doing by the Irish, then the lines also point implicitly to past culpability since the language has now to be learned rather than spoken natively. And the same tone of grievance was used by Nolan in 'A Plea for our Mother Tongue' (an acrostic whose schema is 'Do not despair') which ends: 'Ireland shall weep if this tongue you don't cherish | Repel the disgrace which is yours if it perish' (Nolan 1877: i). James Joyce's response to such a charge is given in *A Portrait of the Artist as a Young Man*, in which Stephen Dedalus rounds on a Gaelic Leaguer who asks him to join the revivalist campaign: 'my ancestors threw off their language and took another....They allowed a handful of foreigners to subject them' (Joyce 1992: 274).[2]

Such recrimination was not uncommon in the period and many attacks were more critical extensions of those made earlier. The Catholic Church, for example, despite the development of its close alliance with the language movement towards the end of the nineteenth century, was again fiercely criticized in O'Donnell's *The Ruin of Education in Ireland and the Irish Fanar*. Arguing that 'Priests kill the Irish language and Irish studies', Frank O'Donnell reiterated the charge that throughout the century 'multitudes of the Irish priests addressed their Irish-speaking congregations in the finest Maynooth English'. His conclusion was that 'the destruction of the national tongue is a serious moment in the existence of any race. When that destruction is precipitated by the priests of the national worship itself, need we wonder that the results may be abidingly calamitous for the race and the religion?' (O'Donnell 1903: 183). But if the church was subject to harsh criticism, by far the most frequent target of blame for the neglect of Gaelic were the leaders of Irish political nationalism.

In 'Politics and the Language'(1918) the nationalist historian P.S.Ó h-Eigceartaigh attributed responsibility for the shift from a Gaelic to an Anglophone Ireland:

It was politics which brought about that change: which enabled the English Government to establish and maintain in Ireland conditions which gave the Irish-speaking Irishman the choice of learning English, and using English, or of being shut out from every public function of life in his own country. There was no Irish leader from 1793, when the peril began, sufficiently clear-headed to see what was happening, and so a refusal to work the machine, the one thing which could have stopped it, was not forthcoming, and Irish gradually faded (Ó hEigceartaigh 1918: 17).

---

[2] Flann O'Brien repeated the criticism later: 'The present extremity of the Irish language is mainly due to the fact that the Gaels deliberately flung that instrument of beauty and precision from them, thrashed it out of their children and sneered in outlandish boor's English at those who were a few days slower than themselves in getting rid of it' (Bartlett et al 1988: 99).

Hyde made the exaggerated claim that 'the ancient Gaelic civilisation died with O'Connell' (Ó Conaire 1986: 158) because O'Connell's lead had been followed with few exceptions by the other leaders of political nationalism. It is open to question whether O'Connell had a developed sense of the consequences of the process which was underway, though he was certainly indifferent to the fact that Irish might fall into disuse. What is beyond doubt is that O'Connell did not 'work the machine' of constitutional politics in favour of the language, and for that he was repudiated by the language revivalists. Other politicians and their political parties were also charged with betrayal of the language cause. The fact that the first meeting of the Land League, in the Mayo Gaeltacht, was addressed in English by an Irish-speaking native of the area, Michael Davitt, was the subject of critical comment (Ó Loingsigh 1975: 14). And in 1901 the journal of the Gaelic League, *An Claidheamh Soluis* (The Sword of Light) described Redmond's Irish Parliamentary party as a 'huge anglicising agent' despite its adoption of resolutions in favour of the language movement. To prove its impartiality the paper also criticized the United Irish League for the same reasons; it observed that at a meeting in the Irish-speaking area of Dungloe, a resolution supporting the revival of Gaelic was passed in English (Ó Fearail 1975: 16).

In a claim calculated to appeal to those who remembered Irish political nationalism's history of treachery, D. P. Moran, author of *The Philosophy of Irish Ireland*, saw the language movement as holding an edge over political organizations:

There is one great advantage which a language movement has over a political agitation, an advantage which must appeal to a people sick to despair with disappointed hopes—it cannot be betrayed by its leaders... A movement of this kind stands like a cone upon its base, not like so many of our disastrous agitations, a cone upon its apex with one man holding it in place (Moran 1905: 27).

The disappointments and disasters which surrounded political nationalism, particularly in relation to the fall of Parnell, opened up a space for cultural nationalism to operate—political nationalism's difficulty was, to coin a phrase, cultural nationalism's opportunity. Yeats made the historical observation that 'the modern literature of Ireland, and indeed all that stir of thought which prepared for the Anglo-Irish war, began when Parnell fell from power in 1891. A disillusioned and embittered Ireland

turned from parliamentary politics' (Yeats 1955: 559). And in a letter to
*The Leader* written in 1900, he argued for precisely such a shift from a
purely political nationalism 'to a partly intellectual and historical nationalism ... with the language question as its lever' (Yeats 1975: 237).

Moran's view of the language movement, as an organization firmly
rooted in social, cultural, and historical tradition rather than the mundane exigencies of politics, became central to the cultural nationalist
movement's view of political nationalism. In essence the cultural activists accused the politicians of a mistaken understanding of nationalism;
it was an important idea which had two significant consequences. First,
it allowed the cultural nationalists to undermine their political colleagues
by charging them with acting against the interests of Ireland while
appearing to be fighting for it; the politicians took their revenge against
the cultural nationalists for this in the twentieth century. Second, it
allowed the cultural nationalists to claim that they did not have political
intentions. The fact that the principal organizing body of the cultural
nationalist movement, the Gaelic League, held to this principle for
twenty-two years before finally rescinding it is testimony both to the
tenacity of the belief and the wilful blindness of those who held it.

Political nationalism's historical mistake was outlined in Moran's
'The Battle of Two Civilisations':

since Grattan's time every popular leader, O'Connell, Butt, Parnell, Dillon and
Redmond, has perpetuated this primary contradiction. They threw over Irish
civilisation whilst they professed—and professed in perfect good faith—to
fight for Irish nationality. What potential genius that contradiction has choked,
what dishonesties and tragedies, above all what comedies, it has been responsible for (Gregory 1901: 27).

In *The Philosophy of Irish Ireland* Moran argued that it is 'not true that
politics is the only manifestation of nationality' and asserted that 'the
fact of being a sound political nationalist of any stamp, from a constitutional Home-Ruler to a fire-eating revolutionist, does not necessarily
mean that one is Irish at all' (Moran 1905: 69).

Other commentators too warned against the confusion of nationality
and politics:

A movement free from all political bias and outside of party spirit, may yet be
the national movement of the country; and such the Irish language revival
claims to be. Political weapons are not to be despised, nor can they well be
dispensed with; but we must not forget that politics are but a means to an end,

and that end is nationhood; nor must we forget that the political ideal may fall short of nationhood (O'Farrelly 1901: 3).

This prompted the key question as to what nationality entailed and in the first pamphlet published by the Gaelic League, *The True National Ideal,* Fr. O'Hickey attempted an answer:

It is the outcome, the resultant, the culmination of many things, of which political autonomy is but one—very important doubtless, but by no means the only or even the chief, thing to be considered. You may have a nation without political autonomy—not, I admit, a nation in all its fullness and integrity; but I emphatically insist that autonomous institutions, failing all other elements and landmarks of nationality, do not constitute a nation in the true sense (O'Hickey 1900: 1–2).

In other words, political independence would guarantee nothing except green flags where there used to be Union Jacks, Gaelic symbols on postage stamps rather than Victoria's visage, and Irish rather than British politicians. Political autonomy could even be achieved at the cost of Irish nationality if it meant the loss of the one factor which above all would guarantee national identity: the language itself. The problem with nineteenth-century political nationalism was that 'with its repeal Movements, Young Irelands, Fenians, National Leagues, and what not, that were put on foot to make Ireland free, no provision whatever was made or attempted to enable men and women born in this country to grow up Irish' (Moran 1905: 71). Political nationalism's failure was its neglect of the constitutive element of real Irishness; what cultural nationalism had to rectify was political nationalism's deficit. Its task was to supply the means by which the children of Ireland could 'grow up Irish'.

In a fateful emphasis it was education which was identified as the principal focus for the cultural nationalist project. Thomas Davis had coined the slogan 'educate that you may be free' and the idea that the Irish future lay in an education in the past, specifically the Irish language past, became a central doctrine. As part of this development the colonial scheme of education was largely blamed for the decline of the Gaelic language.[3] Yet as noted in the previous chapter, it would simply be wrong to claim that the colonial education system was used as the

---

[3] The most stringent critique of the education system was Pearse's 'The Murder Machine' (Pearse 1952: 5–50). His own position on the language question was bilingual education as a way of restoring Irish.

instrument to foist the English language on an unwilling populace. A more accurate account would be that the educational system played its part in the 'British policy of assimilation [which] was strengthened by the desire of Irish people, springing to a large extent from economic necessity, to learn English' (Kelly 2002: 4). However, once colonial education had been identified as the means by which English had triumphed, it appeared to be a corollary that an Irish education could lead to the successful revival of Irish.

An interest in the Gaelic past and the Gaelic language had been stimulated amongst the Anglo-Irish Ascendancy in the late eighteenth and early nineteenth centuries. This was largely based in the work of the Royal Irish Academy, particularly in the research undertaken by the Irish Ordnance Survey Commission after 1824. In the mid nineteenth century, by dint of the restricted nature of membership of the Academy, various scholarly societies appeared which served to stimulate wider interest for such research and this resulted in the publication of editions of Irish texts which had existed previously only in manuscript form. In addition, European academic interest in the Celtic languages, Irish in particular, was transformed by the publication of Zeuss's *Grammatica Celtica* in 1853, and such work outside Ireland further encouraged native study of the language and texts of the past. But interest in Irish was largely academic and historical rather than concerned with the language in the present. There were exceptions: the Ulster Gaelic Society had aimed to preserve ancient Irish literature, to maintain 'teachers of the Irish language where it most prevails', and to publish 'useful works in that tongue'.[4] And two commercial venturers had also taken an interest in the contemporary language. Philip Barron published *Ancient Ireland* in 1835, with 'the purpose of reviving the cultivation of the Irish Language and originating an earnest investigation into the Ancient History of Ireland', and founded an unsuccessful Irish college in Waterford (Barron 1835*a*). Richard D'Alton published *An Fíor Éirionnach* in 1862. However, the success of both projects reveals much about prevailing attitudes to the Irish language and attempts to preserve or revive it: Barron's magazine was published five times and folded while D'Alton's lasted for seven issues. Interest in the Gaelic language at the time was academic in both senses of the term: it was confined to scholars and it was otherwise redundant.

---

[4] The society published translations of Maria Edgeworth's *Forgive and Forget* and *Rosanna* in 1833.

In 1876 a society was founded which, though it was to have a limited existence, was to play an important part in the alteration of that situation. David Comyn wrote to *The Irishman* proposing the idea that those living outside the Gaeltacht areas should learn 'the historic language of Ireland' and attracted enough support to hold a meeting at which it was agreed to found a Society for the Preservation of the Irish Language (SPIL). The advertisement for the formation of the Society revealed its agenda:

To create such a tone of public feeling as will utterly banish the ignorant and unpatriotic notion (of foreign origin), that our native tongue is one which no Irishman of the present day should care to learn, or be willing to speak. If once the Irish people determine that their language shall not die, it will soon be taught in our primary and intermediate schools, especially such as are situated in those parts of the country where it is still spoken (SPIL 1880: 1).

The aims of the society, and the methods to achieve them, were published on St Patrick's Day 1877 and the first rule was that 'This Society is instituted for the Preservation and Extension of the Irish as a spoken Language' (SPIL 1880: 1). The methods included the encouragement of the use of Irish by those who knew it; the formation of classes and parochial associations for teaching it to adults; the teaching of the language in schools, especially in Irish-speaking areas; the publication of cheap basic works in the language; and the fostering of a modern Irish literature 'original or translated'. Such means would avoid the 'national reproach' engendered by the neglect of the language, and 'the universal disgrace which the loss of the living language of Ireland' would entail. Though culturally revolutionary (and at the time hopelessly idealist) the Society was supported by large numbers of the great and the good: Archbishop MacHale was its patron, Lord Conyngham was its President, and both Isaac Butt and the O'Conor Don were vice-presidents in its first year. When the Society issued a memorial to the National Commissioners of Education in 1878 urging that Irish be permitted in the national schools curriculum, there were 1,300 signatories including the Primate of All Ireland and members of the hierarchies of the Catholic Church and the Church of Ireland, the Lord Mayor of Dublin, and forty Members of Parliament as well as prominent members of the Society itself such as Hyde, Michael Cusack, and Fr. John Nolan (Ó Cuív 1996: 399). The response of the Government was to give Irish the status of a marginal extra subject for the purposes of results fees (the language, 'Celtic' as it was called, was introduced into the secondary schools when the Intermediate Education Board was set up, though it carried lower marks than other language subjects). Significantly it was through these concessions that the Irish language for the first time gained a place in the educational system. Notwithstanding the state's niggardliness, Comyn hailed the breakthrough as the most important advance in Ireland for six hundred years (evincing a tendency to hyperbolize its achievements which was to prove typical of the language movement). Ten years later Irish, an additional subject and thus only available outside school hours, was taught in fifty-one national schools (Greene 1972: 17) and such low take up was met with impatience on the part of a number of the language activists such as Canon Bourke, Thomas O'Neill Russell, Hyde, and Comyn. Criticizing SPIL as too intellectual and academic in its interests, they formed an alternative organization, the Gaelic Union (Aondacht na Gaedhilge) in 1880. With a more radical attitude towards retention of the language in Gaelic-speaking areas and its extension amongst the non-Gaelic speaking population, the new organization established *Irisleabhar na Gaedhilge/ The Gaelic Journal* under the editorship of Comyn in 1882. There had been earlier attempts at publishing selected items in Irish: Barron and D'Alton were mentioned above, the *Shamrock* published Irish songs and 'Lessons in Irish' between 1866 and 1882, and *Young Ireland* and *The Irishman* carried Irish-language contributions (Ó Cuív 1996: 399); in New York *An Gaodhal* (The Gael) was dedicated to 'the Preservation and Cultivation of the Irish language and the Autonomy of the Irish Nation' (O'Leary 1994: 7). But *Irisleabhar na Gaedhilge/The Gaelic Journal* was the first magazine in Ireland 'exclusively devoted to the interests of the Irish language' (Gaelic Union 1882: 17). The rejection of antiquarianism and the positive attitude towards the modern Irish language which the *Gaelic Journal* espoused marked a turning point in the language movement's history.

One of the contributors to the first issue of the *Gaelic Journal* was Douglas Hyde, the son of a Church of Ireland rector who learnt Irish during his childhood in Roscommon and his student days at Trinity. It was Hyde who made perhaps the most important speech in the history of Irish cultural nationalism, 'The necessity for De-Anglicising Ireland', to the National Literary Society in 1892. Though presented by a somewhat unlikely revolutionary, the ideological ramifications of the talk were far-reaching; Hyde's address set an agenda for cultural nationalism, and by default political nationalism, which was to have effects that stretched far into the twentieth century. Yet the immediate reception given to the talk was little less than incredulous. After its initial delivery Hyde prepared to reiterate his ideas at the Contemporary Club a week later but the chairman of the debate ruled that they should move instead to another topic 'which has a greater appearance of reality attached to it' (Ó Fearaíl 1975: 2). Ireland in the early 1890s did not seem quite ready for the idea that the linguistic effects of seven centuries of colonial rule could be, or even should be, cast off for the betterment of the nation. Apart from a small band of language enthusiasts almost everybody, from the leaders of Ireland's Home Rule campaign to the poorest inhabitants of the Gaelic-speaking areas, believed that English was to be the future language of Ireland. Hyde's speech aimed at reversing that belief and it was a masterpiece of its kind.

The argument began by stating that it was not 'a protest against what is *best* in the English people, for that would be absurd', but that the aim was 'to show the folly of neglecting what is Irish, and hastening to adopt, pell-mell and indiscriminatingly, everything that is English, simply because it *is* English' (Ó Conaire 1986: 153). Hyde's point was to demonstrate Ireland's 'most anomalous position, imitating England and yet apparently hating it' (Ó Conaire 1986: 154). Ireland, apparently on the verge of Home Rule, was in the contradictory position of neither being faithful to its own history nor embracing a role within the British Empire. Hyde's explanation for this curious paradox was challenging and based on the charge of self-neglect:

What the battleaxe of the Dane, the sword of the Norman, the wile of the Saxon were unable to perform, we have accomplished ourselves. We have at last broken the continuity of Irish life, and just at the moment when the Celtic race is presumably about to largely recover possession of its own country, it finds itself deprived and stript of its Celtic characteristics, cut off from the past, yet scarcely in touch with the present (Ó Conaire 1986: 157).

The remedy was both simple and radical: to reverse the process of Anglicization by removing the material effects which it had left behind. For example, colonial legislation of 1495 had ordered that the Irish should adopt English surnames, and Spenser had recommended the reinvocation of the statute in the 1590s, taking its purpose as the encouragement of individual rather than clan-based or national identity:

each one should take upon himselfe a severall surname, either of his trade and facultie, or of some quality of his body or minde, or of the place where he dwelt, so as every one should be distinguished from the other, or from the most part, whereby they shall not onely not depend upon the head of their sept, as now they do, but also in time learne quite to forget his Irish nation (Spenser 1633: 109).[5]

For Hyde the process of learning to forget Irishness had to be reversed and the Irish names which had been changed now needed to be altered back: Maud to Mève, Eileen to Eibhlin, Daniels to O'Donnell, Bradley to O'Brollahan, and so on. Topography too was another casualty of colonialism, since for Hyde Irish place-names had been treated 'with about the same respect as if they were the names of a savage tribe which had never before been reduced to writing . . . as vulgar English squatters treat the topographical nomenclature of the Red Indians' (Ó Conaire 1986: 157). Thus, among other examples, the river Nore had to be re-named the Feóir, Lock Corrib Loch Orsen, and Telltown Tailtin. The Anglicization of music had to be halted, and the harp, pipes, and fiddles reintroduced. And sport was also included since the *Statute of Kilkenny* (1366) had ordained that the colonizers 'do not, henceforth, use the plays which men call horlings, with great sticks and a ball upon the ground, from which great evils and maims have arisen, to the weakening of the defence of the said land' but adopt instead the 'gentlemanlike games' of the English (Irish Archaeological Society 1843: 23). The nationalist response had to be to restore or codify Gaelic games (the rules for Gaelic football were first registered in 1885) through the politically important institution of the Gaelic Athletic Association.

There were two major factors above all others which needed to be addressed in the de-Anglicizing process. The first was literature and Hyde stressed the need to encourage the reading of 'Anglo-Irish literature' instead of English imports, particularly English magazines. Against the debasing influences of contemporary English writing only such stalwarts of national sentiment as Moore's *Irish Melodies* (first published in two volumes in 1808) and the writings of Thomas Davis could prevent the vulgarization of Irish taste. The second element in de-Anglicization, and in Hyde's view the most important, had to be the revival of the national language:

---

[5] For details of the 1495 legislation see Chapter two.

I have no hesitation at all in saying that every Irish-feeling Irishman, who hates the reproach of West-Britonism, should set himself to encourage the efforts which are being made to keep alive our once national tongue. The losing of it is our greatest blow, and the sorest stroke that the rapid Anglicisation of Ireland has inflicted upon us. In order to de-Anglicise ourselves we must at once arrest the decay of the language (Ó Conaire 1986: 160).

For Hyde the Gaelic language was the link to the Gaelic past, to that period when Ireland was central to European culture and learning; it was the means by which the Irish had distinguished themselves in history both in terms of their achievements and with regard to their unique identity; it was the only barrier to the complete eradication of the Irish nation in terms of its past manifestations and its present and future potential. Once the language was lost, cultural nationalism would be but a sad, oxymoronic phrase, and Irish culture itself would be nothing more than an empty parody of its English counterpart. Such dispossession would be irreparable and thus Hyde appealed to all shades of Irish opinion, laying claim both to 'the sympathies of every intelligent Unionist' and to radical political nationalism (his call for activities based on a 'house-to-house visitation and exhortation of the people' was a reference to the Fenian leader James Stephens). The claim was based on the ideal of a deep common identity which endured in spite of superficial differences: 'in a word, we must strive to cultivate everything which is most racial, most smacking of the soil, most Gaelic, most Irish, because in spite of the little admixture of Saxon blood in the north-east corner, this island *is* and will *ever* remain Celtic to the core ... (Ó Conaire 1986: 169). The shared 'racial' identity (in which Irish was conflated with Gaelic which was in turn conflated with Celtic) was the basis upon which various odd fellow travellers could gather under the banner umbrella of cultural nationalism for an extended period. It was also the foundation which, when it ultimately proved unstable, provoked the beginning of the end of the cultural project which was supposed to hold the nation together. Hyde's belief in the common ground was articulated as a call to unity:

I appeal to every one whatever his politics—for this is no political matter—to do his best to help the Irish race to develop in future along Irish lines, even at the risk of encouraging national aspirations, because upon Irish lines alone can the Irish race once more become what it was of yore—one of the most original, artistic, literary, and charming peoples of Europe (Ó Conaire 1986: 170).

Cultural nationalism was simply the return to the Gaelic cultural past in order to guarantee the continuation of the Irish nation; in that sense it could be promoted as apolitical and a force for unity rather than as politically divisive. That claim to apolitical status was to be at once cultural nationalism's greatest strength and in the end one of its most profound weaknesses.

The basic tenets of Hyde's argument were repeated often, sometimes directly, sometimes obliquely, and were in essence that: Ireland had declined from a previous glorious Gaelic past; the decline was attributable to Anglicization; Anglicization was the result of both colonialism and Irish imitation; English popular culture was a particular danger to Irishness; Anglicization needed to be reversed by a return to Gaelic customs and traditions; the Irish language was the key to the restoration of Ireland's Gaelic greatness; the language was part of the common shared inheritance of all of the people of Ireland; the language question was thus non-political and unifying rather than a cause of division. These were the beliefs of which Hyde attempted to persuade his listeners at the National Literary Society in 1892 and they were in the main unconvinced. But though he could not have known it, that evening Hyde was unleashing revolutionary forces in Irish history.

In March 1893 Eoin MacNeill, an Ulster Catholic, issued 'A Plea and a Plan for the Extension of the Movement to Preserve and Spread the Irish Language' in the *Gaelic Journal*. Noting that previous movements to preserve Irish had been limited to educators and the middle classes, and that there was 'among the mass of the people . . . an attitude of indifference', he proposed that it was time 'to appeal directly to the masses through a movement organised on a parochial basis and addressing itself to units made up of small numbers' (McCartney 1973: 79). This led directly to the formation of Conradh na Gaeilge (The Gaelic League) and the inaugural meeting was held on 31 July 1893. Among the founding members were MacNeill, Hyde (President), and Thomas O'Neill Russell and the membership soon included Cusack, Comyn, the Rev. Euseby Cleaver, Fr. Eugene O'Growney, and Fr. Michael O'Hickey.[6] The aims of the League echoed those of the Society for the Preservation of the Irish Language and were: '1. The preservation of Irish as the National language of Ireland, and the extension of its use as

---

[6] The early membership of the league was notably interdenominational; see Greene 1972: 9–19.

a spoken language. 2. The study and publication of existing Irish literature, and the cultivation of a modern Irish literature in Irish' (Ó Fearaíl 1975: 6). Despite what many Leaguers thought, however, the aim of preserving and extending Irish was precisely not a project to restore the language as the spoken tongue of the whole country, and in this the Gaelic League was following the lead given by earlier revivalists. In 1843 Davis countered an objection to 'attempting the revival of Irish' by replying that any effort to introduce the language through the schools or courts in the eastern side of Ireland 'would certainly fail, and the reaction might extinguish it altogether'; such a project was therefore not proposed, 'save as a dream of what may happen a hundred years hence'. But, he continued, 'it is quite another thing to say, as we do, that the Irish language should be cherished, taught, and esteemed, and that it can be preserved and gradually extended' (Davis 1914: 105). In 'The Irish Language', an address delivered in 1891, Hyde argued for a comparable limited task:

I do not for a moment advocate making Irish the language of the country at large, or of the National Parliament. I do not want to be an impossible visionary or rabid partisan. What I wish to see is Irish established as a living language, for all time, among the million or half million who still speak it along the West coast, and to insure that the language will hold a favourable place in teaching institutions and government examinations (Ó Conaire 1986: 152).

He justified this pragmatic vision in part on the ground that 'a bilingual race are infinitely superior to a race that speaks only one language'.

The effects of the Gaelic League's activities, however, cannot be overestimated; Pearse, announcing what he considered to be the league's epitaph in 1913, declared that when its founders had met twenty years previously 'they were commencing...not a revolt, but a revolution' (Pearse 1952: 95). Though the league was modelled to a great extent on previous mass participation movements such as the Land League and the Gaelic Athletic Association, its methods were novel and radically modern. Rather than the debating chamber favoured by the Irish parliamentarians, or even popular agitation in the form of the 'monster meetings' which had been favoured by O'Connell, though it used both, the Gaelic League chose propaganda as its weapon and education as its battlefield. Hyde made the priorities clear at an early stage: 'we can, however, insist, and we *shall* insist if Home Rule be carried, that the Irish language...be placed on a par with—or even above—Greek, Latin, and modern languages, in all examinations held under the Irish Government' (Ó Conaire 1986: 161). Political freedom was desirable but without cultural independence it was empty; and cultural independence depended upon the education of the Irish people. Rather than being free in order to educate, the Gaelic Leaguers remained faithful to Davis' project of educating for freedom.

The extent of the league's educative and propagandist mission can be seen in its popular publications and activities. Having taken over *The Gaelic Journal* in 1893, the league established its own official bilingual organ *An Claidheamh Soluis* (The Sword of Light) in 1899.[7] It published O'Growney's *Simple Lessons in Irish* (1894), the first part of which sold 360,000 copies by 1904 (Ó Cuív 1996: 427). And at the turn of the century it established a publishing scheme for collections of short stories, folktales, a number of novels and plays, translations from English, and editions of prose and poetry from manuscript sources. In 1900–1901 it put out over one hundred thousand copies of various pamphlets broadly concerned with educational issues. The pamphlets included among others O'Hickey's *The True National Ideal* and *The Future of Irish in the National Schools*; Butler's *Irishwomen and the Home Language*; Hyde's *A University Scandal*; Kavanagh's *Ireland's Defence—Her Language*; O'Reilly's *The Threatening Metempsychosis of a Nation*; Martyn's *Ireland's Battle for Her Language*; and the evidence from the contentious debates on the role of Irish in schools in *The Irish Language and Irish Intermediate Education*. As can be seen from the titles, the formal education system subsidized by the State was one of the league's principal targets in its campaigns. The belief was that since the colonial education system had contributed to the plight of the Irish language in the past, then for the Gaelic League the very same system must be made to support its revival. The stress on education as the chief means of preserving the language was to have important consequences in the twentieth century.

The league's battles with various arms of the educational establishment were important both in terms of its own aims and in cultivating the esteem in which it was held by the majority of the Irish population. One of its first public successful debates was with T. W. Rolleston, Trinity College graduate, poet, and founding editor of the *Dublin University Review*, whose charge was the same that had been laid against the English

---

[7] The first political paper published in Irish was Pearse's *An Barr Buadh* in 1912.

language in the Renaissance period: that Irish simply was not copious enough for modern intellectual thought and culture.[8] The major educational contests, however, were more protracted and acrimonious, and although they attracted a great deal of publicity and many more adherents to the cause, they also revealed the types of division which were later to bedevil the language movement. The first campaign which saw the league at the forefront of public attention was its submission to a Royal Commission investigation of the intermediate school curriculum. Eager to build on the limited gains made by the Society for the Preservation of the Irish Language some twenty years earlier, the league was concerned to enhance the status of Gaelic in the Intermediate Schools. Its chief opponents were two Trinity dons, Professors Mahaffy and Atkinson, both of whom disparaged Irish in their evidence to the commission. Atkinson, Todd Professor of Celtic Languages at the Royal Irish Academy and an editor of facsimile versions of Irish texts such as the *Book of Leinster*, the *Book of Ballymote*, and the *Yellow Book of Lecan*, asserted that 'it would be difficult to find a book in ancient Irish in which there was not some passage so silly or indecent as to give you a shock from which you would not recover during the rest of your life' (O'Leary 1994: 223). If this was the triumph of ideology over knowledge, then Mahaffy's evidence was the victory of ideology over ignorance. Knowing nothing of the language, Mahaffy's comments veered between condescension and contempt. Questioned whether the real utility of Irish was simply philological, Mahaffy's answer was that 'it is sometimes useful to a man fishing for salmon or shooting grouse in the West. I have often found a few words very serviceable'. Asked his opinion of 'Celtic' as a school subject, Mahaffy opined that 'it is a mischievous waste of time' (Gaelic League 1901: 12). The Gaelic League's successful response was led by Hyde and rested on the evidence of a formidable cohort of leading European scholars (Zimmer, Windisch, Meyer, Pedersen, Stern, Dottin) attesting to the academic and cultural advantages of the study of Irish. The league's victory was two-fold. First, it gained concessions from the commissioners; Irish could be taught as an

---

[8] Rolleston's challenge was to present a passage of scientific prose to the Gaelic League for translation into Irish. The piece would then be given to an Irish speaker for translation back into English, and the translation and the original could then be compared for intellectual coherence. Accepting the challenge Hyde translated into Irish and MacNeill worked the piece back into English; after comparison Rolleston was convinced and later joined the Gaelic League (Ó Fearaíl 1975: 5).

ordinary school language provided it did not hinder the teaching of other subjects. Second, it attracted widespread publicity and public support for the language movement. Mahaffy's patrician disdain did the Gaelic League more good than harm; not for the first or last time, the enemy's intransigence and contempt contributed greatly to the success of the nationalist movement.

A further campaign for bilingual education, supported by a Gaelic League pamphlet by Archbishop Walsh, the Catholic Archbishop of Dublin, was successful in 1904; the bilingual programme ordained a curriculum in Irish and English which could be used in Irish-speaking or bilingual districts. Other battles were more difficult, however, and one in particular demonstrated the league's undoubted steadfastness to its ideals and willingness to take on powerful enemies; it also evinced the first public divisions between the forces gathered under the league's tent. The controversy arose as a result of the government's decision to establish the National University of Ireland in 1908, a move greeted by the league with a demand that Irish be a requirement for matriculation. In *Irish in the National University of Ireland* (1909) MacNeill summarized the issue:

1. Should the National University of Ireland require a preparatory knowledge on the part of its students at entrance of some special and distinctively Irish branch of knowledge, by virtue of which the University and its studies will be differentiated in character from those of non-Irish universities?
2. If so, what is the distinctively Irish branch of knowledge that will suffice for the purpose? (MacNeill 1909: 14).

For the Gaelic League the answer to the first question was undoubtedly yes, and to the second the reply was that there could be no subject 'that can effectively take the place of the Irish language with a view to conferring a distinctively Irish character on the work, the "atmosphere", and the future *personnel* of the members of the university' (MacNeill 1909: 14). The hierarchy of the Catholic Church (supported by Redmond and Dillon, the leaders of the parliamentary party), however, opposed 'compulsory Irish' principally on the grounds that it would drive those who did not have the required language qualification to (Protestant) Trinity College instead. Hyde, though at the forefront of the campaign, also noted that it would alienate the Catholic middle class (Garvin 1987: 59). The bitter controversy which followed damaged the language movement in various ways: several important public supporters left the Gaelic League; others paid high personal costs for their involvement; and a division was made between hard-liners and moderates. The debate sank to a low tone. One of the respondents to the campaign against the Irish matriculation requirement was the Maynooth Professor of Irish and prominent Gaelic Leaguer, Fr. Michael O'Hickey, whose contributions to the debate were at best intemperate, at worst simply damaging. Commenting on the objectors to compulsory Irish (with the exception of Archbishop Walsh) O'Hickey asserted that 'to be opposed by the colonists is one thing we are accustomed to; to be opposed by a section of our own, no matter how worthless and degenerate, is not to be endured' (Ó Fiaich 1972: 72–3). The tenor of O'Hickey's comments led to a demand for his resignation from his Chair by the hierarchy, a demand which once refused was followed by dismissal. Nonetheless the Gaelic League won the argument about Irish for matriculation purposes when in 1909 the general council of the county councils threatened to make their university scholarship scheme dependent on the policy. But the campaign had witnessed accusations concerning degeneracy, worthlessness, proper Irish behaviour and opinions, and a proposal for blacklists.[9] One positive aspect of the league's success was an increase in the number of students taking Irish in the secondary schools; a negative effect was the further propagation of definitions of Irish identity which were exclusive and divisive.

Though victories in debates about the provision of Irish in formal educational contexts were noteworthy, they were as nothing compared to the Gaelic League's wider success in establishing the language as the key to the nationalist movement's project. If the answer to Yeats' question in 'The Man and the Echo', 'Did that play of mine send out | Certain men the English shot?'(Yeats 1957: 632), was, as Paul Muldoon has bluntly asserted, '"Certainly not". | If Yeats had saved his pencil-lead | would certain men have stayed in bed?' (Muldoon 1987: 39), then a more qualified assessment might be given of the effect of the Gaelic League's work. To put it in the terms of Antonio Gramsci, a contemporary political theorist and a keen (doctoral) student of language questions, what the league achieved in the early twentieth century was the formation of a new cultural hegemony. It played a crucial role in the revolution in thought which was central to the overthrow of colonial

---

[9] To his opponents O'Hickey's most objectionable act was his mention of the record of those who had voted for the Act of Union and his call for a similar blacklist of those voting against compulsory Irish.

rule in Ireland; of that there can be no doubt whatsoever. As Pearse claimed in 1913, the 'coming revolution' was to be undertaken by 'the men and movements that have sprung from the Gaelic League' (Pearse 1952: 91).

As demonstrated in Chapter five, the relationship between language and national identity had been a key concept for European cultural nationalism in the late eighteenth and early nineteenth centuries. In Ireland such a relationship had been posited much earlier and there were two aspects to this which need to be understood in the light of colonial history. From the colonizer's view, the danger was that the Irish language embodied and ensured radical difference and acted as a barrier to cultural and political assimilation, hence Spenser's warning that 'the speach being *Irish*, the heart must needes bee *Irish*' (Spenser 1633: 48). From the point of view of the colonized, the problem was that the language was the only sure warranty of Irish identity, hence Donlevy's definitive comment that '*Irish-Men* without *Irish* is an incongruity, and a great Bull' (Donlevy 1742: 506–7). What both the colonizers and the colonized agreed upon was the central belief that the Irish language was the key to a distinct, in fact radically separate, sense of Irishness: for the one Irish was a problem, for the other it was a necessity. And that was a lesson which the Gaelic Leaguers took on board and made a central doctrine.

In *The True National Ideal* (1900) O'Hickey asked the questions which were crucial to the enterprise of forging a new Ireland: 'what is a nation? Or, in other words, what is nationality?' The answer was that nationality was compounded of several elements such as tradition, history, language, literature, and institutions, but of these features, some are more important than others and 'none is more fundamental, none more important, none strikes deeper roots, none is more far-reaching in its results than a national language. This truth the Dutch clearly grasped, and have enshrined in a proverb—"No language, no nation"' (O'Hickey 1900: 2). A version of that truth became the Gaelic League's own motto: 'Tír is Teanga' (the Nation is the Language). As a mode of truth, the doctrine was open to the scientific gaze of the late nineteenth century and to description in its legitimating discourses such as that of Ethnology. Ethnology in particular, the Reverend Patrick Forde argued, was of interest because it enquires into 'the laws which govern the origin and growth of racial diversities, how the many races of men who now inhabit this globe differ, and came to differ'. This was of relevance to the

Irish because one of the fundamental racial differences was that 'each nation has a character and a language of its own, has its own peculiar and characteristic gifts of body and soul, of mind and heart'. Thus when studying national characters, the national language is of unique benefit to the ethnologist since 'scientists find a real intrinsic connection between the two'. To appreciate the significance of this point, Forde told his readers, 'you should bear in mind that science deals with the fixed laws of nature, not with accidental or random conventions (Forde 1901: 2). Rather than looking to history for an explanation of the link between the language and national identity, Forde claimed to find something more reliable: the link is a fact of nature rather than a socially and historically constructed connection. While it may strike some as odd that a Catholic priest should use the rhetoric of scientificity in this way, it needs to be remembered that from this perspective the fixed laws of nature were ordained by a higher power. The linkage between language and nation existed not simply as a natural fact, but as part of the Deity's order: 'Each nation has its own country and its own soul, its own language and its own liberty given to it by Almighty God, as the means whereby the Divine plan is to be wrought out' (Forde 1901: 2).

Yet if the link between language and nation were abstract and formal, fixed by nature and God, validated by science and theology, the realization of the link was precisely historical. In fact nowhere else could the history of the nation be more reliably discovered:

A people's language tells us what they were even better than their history. So true is this that even if the people had perished and their history had been lost, we might still learn from their language—and in language I include literature—to what intellectual stature they had attained, what was the extent and direction of their moral development, and what their general worthiness (Kavanagh 1902: 1).

Unsurprisingly, given that the authors of many of the Gaelic League pamphlets were clerics, there is a constant slippage in such texts between the metaphysical and the historical realms. God ordained the nation, gave it its language, and then human beings, endowed with free will, created the national history which in turn was reflected back in the language. History itself, however, was not considered in terms of the categories of discontinuity and rupture, tragedy and disaster, which more radical commentators used at the time. In the language wing of

cultural nationalism, history, or at least proper Irish history, was conceived in terms of the idealist sense of tradition: of continuity and
simple transmission, of endurance through time, of the triumph of
eternal values over the contingencies of material fact. Thus when a
father teaches the Irish language to a child, there is more occurring than
a simple education in language: 'he makes his infant child a denizen of
an empire that embraces the past and present, he makes him heir to the
thought, the wisdom, the imagination, the melody of his ancestors, he
supplies him with a medium in which he can continue the interrupted
conversation of those that went before him' (Dinneen 1904: 12). It was a
conception of history and society couched in the idealist terms which
Edmund Burke had used more than a century earlier: 'a partnership not
only between those who are living, but between those who are living,
those who are dead, and those who are to be born' (Burke 1790: 195).

There were others who shared this vision of the nation and its
traditions, particularly with regard to the centrality of language. One
commentator, for example, noted that the defining characteristic of a
nation was not racial identity, or land, or even 'the physical fact of one
blood'. The nation is united through 'the mental fact of one tradition'
and,

just because a nation is a tradition of thought and sentiment, and thought and
sentiment have deep congruities with speech, there is the closest of affinities
between nation and language. Language is not mere words. Each word is
charged with associations that touch feelings and evoke thoughts. You cannot
share these thoughts and feelings unless you can unlock their associations by
having the key of language. You cannot enter the heart and know the mind of a
nation unless you know its speech (Barker 1915: 13).

The irony is that this was not written by a member of the Irish language
movement, but by a leading English cultural nationalist with reference
to the English language. In England, during the social and political crisis
engendered by the First World War, cultural conservatives turned to the
language as the repository of national traditions and national identity. In
Ireland much the same reflex occurred, though with radically different
ends since in Ireland both the language and the nation were under
threat. Thus O'Farrelly drew attention to the 'internal cancer that is
eating away the heart and soul of Ireland' and diagnosed that 'the root of
the cancer is in the English language, or rather, in the loss of the Irish
language, and the sole use of English over the greater part of the

country' (O'Farrelly 1901: 3).[10] In an interesting argument which is essentially an attack on 'cosmopolitanism', she defended the right of independent small nations to uphold their own cultures and traditions:

In being true to the duties which come in our own way in our own corner of earth we are thus working for the general good . . . It means that having fulfilled our duties to ourselves and to the land where God has thrown our destinies, we are ready to stretch the hand of friendship to all men. It means that having developed the individualism that is our birthright we are ready to give and take in the mutual action of nations (O'Farrelly 1901: 2).

In an argument which still has force in the context of neo-colonialism and 'globalization' Trench extended the point:

The mingling of races, the increase of communication, may cause national languages to disappear or be merged in a universal speech. If this is to take place through a gradual process of evolution no one will oppose its consummation. National language movements are not as a protest against the abolition of barriers of race in the interests of human solidarity, but against the forcible extermination of a racial genius through the pressure of political and economic circumstance (Trench 1912: 29).

Trench's essay is in part concerned with the relationship between language, thought, and politics. It was a connection which the colonizers made in the early modern period, as noted in Chapters three and four, but in the twentieth century it became central in the theory of linguistic determinism, a strain of thought ranging from the Sapir–Whorf hypothesis, through George Orwell's depiction of the dystopian future in 1984, to contemporary concerns with political 'spin'. Citing the example of the Irish and English words for the bird 'pilbín' (plover), Trench noted their distinct effects on the mind of an Irishman and concluded that 'it raises the interesting question as to whether an Irish word has not a greater inherent power of drawing forth an Irish mind than attaches to the word in any other tongue, quite apart from the question as to whether such a mind has acquired a previous knowledge of the Irish language'. Even a recent learner of the language, he argued, would confirm 'that "pilbín" expresses his meaning with a truth to which the English "plover" cannot attain' (Trench 1912: 27). Unlike the neo-Kantian belief that language determines mind, Trench's postulated

---

[10] O'Farrelly's rhetoric of disease was a return to that used during the Plantation period and the Famine; see Chapter two, note nine.

linkage is more complex: the Irish mind pre-exists language, but it can only be fully expressed when articulated in its own natural medium, the Gaelic language. Given this constitutive role, it is unsurprising that Irish was constructed rhetorically as being both essential to the nation and in grave danger. In *Ireland's Defence—Her Language* Kavanagh claimed that 'an enslaved nation can call nothing of its own but its mind, but the mind of a nation must in time follow its language, and when the national language is lost the national mind cannot long survive. When both are lost it is easily absorbed and assimilated by its enslaver'(Kavanagh 1902: 2). And the function of language in offering resistance to colonial assimilation was reiterated by Moran. When young Irish men and women, he claimed, could speak Irish as well as English, 'then there will be a genuine Irish nation—whoever may be making the laws—which economic tendencies, battering rams, or the Queen's soldiers will be powerless to kill' (Moran 1905: 27). Moran's faith in the political power of culture as a form of national resistance to colonial domination was widely shared in the language movement. What the cultural nationalists were arguing in essence was that language, as the central element in Irishness, was the key to all of the debates taking place within Ireland, be they cultural, political, or economic. 'Gan teanga, gan tír' (no language, no nation): the disappearance of the language would mean the end of conflict since, quite simply, there would be nothing to fight over.

One tactic deployed by the cultural nationalists in their campaigns was the re-inscription of the cultural binary divide between the Irish and the English (a division which the colonists had created). There have been recent readings of this manoeuvre which have attempted to read it as mere polemic and which have stressed that the excesses in which certain proponents indulged were uncharacteristic. O'Leary, for example has argued, properly, that the language movement's rhetorical strategies were varied and complex, with even the same people on different occasions espousing contradictory viewpoints (O'Leary 1994). Kiberd has also proposed, less convincingly, that the use of stereotypes by the language revivalists was 'an inevitable, nationalist phase through which they and their country had to pass *en route* to liberation' (Kiberd 1996: 32). It is not quite clear why this was inevitable but be that as it may, it is certainly the case that the stereotyping was crude and offensive, as well as effective and durable. The division was radical: Kavanagh described the English as 'a people with whom [the

Irish] have nothing in common but a common humanity' and added that between them 'nature itself has drawn a broad line of separation, I must say a triple line, geographical, moral and intellectual' (Kavanagh 1902: 10). Others were less reserved; an editorial in *An Claidheamh Soluis* in 1917 asserted simply that 'An Irishman, however bad, is better than an Englishman, however good' (O'Leary 1994: 211).

One mode of distinction was drawn up on the grounds of taste and decorum. Yeats described the Irish language as 'the only barrier against the growing vulgarity of England' (Yeats 1975: 45). Dinneen couched the situation in the more common apocalyptic language: 'the struggle between the languages, is a deeper, a more far-reaching struggle than appears on the surface, it is a struggle between the civilisations which these languages represent' (Dinneen 1904: 28). The danger was that the English language, if its pervasive influence in Ireland were not resisted by the revival of Gaelic, would bring with it modern English values and habits, as embodied in English literature in its various modes:

The English language is overrun with the weeds of triteness and vulgarity. Its vocabulary is being daily increased in all directions. Science, art, history, economies, industries, athletics, horse racing, gambling, and the rest are claiming to be heard. The quality of poetry has declined; the quality of the drama has declined. Prose in its richest domains has declined; the novel, a plant of recent growth, has lost its strength and flavour and lives on sensation, pruriency or mawkishness (Dinneen 1904: 26–7).

Following Hyde's lead in 'De-Anglicising Ireland', there was a repeated focus on the corrupting effects of English popular culture. O'Farrelly drew attention to the consequences of cheap English literature in cities, railway stations, and country towns and the horror of 'the purity of the Celtic mind coming into contact with London's exhalations' (O'Farrelly 1901: 6–7). The result was apparent: 'we are being touched by the influence of a material race. Here we can see the evils of commercialism without any of the solid benefits'. The only answer was, as Butler termed it, 'a war to the death between Irish ideals and British sordid soullessness' (Butler 1901: 2). Of particular concern for many writers was the music hall, probably because its reach was not dependent upon literacy. Moran, noting that the English poor are 'largely composed of the dregs of their race' while the rich amount to no more than Caliban with manners (a neat inversion of colonial stereotypes), warned that 'there are worthier things between heaven and earth than English music halls,

May meetings, company promoters and bean feasts' (Moran 1905: 44–5). These, and things like them, he argued, 'may represent some of the highest points of English civilisation', but any culture worthy of the name would treat them with contempt (Moran 1901: 26).

Even making allowance for rhetorical excess, the postulated opposition between the Irish and the English in such arguments spoke both of a confidence in the Gaelic revivalist position and yet also a desperate fear that Anglicization was rapidly succeeding; it was a reverse image of the fears of the Renaissance colonists. What the revivalists often did in fact was to take colonial stereotypes of the Irish and invert them for positive effect (superstition became spirituality, pugnacity a sense of self-pride, lying the tradition of oral story-telling); in doing so they often turned the Irish into versions of the respectable Victorian middle classes, values and prejudices included. And they also produced their own versions of the English. Moran described 'the English mind' as 'narrow and bigoted by nature' and 'bloated by the fat traditions of success' (Moran 1905: 45). O'Reilly was more detailed in his account:

It is a fleshy spirit, bent towards earth; a mind unmannerly, vulgar, insolent, bigoted; a mind to which pride, and lust, and mammon are the matter-of-course aims of life, the only conceivable objects worthy of pursuit; a mind to which real Christian virtue is incredible, and sure to be set down as clever hypocrisy or stark imbecility; a mind where every absurd device, from grossest Darwinisim to most preposterous spiritualism, is resorted to and hoped in, to choke the voice of eternity in the conscience (O'Reilly 1901: 4).

What this produced were two opposed racial types. As Séamus Ó Grianna formulated it in 1921, it was important to understand that 'there is a world of difference between the soul of an Englishman and the soul of a Gael—that the Englishman is deceitful, full of faults, scoundrelly, and false; and the Gael is straightforward, honest, and innocent' (O'Leary 1994: 465). Not everyone was taken in by the rhetoric: Shaw mocked that 'when people ask me what Sinn Féin means, I say it is the Irish for John Bull' (Shaw 1962: 149).

As O'Reilly's comment indicates the division between the Irish and the English was not simply cultural, it was more significantly religious. That this element should be stressed is predictable, given the overwhelmingly Catholic nature of the language movement's membership (despite the significant role of Protestants in the Gaelic League such as Hyde the Catholic church was central to the organization's development and activities). Morris, in an essay in the league's organ *Fáinne an Lae* entitled 'The Loss of the Irish Language and Its Influence on the Catholic Religion in Ireland', asked Catholics to consider, 'is it their duty, is there any moral obligation on them to preserve the Irish language merely and solely *for the sake of their religion*'. He continued:

I will not speak here of the baneful effects of English literature—Protestant, infidel, immoral; or of subjecting the intellect of a soulful, spiritual people like the Irish to that of a sordid, wordly race like the English by adopting their language and literature...Irish is pre-eminently the language of prayer and devotion. Its dignity and impressive majesty admirably suit the themes of religion...it has for Catholics an altogether peculiar interest common to themselves alone (Morris 1898: 8).

There were others who argued that the Irish language and Catholicism were inextricably entwined, including one of the Gaelic League's founders, Eoin MacNeill: 'When we learn to speak Irish, we soon find that it is what we may call essential Irish to acknowledge God, His presence, and His help, even in our most trivial conversation' (Lyons 1979: 80).[11] Ó Braonáin made clear the relative merits of the English and Irish languages with regard to the Catholic faith and, implicitly, the future of the Irish nation:

English is the language of infidelity. It is infidels who for the most part speak English. It is infidels who for the most part compose literature in English. Infidels have most of the power in the English-speaking world...The sooner we discard English and revive our own language, the better off the faith will be in Ireland (O'Leary 1994: 24).

The message that Irish had an interest peculiar to Catholics was of course contrary to the principles of the Gaelic League (and was repudiated by it) and flew in the face of a history of Protestant involvement with the language.[12] But it was a message which gradually came to dominate. Against his characterization of the English mind as material and worldly, O'Reilly posited even pre-Christian Ireland as 'emphatically and eminently a mind inclining towards religion. It was chaste, idealistic, mystical. It was spiritual beyond the ways of men' (O'Reilly 1901: 1). In order to preserve the Irish mind and to resist the English

---

[11] 'Dia dhuit', an Irish greeting, can be translated etymologically as God be with you; but then so can 'goodbye'.

[12] For overviews of Protestant engagement with Irish see Blaney 1996, Ó Glaisne 1981, and Ó Snodaigh 1995.

mind, O'Reilly saw only one possibility: 'if this nation is to live on, or the Church of this nation, the Irish mind will have to be preserved; and to try to preserve it without the Irish tongue, is to endeavour to hold it while choosing the best means for letting it go' (O'Reilly 1901: 5). Against any attempt to propose a form of secular nationalism, typified by the slogan, 'no priests in politics', O'Reilly asserted that such a sentiment 'could not be rendered into Irish idiom. The genius of the Gaelic tongue could no more assimilate it, than the human system could assimilate a dagger in the stomach' (O'Reilly 1901: 5). The truth was, however, that the explicit linking of the Catholic faith and the Gaelic language was a relatively recent occurrence. Ó Cuív rather generously asserts that 'there seems to be no evidence that the Irish hierarchy ever planned collectively to ensure that the clergy would be competent in both Irish and English' (Ó Cuív 1996: 392). As noted in the previous chapter, a more accurate assessment would be that in the nineteenth century the Catholic Church to a large extent, and with a few notable exceptions, ignored the language at best, and in truth often acted against it until it became involved with, some would say hijacked, the language movement in the last decades of the century.

It is now a commonplace that nations are imagined communities and it has been demonstrated how Irish cultural nationalism imagined a version of Irishness which was based on a vision of the Irish as the binary opposite of the English colonists. Using the Irish language as the key to Irish nationality, a type of Irishness was constructed which was pure, spiritual, largely anti-modern, and Catholic. Of course, as O'Leary has demonstrated, there were many counter-voices to this construction within the language movement and without, but it was a model which was to become popular, hegemonic, and durable.[13] One further element to this definition of Irishness was that of 'race'. Lee makes the important point that the meaning of this term in the period needs careful analysis since 'only rarely did it carry the full range of subsequent sinister connotations' and 'it was still often used as an innocent synonym for nation or people' (Lee 1989: 3). The use of the term in these senses at the time was common enough in Ireland; Stephen Dedalus's declaration at the end of *Portrait of the Artist as a Young Man*, that he will 'forge in the smithy of my soul the uncreated conscience of my race' is

---

[13] For an analysis of the contradictory tendencies in cultural nationalism, particularly the clash between 'nativism' and progressivism', see O'Leary 1994: chapter one.

a good example of it. But there were the sinister uses too, many of which were evident in the texts of the language movement, which is unsurprising, since the revivalists, as noted earlier, often used precisely the same discourse as the colonists, even though the inflections were different.

In the 1840s Davis had elided culture and biology in his assertion that the language of a specific people is 'conformed to their organs'. And in the early twentieth century this idea was reproduced by Trench when he asked: 'is it to be believed that in fifty years the Irish brain has ceased to be convoluted in accordance with the subtle architecture of the Gaelic sentence, or that the Irish larynx has ceased to be the counterpart of Gaelic phonetics?' (Trench 1912: 27). Such confusion can of course be accounted for in terms of a basic misunderstanding of biology, but then it is precisely such misconceptions which were and are at the heart of the discourse of racism. In Trench's work such thinking led to the use of an idea crucial to that discourse as he addressed the various groupings within Ireland (Firbolg, Milesian, Gael, Cromwellian Planter, Catholic, Protestant, Dissenter) with the question: 'Are you or are you not predominantly Irish, and do you not wish to live in an Ireland which reflects your racial type?' If the answer is yes, he declared, 'you will support the language which expresses the Irish nature and which will keep the Irish nation true to itself in all that it sets its hand to accomplish' (Trench 1912: 32). Over and above the cultural and historical differences between the distinct constituencies, there is the unity of the racial type which embodies the truth of Irishness. The logic of the argument is that the only way of ensuring the maintenance of the racial type, and thus the proper nature of Irishness, is to support the Irish language, its essential sustaining medium.

The clearest rendering of racist discourse in these debates is Forde's *The Irish Language Movement: Its Philosophy* (1901), in part an essay on the implications of ethnology for the language movement. Forde presented the central doctrine of the 'racial type' as the resemblance 'between members of the same race, a likeness of physical conformation, and a likeness of thought, feeling, general behaviour and deportment'. Taken together such resemblance constitutes 'the peculiar racial endowment in body and soul, in mind and heart' (Forde 1901: 3). The idea of the racial type is often a confusion of the biological and the cultural, in this case physique and behaviour, but as Forde noted, similarity of behaviour depended upon one crucial component: a common language, or what he called 'a racial unity of speech'.

But how is racial unity of speech determined? Members of the same race, as we have seen, have quite the same things to say—the same peculiar thoughts and feelings that demand utterance; and, on the other hand, their organs of speech are alike also, and will, therefore, under pressure of similar inward experiences, be likely to utter similar articulate sounds (Forde 1901: 3).

The fact that a certain group of people living in the same historical location over a period of time will have many experiences in common, and that these will be registered in their language, is incontestable, though of course this will be greatly complicated by other factors such as internal social difference. But the idea that such a group will have peculiar organs of speech which, because of common thoughts and feelings, will therefore produce similar sounds is unscientific nonsense. And it was the sort of nonsense which led to highly dangerous racial beliefs. Forde asked rhetorically whether the Irish are simply second-rate English,

Or are we on the other hand, a totally distinct and wholly superior race, ever zealous for the better gifts that God made the soul of man to desire and enjoy, clinging ever to the spirit-world? ... Are we mere planters and marchmen of the Pale, or are we Celts, Gaels, Irish? Oh, thank God, we know what we are; and may we realise the pressing duty that springs from that knowledge (Forde 1901: 8).

In order to sustain the distinct and wholly superior race it was necessary to avoid specific dangers. George Russell (AE) cited the perils of Anglicization which were leading to 'moral leprosy' and 'racial degradation': 'the songs of the London music halls may be heard in places where the music of fairy enchanted the elder generations. The shout of the cockney tourist sounds in the cyclopean crypts and mounds once sanctified by druid mysteries' (Gregory 1901: 20). The forcing of English culture onto Irish nature could only bring about disastrous results, and in the first Gaelic League pamphlet O'Hickey used the racial theory of miscegenation to describe the consequences.[14] Arguing that the

---

[14] 'Miscegenation' was coined in 1863 in the United States to refer to sexual intercourse or interbreeding between 'whites' and 'non-whites'. Originally a theory which viewed this as socially advantageous, it was soon deployed in arguments which warned of the dangers of degeneracy. For earlier colonial worries about the degeneracy of the English in Ireland, see Chapter two.

cultural assimilation of the Irish to the English was impossible, he proposed that the partial Anglicization of Ireland would produce a 'mongrel race':

We may, to all intents and purposes, cease to be Gaels; we may, in a sense, become West Britons; further we cannot go—Saxons we cannot become. Should the worst befall, it were better, in my opinion, to be something that could be clearly defined and classed; for anything at all would seem preferable to a mongrel, colourless, nondescript racial monstrosity evolved somewhere in the bosom of the twentieth century (O'Hickey 1900: 4).

Such were the stakes involved that Moran, whose historical observations were moulded by a form of Social Darwinism, was induced to defend racial hatred:

Racial hatred is a bad passion at the best, and one which it appears to me, is absolutely unjustifiable on moral grounds, unless in so far as it is impersonal and complementary to a real desire to keep intact the distinctive character, traditions, and civilisation of one's own country (Moran 1905: 67).

Many among the language movement had learned the lessons offered by the colonialists all too well; whilst inflecting them differently, they accepted the terms in which they were couched.

But there were other aspects to the movement too, many of which were highly positive and progressive, and the Gaelic League itself is the best example of the often contradictory tendencies. As demonstrated above, it offered narrow, prescriptive, and proscriptive definitions of Irishness which were to prove durable and which, it should be pointed out, excluded the majority of the Irish people. Yet it was also a mass democratic movement which stressed education as its chosen weapon and adopted modern methods for the achievement of its aims. Its use of teacher education colleges, timirí (organizers), travelling teachers, summer schools, the contemporary modh díreach (direct mode) of teaching, adult education, mixed classes (despite the frequent opposition of the Catholic clergy), the intermingling of traditional dance and music with language instruction, and the stress on the importance of Irish industry (Hyde called the league an educational body tinged with an industrial strain) made the Gaelic League in many ways a progressive and innovative organization. And on its chosen terrain of battle, the formal education system, the league was highly successful: in 1900 it won the concession that Irish could be taught as an ordinary school subject; in

1904 it forced the Commissioners of Education to introduce a bilingual programme; and in 1910 it succeeded in having Irish made a compulsory requirement for matriculation in the National University.

Yet if in many ways the Gaelic League was a successful modern movement it was nonetheless a movement which failed in its central aim. In a speech to Dáil Éireann in 1919 Cathal Brugha argued that Irish was dying. Gaelic League classes, he declared, 'were not coping with the situation, as not five per cent of the persons who attended these classes were able to speak the language afterwards' (Ó Cuív 1969: 129). Arthur Clery compared the league to the Church of England: an institution which had 'a strong hold on the affections of vast numbers in Ireland who but poorly practise its principles' (Clery 1919: 398). The league did in fact have great success with one of its main aims: in 1893 twenty-odd books were in print in Irish, mostly devotional or concerned with grammar or folklore; between 1900 and 1925 the league published some four hundred (Ó Tuama 1972: 27). And in the debate between the classicists and the modernizers, the league supported the successful arguments of those who wanted to make *caint na ndaoine* (demotic speech) the basis for the contemporary written vernacular. In its main objective, however, the league must be said to have failed. Fifteen years after its foundation there were some 950 branches of the league with an estimated membership of 100,000 (Garvin 1987: 40) (there was a fall-off between 1906 and 1915, and then renewed development between 1916 and 1922). Yet such activity did not halt the decline in the use of Irish. In 1851, 1,524,286 people (or 23.3 per cent of the population) were Irish-speaking, of whom 319,602, (or 4.9 per cent of the population) were Gaelic monoglots; in 1911 the number of Irish speakers was 582,446 (or 13.3 per cent of the total population) of whom only 16,873 were monoglot (2.9 per cent of the Irish-speaking population); it was a trend which continued between 1911 and independence. But if it is true that the league failed in its primary aim of preserving and extending Gaelic as a spoken language, it is also true that through its activities it forged a new cultural hegemony. In many respects that cultural order was deeply reactionary, but there can be no doubt that the league played a central part in the overthrow of British colonial rule in Ireland. Officially it adhered firmly to its apolitical stance until 1915, when rule two of the constitution was slightly altered to read 'Connradh na Gaedhilge shall be strictly non-political and non-sectarian, and shall devote itself to realising the ideal of a *free* Gaelic-speaking Ireland' (italics added). But the league's stance was in essence always political and could not have been otherwise given the historical circumstances, a fact bolstered by the influx of new recruits after 1916. In 1907 Canon Hannay, a Protestant member of the league (also known as George Birmingham, the novelist) warned Hyde that he understood 'the Sinn Féin position to be the natural and inevitable development of the League principles' (Kiberd 1996: 149). The British authorities thought much the same: on 3 July 1918 Sinn Féin, The Irish Volunteers, Cumann na mBan, and the Gaelic League were proscribed; the league was not banned merely because the British thought that it threatened linguistic revolution.[15]

The spread of the English language was of course the Irish language movement's greatest enemy, and as with the binary opposition between Irish and English culture in general, attitudes towards the English language were often derogatory. Despite Joyce's claim that he stopped his Irish classes because his teacher exalted Irish by denigrating English, his tutor, Pearse, delivered a measured judgement of the matter. Rejecting the 'indiscriminate abuse of English', he made a simple point: 'The English language is not *our* language: in stating that fact we have stated our whole case against it' (O'Leary 1994: 66). Others were less judicious. George Moore prophesied that 'the English language in fifty years will be as corrupt as the Latin of the eighth century, as unfit for literary usage, and will become, in my opinion, a sort of volapuk, strictly limited to commercial letters and journalism' (Moore 1901: 49).[16] Fr. Peadar Ua Laoghaire, one of the leading Gaelic Leaguers and campaigner for *caint na ndaoine*, argued in 'Is the English language poisonous?', that contemporary English usage is 'rotten language, as rotten as anything which is corrupt. It is unwholesome. It ruins the mental health of those who read those English "navvils" . . . Their faith becomes weakened. So does their patriotism' (O'Leary 1994: 61). For the more extreme holders of this position, the answer was 'Bás don Bhéarla' (Death to the English Language), a position which depended again on the type of binary thinking considered earlier. And a great fear among such thinkers was precisely the possibility of 'mongrelism', or hybridity—the product of the fusion of two distinct 'types'. The danger of this aspect of

---

[15] Ó Fathaigh's *Recollections of a Galway Gaelic Leaguer* makes clear the common membership of the league and political revolutionary organizations.

[16] Volapuk was an artificial language invented in 1879 as a medium of international communication.

Anglicization was the potential it brought for a new, mixed language which was neither simply Irish nor simply English but a combination of both. And as a matter of historical irony, this possibility was ably articulated at exactly the moment of the Gaelic League's greatest activity. Though Hiberno-English had been in the process of formation for centuries, the earliest attempts at representing the language in any proper sense were made in the 1890s; another irony is that they were written by none other than Douglas Hyde, President of the Gaelic League.[17]

In 1890 Hyde published *Beside the Fire*, a collection of prose translations which included renditions of folk tales contained in his earlier *Leabhar Sgeulaigheachta* (1899) into Hiberno-English. In 1893 *Abhráin Grádh Chúige Connacht or The Love Songs of Connacht* appeared, a development which Ó hAodha asserts 'marked a turning-point in the Irish Literary revival and revealed a new source for the development of a distinctive Irish mode in verse and poetic prose' (Ó hAodha 1969: v). Yeats asserted that Hyde's Hiberno-English represented 'that English idiom of the Irish-thinking people of the west', 'which mingles so much of the same [English] vocabulary with turns of phrase which have come out of Gaelic'; he described it as 'the coming of a new power into literature'(Yeats 1902: 8). It was in a sense the fulfilment of Keenan's prophecy of the result of bilingual education of children: by their 'continuing to speak Irish and *learning English through its* medium, the latter language would be enriched by the imagery and vigour of the mother tongue' (Keenan 1856: 75). What was so disturbing about this language for the cultural nationalists was the way in which Hiberno-English disrupted the binarism of their arguments. Joyce, not a cultural nationalist of any recognized type, offered an insight into the peculiar position of an Irish person speaking the English language in the late nineteenth century. After an exchange between Stephen Dedalus and the English Dean of Studies, Stephen reflects:

The language in which we are speaking is his before it is mine. How different are the words *home, Christ, ale, master,* on his lips and on mine! I cannot speak or write these words without unrest of spirit. His language, so familiar and so foreign, will always be for me an acquired speech. I have not made or accepted

---

[17] Representations of Hiberno-English had of course existed since the late sixteenth century (see Bliss 1976) but this new development attempted to articulate an innovative form of language, rather than the defective utterances of Paddy Oirish.

its words. My voice holds them at bay. My soul frets in the shadow of his language (Joyce 1916: 205).

Though Stephen, a Dubliner, confesses to unease with English, he also deconstructs the rigid opposition between the Irish and the English languages. English for Stephen is *both* familiar *and* foreign—it is not simply alien; indeed as we later discover in *Portrait*, for Stephen it is Gaelic which is the exotic language. Yeats put it slightly differently when he argued that Irish may well be his native language, but it was not his mother tongue.

Hyde's work was contradictory in its effects: on the one hand it made both accessible and popular traditional forms of Irish culture and literature; on the other it opened up the idea that English could be the successful medium for an Irish national literature. The form of his work was at odds with the content of his arguments. Hyde's use of Hiberno-English also facilitated the development of Lady Gregory's own literary representation of the language, Kiltartanese, and more durably and significantly, Synge's work. The dangers of such writing from the cultural nationalist point of view were clear, and in response to Lady Gregory's translations from the Ulster cycle, *Cuchulain of Muirthemne* (1902), MacNeill wrote to the author lauding the text in terms which concealed fear behind praise:

A few more books like it, and the Gaelic League will want to suppress you on a double indictment, to wit, depriving the Irish language of her sole right to express the innermost mind, and secondly, investing the Anglo-Irish language with a literary dignity it has never hitherto possessed (Gregory 1974: 402).

Others were more forthright. W. P. Ryan denounced it as 'a half-way house' (Ó Tuama 1972: 49), whilst Ó Rinn proclaimed that Irish language revivalists had to be the 'enemies of the English language and of those cultivating the English language':

I do not understand how it is possible for anyone to have any great love for Ireland if he gives assistance to the English language in gaining a firmer grip on the people of Ireland, and there is no better way to do that than to lure and deceive the people of Ireland with a quasi-Gaelic literature (O'Leary 1994: 481–2).

Such responses reflected the contradictory attitudes towards the Anglo-Irish literary movement in general and the best example of the differing views in the language movement are Pearse's comments on the issue. In

*An Claidheamh Soluis* he denounced the 'heresy...that there can be an Ireland, that there can be an Irish literature, an Irish social life, whilst the language of Ireland is English', and opined that 'if once we admit the Irish literature in English idea, then the language movement is a mistake. Mr Yeats' precious 'Irish' Literary Theatre may, if it develops, give the Gaelic League more trouble than the Atkinson-Mahaffy combination. Let us strangle it at birth'. He added for good measure that Yeats 'is a mere English poet of the third or fourth rank, and as such he is harmless. But when he attempts to run an "Irish" Literary Theatre it is time for him to be crushed' (Crowley 2000: 189). Pearse was nineteen at the time and can be forgiven the rhetorical excess; in 1905 he praised *Cathleen Ni Houlihan* as 'the most beautiful piece of prose that has been produced by an Irishman in our day' and asserted that Yeats 'has never ceased to work for Ireland' (O'Leary 1994: 333).

Yet despite the scattered positive comments towards the Anglo-Irish literary writers, it is nonetheless true that for the most part the dominant attitude of the language movement was hostile. In the face of such opposition the work of Gregory and Synge stood as an act of confident rejection of the binary division favoured by the Gaelic nationalists (and of course the colonists). Rather than Irish *or* English, what those writing in Hiberno-English offered was a new form, hybrid, mongrel even, which was Irish *and* English. For Gregory the act of translating from Irish into Hiberno-English was, as Cronin notes, ironically similar to that undertaken by the translators of Tudor England eager to demonstrate the copiousness of English in relation to the classical languages (Cronin 1996: 139). Hiberno-English at the turn of the nineteenth century, like English at the turn of the sixteenth century, had emerged as a 'modern language', capable of serving the interests of a new nation. Synge, who was critical of Gregory but influenced by her, declared that it was a unique historical moment: 'the linguistic atmosphere of Ireland has become definitely English enough, for the first time, to allow work to be done in English that is perfectly Irish in essence' (Synge 1966: 384). Notwithstanding the attacks by the language movement on this new form, there was one critic who was aware of the historical shift which had taken and was taking place, and whose nationalist credentials could not have been more impressive. A Gaelic League member until he became disillusioned and left in 1909, Thomas MacDonagh was a signatory to the Proclamation of the Irish Republic, took part in the Easter Rising, and was executed by the British. In *Literature in Ireland* (published posthumously in 1920), MacDonagh traced a linguistic history of Ireland under colonial rule from the Elizabethans onwards. His judgement was that through a mingling of the English and Gaelic languages, 'the alien language has stirred to expression on the lips of the native people'. In Ireland, 'English had to be broken and re-made . . . that language, in order to serve the different purpose of the new people, had to go back to the forge of living speech' (MacDonagh 1916: 39). And that forge was the linguistic practice of the Gaelic-speaking peasantry as they adopted and adapted English for their own use; it produced 'a different complication from the modern complication of the central English language' (MacDonagh 1916: 41). The binarism of Irish *or* English was rejected as MacDonagh came to his conclusion that the new language 'at its best is more vigorous, fresh and simple than either of the two languages between which it stands' (MacDonagh 1916: 48). What Irish history had produced was a language neither wholly Gaelic nor purely English, but a language which mirrored the complexity of Irish history and which could serve the nation in the future. The twentieth-century contest of languages in which such views were debated will be analysed in the next chapter.

# CHAPTER SEVEN

# The languages of the island of Ireland, 1922–2004

'We are the brack people...We don't just have one language and one history'

Hugo Hamilton, *The Speckled People*, 2003.[1]

Michael Collins noted the central role which Gaelic had played in the period which ended with the war of independence:

We only succeeded after we had begun to get back our Irish ways, after we had made a serious effort to speak our own language, after we had striven again to govern ourselves. How can we express our most subtle thoughts and finest feelings in a foreign tongue? Irish will scarcely be our language in this generation, nor even perhaps in the next. But until we have it again on our tongues and in our minds, we are not free (Collins 1922: 100).

Collins's caution in forecasting the exact time at which Ireland would be free and Gaelic was prudent. Despite the fact that in the Irish Republic 2002 census some 1,570,894 respondents categorized themselves as Irish speakers (42.8 per cent of the population), the story of the Irish language in independent Ireland has been a dismal one. The level to which the language had sunk is indicated in the title of the parliamentary bill which was intended to clarify the position of the language in 2003. Originally entitled *Bille na dTeangacha Oifigiúla (Comhionannas)/ The Official Languages Equality Bill*, the name was changed to *Bille na dTeangacha Oifigiúla/ The Official Languages Bill* when parliamentarians were reminded that at least in terms of the Republic's

---

[1] 'Brack' is Hamilton's rendering of the Gaelic term 'breac' in *The Speckled People*, an autobiographical story of a child brought up speaking Irish, German, and English (in that order). 'Breac' literally means speckled or spotted; see note 7.

constitution, the two official languages were not in fact equal: Irish has priority over English.[2]

After the sweeping Sinn Féin General Election victory in December 1918, the first meeting of Dáil Éireann took place on 21 January 1919.[3] Though the delegates mostly used Irish in their debates, the cabinet minutes and official documents of the parliament were recorded in English; it was an ominous portent. In October 1919, following a resolution of the Gaelic League Ard Fheis, a proposal was made to the Dáil that a Minister for the Irish language and Minister for Education be appointed. After an initial postponement (both the Gaelic League and the Catholic Church were opposed) the deputy speaker and president of the league, Seán Ó Ceallaigh, was appointed Minister for Irish early in 1920. His Ministry's first report to the Dáil later that year argued that political co-option of the Gaelic League as an official department of government would be politically inopportune, since it would thereby be robbed of its ability to negotiate with the Board of Education and would endanger the British Exchequer's payment for the teaching of Irish (Ó Huallacháin 1994: 79–80). One of the consequences of the league's educational campaigns had been that by the end of British rule, twenty-five per cent of primary and almost two thirds of secondary pupils were learning Irish at school.

The Sinn Féin constitution, drafted in part by the young de Valera, had addressed the reform of education in an independent Ireland by promising 'to render its basis national and industrial by the compulsory teaching of the Irish language, Irish history and Irish agriculture and manufacturing potentialities in the primary system' (Macardle 1968: 916). The stress on education was simply a continuation of the Gaelic League's policies, including that of universal compulsory Irish, a policy on which the league had clashed with the Irish Parliamentary Party in 1913. Once British rule was brought to a conclusion with the

---

[2] Another indication of the low esteem accorded to Irish by the State was the Irish government's advice *against* making the language one of the EEC's working languages when Ireland joined in 1973; Ireland was unique in this. The 1986 Geological Survey Office report on progress in the promotion of Irish in the Civil Service noted that 'a table was set aside in the tea room each Wednesday for those who wish to speak Irish' (Bord na Gaeilge 1986: 72).

[3] The title of the parliament, 'Dáil', as well as that of the new state itself, 'Saorstát' (Free State) was settled upon by a committee charged with providing new terminology and translating official documents (Ó Huallacháin, 1994: 79). Kiberd argues that the adoption of 'Dáil' was a conscious attempt to avoid the English-derived 'Parlaimint' (Kiberd 1996: 484).

Anglo-Irish Treaty in 1922, it seemed a foregone conclusion that the education system would be the focus for the revival and restoration of the Irish language. Cosgrave, President of the executive council, demanded no less in 1923: 'Must we not look to the Minister of Education to mark the gaelicisation...of our whole culture...to make our nation separate and distinct and something to be thought of?' (Lee 1989: 132). Education was to be the key to the linguistic transformation of Ireland because, it was argued, it had served precisely this function in the past. What may be termed the colonial educational fallacy, that it was education and not economic imperatives which caused the Irish language shift, was propagated most influentially by Fr. Timothy Corcoran, who declared that the National Schools had been 'fatal to the national use of vernacular Irish'.[4] Corcoran, whose academic credentials as an expert on education were dubious, though his standing as a cultural nationalist was not, also popularized the corollary of this belief: that the schools of an independent Ireland could rescue the language. Government policy-makers adopted uncritically his beliefs that 'the popular schools can restore our native language. They can do it even without positive aid from the home' and that 'the Irish language will have to be acquired, and thoroughly acquired, as a vernacular within the school' (Corcoran 1925: 387–8).

In 1922 Dáil Éireann enacted the *Constitution of the Irish Free State* (an Irish version of the constitution was passed on the same day) in which Article 4 declared:

The national language of the Irish Free State (*Saorstát Éireann*) is the Irish language, but the English language shall be equally recognised as an official language. Nothing in this Article shall prevent special provisions being made by the Parliament of the Irish Free State (otherwise called and herein generally referred to as the *Oireachtas*) for districts or areas in which only one language is in general use (Ó Catháin 1996: 22).

Constitutional recognition of the language was preceded by the introduction of the curricular scheme for infant and national schools formulated at the First National Programme Conference. The conference discussions included a proviso that the majority of parents would have their preference granted with regard to compulsory teaching of either English or Irish. But whilst the final report retained the

---

[4] In fact as Lee has argued, it was the nature and extension of the state in the nineteenth century which determined the spread of English not the school system (Lee 1989: 662–6).

recommendation, when it was implemented in April 1922 it included the central stipulation that in the national schools, 'the Irish language was to be taught, or used as a medium of instruction for not less than one full hour each day' wherever teachers were competent to teach the language (Kelly 2002: 9). Singing, history and geography were to be taught through the medium of Irish and to make room in the curriculum drawing, elementary science, hygiene, nature study, and domestic studies were dropped. But what caused the most concern, particularly among the teachers, was the recommendation, inspired by Corcoran, that all teaching in the infant classes be conducted in Gaelic (Akenson 1975: 43–4).

The concerns of teachers and parents grew as the policy was implemented and it became clear that both parental preference and the competence of teachers were treated simply as obstacles to the greater goal.[5] In 1924 therefore the Irish National Teachers' Organisation (INTO) attempted to reconvene the National Conference (not least in order to pressure the government to introduce a compulsory attendance bill). Sensing the possibility of political embarrassment, the government took over the conference and ensured that its report, though critical of excessive zeal, nonetheless supported the broad policy while recommending a slight relaxation of the strictures of the first programme (Akenson 1975: 46). The new regulations for infant schools made allowance for teachers' lack of competence in Irish whilst restating the eventual aim of having all children taught entirely in Irish. The rules were to hold whatever the home language of the child; if parents wished for teaching in English, it could take place before or after the normal timetable (this was a simple reversal of the British Board of Education's policy with regard to Irish before 1900). In the primary schools teaching competence was taken into consideration by means of two courses, with higher or lower Irish content, though again this was seen as a temporary measure on the way towards full instruction in Irish. Such revisions were welcomed by teachers and, combined with the introduction of teacher-training colleges geared towards teaching in Irish, summer courses for teachers already in service, and a more

---

[5] Competence was a serious problem. Of the twelve thousand lay teachers in national schools in 1922 only some four thousand held the Bilingual or Ordinary Certificate; in the secondary schools a third of the two thousand teachers had no Irish at all. Even in the Fíor-Gaeltacht areas in 1926 thirty-six per cent of teachers held neither the Bilingual or Ordinary Certificate (Ó Buachalla 1981: 26).

reasonable inspection programme from 1928, they ensured that progress was made: in 1928 1,240 infant schools were all-Irish medium, 3,570 taught in Irish and English, and 373 used English only (Akenson 1975: 47).

The situation in secondary schools was of a different nature, not least because of the numbers involved (in the early 1920s this was around five per cent of the age group—post-primary education remained fee-paying, with scholarship schemes, until 1967). The Commission on Secondary Education was charged with drafting 'a programme which would meet the national requirements, while allotting its due place to the national language' (Ó Buachalla 1981: 26). The result was the Intermediate Act of 1924 and the creation of a Department of Education (education affairs had previously fallen within the remit of the Ministry of Irish). Under the act, which abolished the payment-by-results system, any school seeking state funding (schools were either private or run by the Churches) had to provide an approved course in two languages, one of which was either Irish or English. Grants were introduced to encourage teaching in Irish and schools were categorized according to the level of Irish usage: 'A' schools were effectively all-Irish, 'B' schools taught several subjects through Irish, while 'C' schools taught Irish as an academic subject. Students were examined by means of the Intermediate Certificate (age 15–16) and the Leaving Certificate (two years later). In a crucial development a pass in Irish was made compulsory at the Intermediate level in 1925; from the beginning extra marks were allocated to students who answered in Irish.

The introduction of 'preparatory colleges' for Irish-speaking children, compulsory teaching and examination in Irish, extra payments for teachers of Irish and the extra marks for answering in Irish, were all signs of the government's determination to make education the central focus of its revival policy.[6] It has been argued that one reason for the zeal with which the Free State government engaged in its Gaelicization policy was that the language issue offered nationalist authenticity to its actions, and thereby a defence against republican opposition in the immediate aftermath of the Civil War (Brown 1985: 47). There is no doubt, however, that the policies were both a fulfilment of the pledges

---

[6] National school teachers qualified for payments of up to ten per cent of their salary, while secondary teachers in A and B schools could earn between £15 and £30 more per year. Pupils answering exam questions in Irish were given a ten per cent bonus (with the exception of mathematics, in which the bonus was 5 per cent) (Kelly 2002: 64).

made by the forces which had brought about independence and that there was general support for their introduction amongst the public. Yet not all were in agreement with the government's plans and they met with great scepticism, and indeed resistance, among one section of the community in particular which they were designed to help.

When the government set up the Gaeltacht Commission in 1925, the remit was to decide upon the percentage of Irish speakers in a district required for its categorization as Irish-speaking or partly Irish-speaking, and to identify the extent and location of those areas.[7] In addition it was to inquire into and make recommendations on the use of Irish in the administration of such districts, their educational facilities, and steps to be taken to improve the economic condition of the inhabitants. As Cosgrave made clear, the Gaeltacht was held to have a crucial role in the revival of the language:

We recognise also that the future of the Irish language and its part in the future of the Irish nation depend, more than on anything else, on its continuing in an unbroken tradition as the language of Irish homes. This tradition is the living root from which alone organic growth is possible. For this reason the Irish people rightly value as a national asset their 'Gaeltacht', the scattered range of districts in which Irish is the home language (Ó Cuív 1951: 7).

When published in 1926 the commission's report made unpleasant reading in its depiction of the endemic problems of what the British had called the 'congested districts', and the prospects for the future of the language:

The area in which the language persisted came to be reduced to one in which the economic problem was so acute that the surplus population had continually to look for a living outside, while those who remained at home lived in grinding poverty. The economic conditions then became an important and a growing factor in the decline of the language. We are now in the full tide of that destructive effect (Rialtas na hÉireann 1926: 371).

Yet what ought to have been more disturbing for the language revivalists and government policy-makers were the attitudes of the Gaeltacht

---

[7] When the Gaeltacht was first officially demarcated by the Irish state in 1926 it was divided into the 'Fíor Ghaeltacht' (the Gaeltacht proper, or 'Irish-speaking districts', in which eighty per cent or more of the population had ordinary conversational knowledge of the language) and the 'Breac Ghaeltacht' (the 'partly Irish-speaking districts' in which at least twenty-five per cent of the population had such knowledge). The terms are no longer in use, a fact significant in itself.

people themselves, as revealed in the minutes of evidence to the commission which were published daily between April and October 1925.

Some of the evidence simply reflects the history of the language shift which had taken place in the Irish-speaking areas. A primary school teacher from Sáile, Acaill, offered an analysis of life on Acaill Bheag:

The people know Irish, but they had a greater partiality for English. They thought it was more fashionable. The situation of the locality had much to do with it. The people situated along the public road were brought into contact with strangers coming into the island. That gave them an opportunity of picking up English that the people remote from the public road did not get (Walsh 2002: 49).

Here in microcosm are some of the forces acting for and against Irish: remoteness and lack of contact as a preserving force, communication, traffic, and fashion as destructive tendencies. Other testimony bears witness to the fact that state officials and professionals such as doctors and lawyers appeared to see Irish as inferior or unnecessary, prompting Irish speakers 'instinctively [to] feel that English is the proper language for those with pretensions to education and culture' (Walsh 2002: 86). A sense of shame towards the language was still prevalent; another teacher noted that people regarded the language 'as a badge of backwardness, slavery and poverty' (Walsh 2002: 83). In its report the commission recognized the need to address the problem:

It is necessary to show the people who still speak Irish traditionally, that not only does the State recognise the Irish language as the National language, but that it is determined to redress the disabilities which that language has suffered, and to restore it to its position and prestige. Much propaganda of an educative kind will be necessary before a large number of them will be convinced that it is no longer despised. (Walsh 2002: 85).

As well as the propaganda effort, an attempt had to be made to show that 'Irish is not synonymous with poverty' and the commission argued that no means could persuade public opinion in the Gaeltacht on this as effectively as 'the adoption of Irish by the Government as the language of its administration in those areas'.

The Government's response to such attitudes, which were widely held, was to introduce a series of measures designed to make a qualification in Irish compulsory for certain posts in the public services and thus to demonstrate that Irish was, to put it crudely, cashable. But the difficulty was more complex and demanded solutions of a much more radical nature than that of requiring gardai and postal workers to speak Irish.[8] The root of the problem was economic: without the type of massive investment which the Government was not prepared to provide, the Irish-speaking areas were doomed to remain sites of poverty and emigration. It was a lesson not lost on the people of the Gaeltacht. Another teacher from Acaill argued that,

if it could be brought home to the parents that their children stand to gain something by their speaking Irish to them you might have a remedy. As it is they are opposed to Irish. They see people with English getting all the jobs . . . It is just a question of bread and butter. You cannot blame them because everything practically is denied to them if they don't know English (Walsh 2002: 60).

Observers, often local parish priests, reported parents writing to schools to ask that their children not be taught Irish. The point made by a priest from Killarney was repeated often: 'If you urge Irish speaking the reply is: "What good is Irish in America?"' (Walsh 2002: 102). As the schoolmaster from An Chlochán put it: 'it would be the veriest mockery to say to those people—"Don't speak English, or emigrate: speak Irish, stay at home and starve, cry out yearly for doles, and send your children picking winkles instead of being at school, and earn the contemptuous pity of the world' (Walsh 2002: 101).[9]

Despite such sentiments the government proceeded with its educational innovations, not least because as the Minister for Education, Eoin MacNeill, made clear, the government believed that 'the principal duty of an Irish Government in its educational policy' was to serve the construction of Irish nationality, and the language was central to that project (Brown 1985: 50). In 1928–9 a primary school leaving certificate was introduced, at first voluntarily, and in 1931 the uneasy relations between teachers and the government were upset by a new order to school inspectors to monitor more tightly the abilities and preparedness of

[8] Both Brown and Lee put the argument that the revival of the language called for a much wider and radical transformation of Irish society (Brown 1985: chapters one–four and Lee 1989: chapter two).

[9] There is some evidence that language-learning patterns were dictated by the future prospects of the children. In Galway one teacher noted that 'the mothers speak English to the girls and to the younger boys. The elder boys of ten to twelve years and over speak Irish because these children know Irish better, but the mother endeavours to teach English to them' (Walsh 2002: 126). Girls and younger boys were more likely to emigrate to an English-speaking context, though even the older boys would require some facility in both languages.

teachers with regard to instruction in Irish. The real shift, however, came with the election of the first Fianna Fáil government to power, with de Valera as President and Tomás Derrig as Minister for Education (a position he held almost uninterruptedly for the sixteen years of his party's rule). Derrig, a trained teacher and language enthusiast, made clear the government's impatience with the language revival's lack of success under the previous administration and made a deal with the teachers. Faced with the teachers' concerns, including a resolution at the 1930 INTO annual congress calling for a reassessment of the language policy, the government's response was the 1934 *Revised Programme of Primary Instruction*, a programme which in effect remained in place until 1971 (Kelly 2002: 46). The aim of the revision was not to change the policy with regard to Irish but to strengthen it by easing the pressure on teachers in other areas of the curriculum. In the infant schools English was abolished even as an optional out-of-hours subject, while in the national schools rural science was dropped as a compulsory subject and maths requirements were relaxed. Additional measures included making Irish compulsory for the Leaving Certificate in 1934, and the awarding of the deontas (grant) of £2 per annum to the parents of children in the Gaeltacht areas able to satisfy inspectors that Irish was the home language and that the child had a certain level of fluency and attended school regularly.

The obvious charge against the policy was that it sacrificed the general academic progress of pupils for the sake of achievement in Irish. This objection had been pre-empted before independence by O'Hickey who commented in 1899: 'even though half the subjects in the programme should have to be sacrificed, the language of the country should be taught in all the schools of Ireland. On this question we can have no parley; we can entertain no compromise' (Ó Cuív 1936: 7). When the British authorities had made their concession to the Gaelic League campaign and allowed Irish to be taught in the national schools early in the twentieth century, the rider was that the teacher had to be competent and that other school subjects continued to be taught successfully. De Valera's government made no such stipulation; compromise on such an issue could hardly have been expected from a politician who had once told the Gaelic League that 'it is my opinion that Ireland, with its language and without freedom is preferable to Ireland with freedom and without its language' (Akenson 1975: 36).[10]

[10] There can be no doubting de Valera's sincere commitment to the cause of the Irish language, though he did not even carry his own Cabinet with him, to say nothing of the country

There were arguments for and against the government's measures. The 'preparatory colleges' provided secondary education and gave otherwise unattainable career prospects to some children from the Gaeltacht, the poorest part of Ireland. On the other hand the removal of children to these institutions appeared to favour one group of the nation's children at the expense of others and was strongly opposed by the teaching unions. Those in favour of awarding extra marks for answering in Irish argued that it encouraged interest in the language and that children should be rewarded for the additional effort. Some parents of English-speaking children objected to the fact that their children were disadvantaged academically, whilst others worried that awarding the extra marks distorted the exam system by allowing less academically gifted students to achieve results which did not reflect their ability. Salary supplements were viewed by some as proper recognition of the difficulties of teaching in Irish, particularly in the A and B schools; others viewed them as bribes which undermined the teaching profession itself. Supporters saw the Irish qualifying requirement for entrance to public service posts as evidence of the state's commitment to the language and as necessary for the provision of such services to those who needed them, specifically in the Gaeltacht. Opponents dismissed it as cynical jobbery, a means by which the state could pay lip-service to its language commitments, and as the cause of resentment and hostility towards the language.

There were early doubts even within government circles about the use of the schools alone for the revival of the language. In a memo to the Executive Council in 1924, MacNeill warned prophetically that 'the ministry of education can and will Gaelicise the young people up to eighteen ... but all their efforts will be wasted if the other Departments do not co-operate in keeping them Gaelicised when they leave the schools' (Ó Huallacháin 1994: 87). He also expressed his fears about Irish as a prerequisite for public service employment:

in my opinion the use of Irish by public servants was and would be mainly conditioned by the public attitude on the matter ... purely bureaucratic and official favouring of Irish in the absence of a strongly favourable public attitude,

at large (Lee 1989: 333). There were of course others who put another version of freedom before the language; the socialist Frederick Ryan argued that 'the mere desire to speak another language does not of necessity correlate at all with the active desire for political freedom ... if the people are content to let the substance of their liberty go, for the gew-gaw of a new grammar, so much the better—for the reactionaries' (Eagleton 1998: 263–4).

would lead to no desirable result, nothing more than barren conformity (Ó Huallacháin 1994: 88).

The worst possible scenario would be an educational and employment policy through which all children, whatever their parents' wishes, would be forced to study a subject which would be of no benefit to any except those fortunate to be able to employ it as an entry pass to a state job, in the course of which they would never again be required to use the language. But that was precisely what was achieved.

By the mid 1930s relations between the teachers and the government on the teaching of Irish had reached a low point, and INTO commissioned an investigation which was eventually published as the *Report of the Committee of Inquiry into the Use of Irish as a Teaching Medium to Children Whose Home Language is English* in 1941. The report was a damning indictment of the policy and the figures showed that the only two subjects in which teachers thought that children taught through Irish learnt as much as if they were taught through English, were singing and needlework. It concluded:

parents generally are opposed to a method for the Irish revival which would tend to lower the educational standard of their children according to their values... Many examples were cited of parents who endeavoured to teach their children at home through English, subjects that the same children were being taught in school through Irish, while it was repeatedly urged that complaints from the parents on the low standard of their children's education were widespread (INTO 1941: 60).

The report's complaint that parental attitudes did not appear to have been noted by the educational authorities was not quite accurate. In a complete reversal of the stipulation on parental preference which accompanied the introduction of the policy in 1924, the Minister of Education declared in 1940: 'I cannot see that parents, as a body, can decide in this matter' (Akenson 1975: 176). The report's findings were met with such hostile attacks by the government that INTO responded by making the accusation, in its *Plan for Education* (1947), that 'the general tendency [of the State's policies] is towards making Irish almost a dead language', particularly in view of the stress on competence in written Gaelic rather than facility with the spoken language (O'Connell 1968: 365).

The 1937 Constitution, passed by plebiscite, re-emphasized the place of Irish as the national language:

**Article 8.**

1. The Irish language as the national language is the first official language.
2. The English language is recognised as a second official language.
3. Provision may, however, be made by law for the exclusive use of either of the said languages for any one or more official purposes, either throughout the State or in any part thereof.

**Airteagal 8.**

1. Ós í an Ghaeilge an teanga náisiúnta is í an phríomhtheanga oifigiúil í.
2. Glactar leis an Sacs-Bhéarla mar theanga oifigiúil eile.
3. Ach féadfar socrú a dhéanamh le dlí d'fhonn ceachtar den dá theanga sin a bheith ina haonteanga le haghaidh aon ghnó nó gnóthaí oifigiúla ar fud an Stáit ar fad nó in aon chuid de (*Bunreacht na hÉireann* 1999: 8–11).

In the case of any conflict of intepretation between the two versions of the text the constitution was explicit:

**Article 25.**

4. In case of conflict between the texts of any copy of this Constitution enrolled under this section, the text in the national language shall prevail.

**Airteagal 25.**

4. I gcás gan na téacsanna d'aon chóip áirithe den Bhunreacht seo a bheidh curtha isteach ina hiris faoin alt seo a bheith de réir a chéile, is ag an téacs Gaeilge a bheidh an forlámhas (*Bunreacht na hÉireann* 1999: 82–3).

Though the Constitution was composed for political reasons (at de Valera's insistence) in Gaelic characters and with the antiquated spelling system, measures to standardize the language were initiated in the late 1930s. In 1947, *Litriú na Gaeilge*, a reformed official system of orthography, was produced and in 1958 *Gramadach na Gaeilge*, the official grammar, was published (these are now issued together as *An Caighdeán Oifigiúl*, the Official Standard); in 1959 and 1978 the state sponsored an English-Irish and an Irish-English dictionary; in education between 1964 and 1970 Gaelic script was phased out in favour of the use of roman characters.

With the national role of the language thus firmly enshrined within the constitution, and with the state's revivalist policies in place for a generation, the 1940s might have been a sensible time to take stock. Yet the derision heaped on the teachers and the personal attacks made on any who dared criticize the policy prevented any such reflection; too much ideological effort had been invested to pause for thought. There were, however, clear signs that even activists in the language movement had begun to suspect that the policies were not working, indeed even that they might be counter-productive. Many of the language revival organizations began to be active after almost twenty years of leaving it to the state. The annual cultural celebration, the Oireachtas, was revived in 1939, and along with de Valera's constitution of Comhdháil Náisiúnta na Gaeilge to coordinate activities in 1943, it acted as a spur to new interests. Significant journals for the publication of writing in Irish such as *Comhar*, *Inniu*, and *Feasta* appeared and between 1940 and 1963 some sixteen national organizations were founded, including Na Teaghlaigh Gaelacha, Cumann na Sagart, and the most productive and technologically progressive, Gael Linn (Ó Tuathaigh 1979: 114). But the activity of the voluntary organizations only served to illustrate the ineffectiveness of the state's policies. The truth was that by the late 1940s and through most of the 1950s the language revival, like the Irish economy and Irish society in general was, to put it politely, stagnant; a more frank verdict might be that linguistic, economic, and social policies were causing misery and leading nowhere except to the exit provided by emigration.

The end of the 1950s, and the conclusion of de Valera's leadership of Fianna Fáil, saw the beginning of a period of rapid economic and social change in Ireland, as the prevailing doctrines of self-sufficiency and protectionism were replaced by the policies of foreign investment, openness to the markets of international capitalism, and direct state intervention which the successive Programmes for Economic Expansion encouraged. It was in many senses the end of an era. In the previous forty years Ireland had been established as a post-colonial, conservative, stable, and social democratic state. There had been costs in that process. Emigration had been and remained a running sore inflicting tremendous human damage; the economic war with Britain and Ireland's neutrality in the Second World War had led to insularity and poor economic performance; the influence of the Catholic Church and the Republic's constitutional arrangements had created a Catholic state for a Catholic people; partition remained as a reminder of the failures of the past and present. And the restoration of the Irish language was a goal which remained distant. Two enquiries were undertaken in the mid to late 1950s which demonstrated the depth of the language problem. The first was the attempt to establish the real boundaries of the Gaeltacht and the numbers of people living within them. The 1926 boundaries and figures (some 257,000 Irish speakers, with 110,000 in the Breac-Ghaeltacht) had long since been regarded with suspicion since they had been composed on the basis of linguistic knowledge (rather than use) and the principle of 'potential for restoration of the language'.[11] The 1956 revision was based on the identification of 'substantially Irish-speaking areas' and once the borders of the Nua-Ghaeltacht were taken into consideration the decline of the language became apparent in the 1961 census figures: only around 70,000 Irish-speakers were living in the Gaeltacht. The government reaction to the evident crisis with the language was to set up the *Comisiún um Athbheochan na Gaelige* (Commission on the Restoration of the Irish Language), which reported in 1963. The commission's detailed recommendations prompted publication of a White Paper in January 1965, *Athbheochan na Gaeilge/ The Restoration of the Irish Language.*

At first reading the document appears highly positive towards the language. It asserted that 'the national aim is to restore the Irish language as a general medium of communication'; that 'most Irish men and women instinctively feel an affection for the Irish language and realize its value to the nation and to the individual'; that 'the Irish language is an integral part of our culture'; and that it is only through Irish as a living language that future generations can retain and understand 'the unique and essential elements of the Irish character'. It recognized that 'the Irish language is the most distinctive sign of our nationality' and acknowledged an historical debt:

---

[11] Figures recording Irish-speakers over the past one hundred and fifty years, ranging from the 1851 British census to Irish governmental surveys and the 2001 census of Northern Ireland, have been dogged by the difficulties of interpretation. Sometimes the figures appear to be under-recordings, as in 1851 (see Adams 1975); at other times the figures may have been boosted by a failure to distinguish between some sort of knowledge of the language and actual use; on occasion there is the suspicion that respondents may have exaggerated their knowledge/use for political reasons.

Our present position as an independent State derives in large measure from the idealism evoked by the language movement. The need for this idealism is now as great as ever. A small State has a particular need to preserve its national traditions, to strengthen its independence of outlook and to safeguard its identity (*Athbheochan* 1965: 6).

For this reason,

All sections of the community must share the responsibility of working for the realisation of [the national] aim. The responsibility cannot be discharged by the Government alone, although Government support is essential. The wide-spread, but often passive, public sentiment in favour of the language must be transformed into a willingness to make a sustained personal effort to achieve the national aim (*Athbheochan* 1965: 4–6).

Careful readers of political rhetoric, and there were many among the language movement, might have been assured by the reiteration of the national aim of restoration and the reassertion of the role of the language in the common culture, but they would have been con-cerned by an apparent shift in responsibility for the achievement of the goal from government to individuals. And as they read further into the report feelings of concern would have been replaced by despair. For *Athbheochan na Gaeilge* is a classic example of political evasion and ambiguity. In answer to practical recommendations for state action on the language, the report's response was typically to assert that it would commend others to do something (newspapers to appoint Irish-speaking reporters to cover debates in parliament), agree to set non-demanding targets (telephone calls to State depart-ments and offices to be answered with the title of the department in Irish), take appropriate action (appoint music organizers for the Gaeltacht), consider how far recommendations might be implemen-ted (measure the progress in the extension of Irish to the whole of the Civil Service), accept recommendations in principle, and so on. The response to the commission's call for an annual report detailing the state's efforts towards the preservation of the Gaeltacht and the revival of the language outside the Gaeltacht during the previous year was: 'the Government agree as to the desirability of issuing progress reports at intervals' (*Athbheochan* 1965: 170). What the White paper amounts to is a long (188 page) summary of the Government's stance towards the Irish language which had been developing since the late 40s onwards. In effect the state was withdrawing from its leadership role in the restoration project, despite its acknowledgement of the still integral role of the language in definitions of Irish national identity.

*Athbheochan na Gaeilge* managed both to assert that 'no Irish child can be regarded as fully educated if he grows up without a knowledge of the Irish language' (*Athbheochan* 1965: 12), and to take the first formal step in the relaxation of the compulsory pass in Irish for the Leaving Certificate (candidates who passed all other subjects but Irish should be permitted a second attempt at the language requirement). But calls for the abolition of compulsory Irish had progressed beyond the concerns of parents and were articulated by Fine Gael as part of its 1961 General Election manifesto. The issue was deeply contentious and highly divisive in the 60s. On the one hand there were the revivalists who saw the policy as crucial to their project, essential to Irish national identity, and necessary to safeguard Ireland against the overwhelming forces of Anglo-American culture. They pointed to the fact that at the high point of the schools programme, in the 1940s, large numbers of Irish schoolchildren had learned the language which would equip them for life as educated and integrated citizens of the Irish Republic. On the other hand those who opposed the policy saw it as an unfair restriction on the educational and life chances of those not able to master the language (even if talented in other academic areas), as unwanted by the majority of parents and associated with fear by the children, and as an unrealistic brake on the forces which were modernizing Irish society. The dissatisfaction of this group led to the formation of the Language Freedom Movement, an organization campaigning against compulsory Irish which held an infamous meeting in Dublin in 1966 (the fiftieth anniversary of the rebellion) at which the pro and anti forces clashed.[12] The ultimate causes of the change in the state language policy were general ambivalence among the population (with cynicism and resentment towards the educational and employment consequences of compulsory Irish), the liberalizing tendencies of economic and social strategy in the early to mid 1960s, the great expansion in secondary education, and the

---

[12] Kelly details the bitter divisions which characterized the meeting (Kelly 2002: 140–1). Ó Glaisne, an opponent of the Language Freedom Movement (LFM), gives a taste of the objections against it. He characterizes LFM supporters as Protestants, descendants of those who collaborated with the British, upper-class 'Castle Catholics', those influenced by Anglo-American culture, 'an ambitious stratum within the new Roman Catholic Irish middle class', and people who have failed Irish in the Leaving Certificate examination (Ó Glaisne 1966: 1–2).

publication of the first serious research into the policy.[13] In general people seemed both unprepared to see the language die out and unready to engage in any personal sacrifice to save it (they were even more unlikely to allow the state to make the sacrifice on their behalf). Public attitudes were reflected in the findings of CLAR (the Committee on Irish Language Attitudes Research) whose work covered the early 1970s and represented the opinions of the oxymoronic 'average individual':

The average individual, for instance, in the national population feels rather strongly that the Irish language is necessary to our ethnic and cultural integrity, and supports the efforts to ensure the transmission of the language. At the same time, under present policies and progress, he is not really convinced that we can ensure its transmission. He has rather negative views about the way Irish has been taught in school and has a rather low or 'lukewarm' personal commitment to its use, although in this latter case, the average person has not sufficient ability in the language to converse freely in it. On the other hand, he strongly supports nearly all government efforts to help the Gaeltacht, but at the same time feels that the language is not very suitable for modern life (Committee on Irish Language Attitudes 1975: 24).

In 1973 a Fine Gael/Labour coalition government removed the requirements that pupils pass Irish before gaining the school Leaving Certificate and that a pass in Leaving Certificate Irish was needed for entrance to the Civil Service. Compulsory Irish in the old sense was abolished (though it remained as a mandatory academic subject); one commentator describes it as the act which 'removed the last vestige of state policy on the language' (Ó Tuathaigh 1979: 117).

At this point it is necessary to leave the story of the fortunes of Gaelic in the Irish Republic and turn instead to its fate in Northern Ireland. The 1911 census records some 28,729 Irish speakers in the six counties of the province of Ulster which became Northern Ireland after the Government of Ireland Act in 1920. What partition did to the language in Northern Ireland, however, was effectively to make it a highly political issue. For although Belfast had long been a centre of Irish language activity, and though Ulster Protestantism was represented in the Gaelic League, once the division of the country was made, the Irish language was seen on both sides of the border as a symbol of nationalist,

---

[13] John MacNamara's *Bilingualism and Primary Education* (1966) demonstrated the educational difficulties of children from English-speaking backgrounds forced to learn English and mathematics through Irish; it dealt a serious blow to compulsory Irish.

if not republican, aspirations.[14] The teaching of Irish in schools was the first focus of Ulster Unionism's disdain for the language, and its supporters and attention soon fixed on the fact that as a result of British concessions to the Gaelic League, taxpayers were providing support for the training of teachers in Irish language colleges and paying the salaries of teachers and language organizers. Promises to end this state of affairs prompted a Dublin-financed teachers' campaign designed to gain concessions, some of which were language measures, from the Northern Ministry of Education. The confrontation with the Stormont government proved unsuccessful, however, and by 1923 Lord Londonderry had completed the revision of Irish teaching. Funding for the Irish language teacher-training colleges was withdrawn; the Irish language organizers were abolished; Irish as an ordinary subject was reduced to no more than an hour and a half per week to children of the third grade and higher; and Irish could only be taught as an extra subject outside school hours with fees paid to qualified teachers who taught Irish for at least forty hours per annum. The Protestant state for a Protestant people was also to be an English-speaking state for British people.

Despite these measures the issue continued to be a focal point of Unionists' contempt towards their fellow citizens. Teaching Irish was attacked on the basis that it encouraged sedition, only helped those who wanted to work in the Free State, was impractical, and was in any case alien (in 1945 the nationalist MP Eddie McAteer spoke in Irish in the Stormont Parliament and was shouted down by the Prime Minister and Minister of Education with cries of 'no foreign language here') (MacPóilin 1997*b*: 184). In a debate on the Education Bill in 1923 the Chairman of the Education Committee announced that 'the one thing the Ministry has in mind is to turn out good and loyal citizens—citizens who will respect the flag' (Andrews 1997: 66). It stood to reason therefore that in 1933, under pressure from hardliners and in the guise of a measure taken for financial reasons, all fees payable for the teaching of Irish as an extra subject were finally abolished (their scope had been reduced in 1926). The decision was defended by the Prime Minister:

What use is it to us here in this progressive, busy part of the Empire to teach our children the Irish language? What use would it be to them? Is it not leading

---

[14] Ó Snodaigh provides a history of Ulster Protestant involvement with the Gaelic League (Ó Snodaigh 1995: chapter seven); Ó Buachalla traces the history of language and cultural activities in Belfast in the nineteenth century (Ó Buachalla 1968).

them along a road which has no practical value? We have not stopped such teaching . . . We have stopped the grants simply because we do not see that these boys being taught Irish would make them any better citizens (Maguire 1991: 11).

On both sides of the border children were subject to linguistic education for national purposes: compulsory Irish for the Irish, compulsory English for the British. And lest sectarianism be thought the preserve of the Unionists, it should be remembered that in 1942 the Minister of Education in the Free State introduced a Bill which sought to impose compulsory Irish on Protestants by effectively blocking their right to educate their children in private schools or abroad. Supported by de Valera and passed by both houses of the Irish parliament, the Bill was referred to the Supreme Court by the Protestant, Gaelic Leaguer, and lately President of Ireland, Douglas Hyde; the court threw it out as unconstitutional (Akenson 1975: 130).

The use of Irish in Northern Ireland by individuals was treated with suspicion and hostility and its official use was forbidden. The BBC banned the language for fifty years and the Stormont parliament proscribed street signs in Irish. Despite the official interdiction on Irish, however, the language was taught in Catholic schools and fostered by voluntary organizations. After partition a northern branch of the Gaelic league, Comhaltas Uladh, was set up in order to negotiate with the education authorities on behalf of the language and it has remained active since; one of its former branches, Cumann Chluain Ard in West Belfast, has been a key focal point of Irish language activities since its inception in 1936. In the 1940s, 50s, and 60s, various organizations were formed in Belfast in particular in order to stimulate interest in the language and to offer facilities for its speakers. They included Glún na Buaidhe, Fal (which published a monthly paper *Dearcadh* in the mid 1950s), independent sporting clubs (as well as the Gaelic Athletic Association), an Irish-medium credit union, a shop, prayer groups such as Cuallacht Mhuire and Réalt, a choir, and various literary groups (Maguire 1991: 30–2). But though enthusiastic and determined, such small-scale organizations amounted to little more than a token presence in the face of official disregard. Chluain Ard, however, provided a long-standing meeting place for language revivalists throughout this period and it was there that a small group met whose actions were to have a durable and highly significant impact on the Irish language in Northern Ireland. In 1965 a newspaper article noted that a small group of Irish-speakers intended to found their own Gaeltacht community in Belfast and to open a school. The idea seemed ludicrous at a time when the Irish state itself was beginning to abandon its own language policies by a process of what has been generously described as 'benign neglect' (Ó Riagáin 1997: 23), and when the Northern Irish state offered nothing but implacable hostility. Nevertheless in 1969 the first Irish-speaking family moved into one of a small number of self-built houses on the Shaw's Road in Belfast and in September 1971 the community opened a primary school, Bunscoil Phobal Feirste.[15]

Any objective view of the future for the Irish language on the island of Ireland in the early 1970s would have necessarily concluded that the prospects were poor. In the North the outbreak of war meant a polarization of society in which semiotic paranoia and antagonism at the cultural level was the corollary of sectarian violence. Signs and symbols invested with cultural and political significance for one section of the divided community were met with distrust, resistance, and often hatred by the other. The Irish language was one such symbol. In the Republic the prevailing feeling among language revivalists was one of despair and disillusion; despair at the changes occurring within Irish society which appeared to be incompatible with the traditional precepts of cultural nationalism, and disillusion with the inactivity of the state which in effect meant a policy of favouring English. The Gaeltacht, the well of Irish undefiled, was a particular concern. Throughout the history of the state the Gaeltacht had shared in the continued pattern of emigration as material conditions remained amongst the worst in the country; in 1965 81 per cent of houses were without piped water and 28 per cent had no access to electricity (*Athbheochan* 1965: 54). In addition state policies appeared to exacerbate rather than prevent the process of Anglicization. The creation of the Department of the Gaeltacht in 1956 and Gaeltarra Éireann, a development agency to promote industrialization, in 1958, were in one sense positive changes for the people of the Gaeltacht, but for the language they contributed to overall decline. The spread of the state bureaucracy in the twentieth century, as in the nineteenth century, brought with it the English language; in 1959 despite the Irish entry requirement for the Civil Service, only 14 per cent of the workforce were fluent while a

---

[15] The history of the language revival in Belfast from the 70s to the mid 90s is covered in Maguire 1991; Chapter five renders an account of the origins and development of the Shaw's Road Gaeltacht.

further 50 per cent had a reading and writing knowledge of the language (Lyons 1985: 637). Industrialization, though economically beneficial, also brought immigration and the return of English-speaking emigrants to the area over a sustained period. Economic policies in fact often had more of an effect on the language than the state's official language policies, and Bord na Gaeilge itself commented that 'state intervention in the Gaeltacht areas has been marked by extreme carelessness in respect to linguistic and cultural resources' (Bord na Gaeilge 1988: 3–4, 47). This is not to say that the further weakening of the Gaeltacht was simply met with passivity, since in an important development in the 60s a group of young radical Gaeltacht activists organized a civil rights campaign which wrought concessions from the state, including a revamped and partly elected development authority, Údarás na Gaeltachta, and in 1972 Raidió na Gaeltachta. Despite these improvements, however, the Irish-speaking population of the Gaeltacht continued to decrease; the core areas, which had remained relatively stable between 1926 and 1956, began in the 60s to show signs of significant language shift (Ó Riagáin 1997: 78).

More worrying were the changing social trends which the economic liberalization of the 60s and 70s brought about. Though the Irish language remained a core symbol of Irish national identity, there is no doubt that its role as the constitutive factor of Irishness began to diminish in this period. Of course there were still those who viewed the language not so much as a safeguard of what the Irish were, as a barrier against what they might become. In an essay on the restoration of Irish in 1964 Brennan argued that 'only Irish can prevent us from being levelled into an indistinguishable conformity with the rest of the enormous culturally panmictic population that surrounds us on both sides of the Atlantic' (Brennan 1964: 265). Such lurid fears of cultural hybridity, however, were highly untypical, and were confined to the more extreme edges of a language movement renowned for its reactionary conservatism. In any case they stood little chance of preventing the cultural changes which the opening of Ireland to the influences of international capitalism brought about, particularly through access to Irish and British television. Ireland between the 1960s and the 80s became further and further removed from the dream envisaged by de Valera in 1943:

The home of a people who valued material wealth only as a basis of right living, of a people who were satisfied with frugal comfort and devoted their leisure to the things of the spirit; a land whose countryside would be bright with cosy homesteads, whose fields and villages would be joyous with the sounds of industry, the romping of sturdy children, the contests of athletic youths, the laughter of comely maidens; whose firesides would be the forums of the wisdom of serene old age (Brown 1985: 146).

Irish society underwent rapid and radical social change and the clash between the forces of modernity and tradition imposed defeat on those conservative, insular and self-sufficient values which de Valera idealized. There would be few who would doubt that the economic changes which took place were for the better, particularly given the effects of the economic boom of the Celtic Tiger in the 1990s (though the affluence created by neo-liberalism has been very unevenly distributed). Whether all of the social and cultural effects of the transformation of Irish society were beneficial, however, is very much open to question.[16] The debate over the rejection of traditional values is ongoing; to a large degree it hangs on what is meant by conservatism and self-sufficiency.

If public attitudes in the 70s and 80s were at best ambivalent towards Irish itself, then the stance towards measures to revive the language appeared unambiguous. Kelly argues that already by the 60s, 'the revival policy, if not the language, had become a divisive element in the concept of nationhood' (Kelly 2002: 141). Such antipathy towards the policy was caused in part by the resentment felt by those who had been excluded from the benefits which accrued to those who had achieved success in Irish in education and consequently in the labour market. Another cause was the widespread cynicism towards measures which were imposed upon children and not reinforced at any other level of society, particularly at upper levels such as parliament; in one instance a government minister was coached phonetically to give a parliamentary answer in Irish in order to avoid political embarrassment (Kelly 2002: 113–14). Telling too was the association of compulsory Irish in schools with authoritarian, crude, and ineffective methods of education: 'Irish had become identified in the popular mind with trouble at school, irregular verbs and tight-faced schoolteachers' (Kiberd 1981: 5). Yet although the

---

[16] For a discussion of the negative effects of the Celtic Tiger economy on Irish culture and society, see the essays in *Reinventing Ireland* (Kirby et al 2002).

failures of the state's actions were largely to blame for attitudes towards the revival project, Kelly's comment that the revival and perhaps even the language itself had become problematic rather than unifying factors in the figuration of nationhood is significant. Its importance lies in drawing attention to the fact that Irishness itself changed in the period between the 60s and the end of the century.

In 1988 a Bord na Gaeilge report, *The Irish Language in a Changing Society: Shaping the Future*, offered a stark insight into the state of the language and offered radical proposals to guarantee its future. Central to the report was a statement of an altered structure of feeling with regard to the significance of Irish:

> the meanings assigned to the language, before and after the establishment of the state, no longer carry the same power to mobilise public action. The changes in the nature and structure of our society over the last quarter of a century have been so dramatic that the previous mobilising rhetorics do not operate in the same way, or as effectively as in the past. The ways in which earlier understandings became incorporated into Irish national life have not turned out to have been entirely beneficial to the language. They have encouraged a widening gap between the symbolic significance attached to Irish as an official emblem of national identity, and its use as a richly expressive vernacular in everyday life (Bord na Gaeilge 1988: xvi).

The changes had produced feelings of antipathy towards the language which, combined with a complacent assumption that the language would survive, had enabled governments of all descriptions 'to ignore the need for legislative or other interventions to ensure that those who do speak Irish can actually carry out their daily business in that language' (Bord na Gaeilge 1988: xviii).

The importance of the symbolic role of Irish remained: a clear majority in national surveys in 1973, 1983, and 1993 agreed that 'no real Irish person can be against the revival of Irish', that 'Ireland would not really be Ireland without Irish-speaking people', and that 'without Irish, Ireland would certainly lose its identity as a separate culture' (Ó Riagáin 1997: 174–5). Yet in an indication of the attitudinal shift which had taken place, the same surveys recorded almost a twenty per cent drop in those who believed that 'to really understand Irish culture, one must know Irish', with a majority disagreeing for the first time. Social and economic change had produced cultural change and, for all the dire warnings of those who believed the concept of Irish national identity without the language as its central component to be a nonsense, Irish national identity in the 80s and 90s was reformulated.[17] Traditionalists may not have liked it (and they did not) but Irishness became associated less with comely maidens, athletic youths, and moral idealism than with Christy Moore, U2, The Pogues, popular versions of traditional music, the Irish football team's exploits at major championships, the image of their partying, friendly fans, famous Seamus Heaney, Dublin's Temple Bar, the commercial trendiness of versions of Irish culture in Britain, and in the 90s at least the boom of the Celtic Tiger economy. A young and educated population met the scandals of political corruption and sexual and physical abuse which finally caught up with traditional bastions of patriarchal authority with scepticism and scorn. And the gradual inching towards a settlement in Northern Ireland began to change perceptions of the British (who also, it should be said, changed rapidly during the period). Essentialist nationalism was exposed as what it perhaps always was: an attempt to make a complex social formation fit a particular mould which had long since been fractured. The more the conservatives lamented the loss of traditional Ireland (and neo-liberal economic policies did more than anything else to destroy it) the more it became clear that 'Real Ireland' was lively, contentious, and often divided on specific issues even if still in many ways and perhaps surprisingly, socially consensual; it was a rapidly changing, globalizing, and glocalizing society which was struggling again with that old problem of reconciling traditional and modern values and ways of living.[18]

Where did all this leave the Irish language? Some commentators argued that an important shift had taken place in the understanding of the role of the language in the nation. Tovey, for example, a member of the committee which compiled *The Irish Language in a Changing Society*, argued that from the 70s Irish was no longer considered 'our language' but simply 'part of what we are'—an important part, no doubt, as Ó Riagáin's findings showed, but just one factor among others. What

---

[17] Ó Tuama argued that if the Gaeltacht died, 'the whole notion of an Irish nation will be beyond recall' (Ó Tuama 1972: 101). The Bord na Gaeilge report recorded that 'the belief that the Irish nation has a future seems to many to be fading away' (Bord na Gaeilge 1988: xviii); in an argument which gained national attention, Lee proposed that 'it is hardly going too far to say that but for the loss of the language, there would be little discussion about identity in the Republic' (Lee 1989: 662).

[18] An example of glocalization is the Sult club in Dublin, opened in 1999; catering for Irish language speakers and learners, and those interested in traditional culture, its programme has also included jazz, samba, tango, salsa, flamenco, modern dance, and ballet.

such a change had produced, Tovey proposed (though it is debatable whether the change followed the policy, or the policy the change), was a largely undeclared state policy of bilingualism according to which Irish and English would function together within the integrated community of the nation with the choice of language being left to individuals in particular contexts (Tovey 1993: 15). What this meant for the Irish language, predictably given the historical trends, was the hard but unavoidable conclusion that 'if it is to survive at all it will be as a second language rather than as the main language of society' (Ó Riagáin 1997: 173). Yet, and this is an important rider, two further developments occurred in the 90s which offered hope for the future of the language. The first was a great revival of interest in Irish across Irish society, primarily located amongst the 'new Irish' and particularly the urban young. The precise causes of this development are as yet not certain but they include: the reaffirmation of a specific cultural identity in the face of globalization (more counter-cultural than nationalist in its origins); the social and economic confidence brought about by the expansion of the period; a sense of social maturity as a younger generation dropped the shackles which held back its predecessors; pride and confidence in Ireland's place in Europe and in its popularity there; immigration and the return of emigrants; the ending of the war, and the growth of the language movement in Northern Ireland. Whatever the reasons, over the past fifteen years or so there has evidently been another distinct shift in the structure of feeling towards the language, this time in its favour. For better or worse, to take one aspect of this change, Irish, once the language identified with the peasantry, backwardness, and poverty, has now become popular with, and is often associated with, middle-class, well-educated Dubliners.[19] Notable for being led by voluntary groups of citizens rather than the state, the revival is socially and geographically widespread: from Irish language and music clubs in Dublin to the vibrant Gaelic scene in Galway, from Irish classes in working-class areas of Dublin to the country-wide expansion of all-Irish schools and the creation of third-level degree courses in Irish. Even the very poor record of broadcasting has been considerably improved; Raidió na Gaeltachta broadcasts nationally twenty-four hours a day, while Dublin community-based Raidió na Life offers daily programming to

---

[19] See Ó Riagáin 1997: Chapter nine, for an examination of Irish-speaking networks in urban areas, particularly Dublin. Some commentators believe that the Dublin 'Gaeltacht' is in a healthier state than the officially designated territory (Bord na Gaeilge 1988: 27).

Dublin and the Leinster area. In television the situation has improved drastically since the time when one commentator argued that 'state-controlled television has worked steadily against' Irish (Ó Tuathaigh 1979: 115); in 1996 the Irish language station Teilifís na Gaeilge was launched (now re-named as TG4).

There has been a revival of interest in the language in ways which were simply not conceivable even fifteen years ago. It is, however, necessary to reserve judgment on the durability of the current popularity, goodwill, and activism with regard to Irish. For though wide, the revival is not yet deep and it is open to question whether it will continue at the same pace. Despite the fact that more people claimed to be able to speak Irish in 2002 than did in 1851, it is clear that patterns of use (as opposed to ability) do not bode well for the future and consist largely of passive bilingualism.[20] Bilingualism proper may in fact be weak outside small areas of the Gaeltacht and limited social networks among the Dublin middle class, and even the linguistic distinction between the Gaeltacht and the rest of the country is diminishing. For some such patterns indicate that 'the long-term future of the Irish language is no more secure now than it was sixty years ago' and that the language 'appears to be in serious danger of disappearing as a community language' (Ó Riagáin 1997: 26). This may be true, even if it is too early to say what effect the revival will have (and all supporters of the language agree that there can be no survival without revival), but it certainly appears to be the case that Irish has regained some of the cultural capital which it had earlier in the century and has lost the stigma associated with it for so long. This in turn feeds into the second development which has begun to favour the language, which is part of the reconfiguration of the nation noted earlier. Tovey has argued that,

[20] In the 1851 census 1,524,286 Irish speakers were recorded out of a population of 6,552,365 (23.25 per cent), though this may have been an under-recording; the 2002 census figures are 1,570,894 Irish speakers from a population of 3,750,995 (42.8 per cent); in 1851 there were 319,602 Irish monoglots, today there are none. The 2002 figures do not of course include Northern Ireland. The 2002 census attempted to measure use as well as ability. Of the recorded Irish speakers 21.6 per cent use the language daily (76.8 per cent in the 5–19 school age group), but almost two-thirds do not use the language at all, or use it less than weekly. In the Gaeltacht areas, 62,157 out of a population of 86,517 were recorded as Irish speakers (72.6 per cent), a slight fall from 1996; the proportion of Irish speakers in the Gaeltacht declined in all areas except the Meath Gaeltacht. Usage figures were: daily 33,789 (54.3 per cent), weekly 6,704 (10.8 per cent), less often 15,811 (25.4 per cent), never 4,515 (7.2 per cent), not stated 1,338.

The result of trying to sustain the connection between the language and the identity of the nation, but also to accommodate growing pressures for pluralism, was that the language policy-makers ended up with what could be called a mix-and-match, consumer-oriented version of national identity combined with a 'heritage' concept of the Irish language (Tovey 1993: 15).

Such a conception of Irish national identity and the role of the Irish language in it is of course highly problematic, and recently it has been undermined by an act of legislation which has major implications. The new view is a direct challenge to the traditional form of nationalism which took the nation to be a culturally defined ethnic space.

*The Irish Language in a Changing Society* called for the state to undertake 'legal and administrative changes which would effectively secure the legal status of Irish and English, and determine the basic rights of Irish speakers vis-á-vis the state and its agents' (Bord na Gaeilge 1988: xlii). Although this may look like a simple appeal for state action to support the language, its radical import lay in the demand for state recognition of the rights of users of the language which was, in a sense, a continuation of the Gaeltacht civil rights campaigns of the 60s and 70s. Whereas the 1937 constitution enshrined the status of the language, it did nothing with regard to legal protection of the right to use the language (and there has been remarkably little case law to test the constitution on such matters).[21] Most significant, however, is the definition of the nation which the report's proposal implied. For in it the nation is constituted not as a single, homogeneous group united by a common linguistic and cultural heritage, but rather as composed of two distinct groups which are at least potentially divided by language and which are therefore both in need of protection and legal rights. And once the nation is conceived in terms of citizens (individuals or in groups) with rights, rather than as culturally-defined members of a communal group, which is to say that once the republican ideal is followed through, then various problems with regard to exclusivity, authenticity, and 'real Irishness' can be set aside.

The decision to introduce language legislation in the Republic was taken in 1997, though the bill was not published until 2002 (given that Irish was given official status in the 1922 constitution, the bill was

---

[21] Ó Catháin notes that until the mid 1990s there had been some twenty references to the use of the Irish language in the acts, statutory instruments, and ministerial orders enacted since 1922, with fifteen examples of case law (Ó Catháin 1996: 24–7).

precisely 80 years a-growing). There were a number of immediate reasons for its conception, including the state's acknowledgment of campaigns for the Irish language which had been conducted over a long period, the significance accorded to language issues in *The Belfast Agreement*, and a timely reminder by the Supreme Court that the Irish State was failing in its constitutional obligations with regard to the language.[22] *Acht na dTeangacha Oifigiúla/The Official Languages Act* (2003), which will be enforced not later than three years after its passing, includes measures which guarantee: that members of either house of the Oireachtas can use either or both of the official languages; that Oireachtas proceedings and reports will be published in both languages; that all Acts of parliament are to be published in each of the official languages at the same time; that either language may be used in court proceedings (without expense or disadvantage), including documentation; that public bodies prepare draft schemes (to be approved by the Minister for Community, Rural and Gaeltacht Affairs) which specify the services available in both of the official languages, and plans to ensure that services not yet provided in Irish will be introduced in future without cost to service users (including the employment of sufficient Irish-speaking staff to ensure provision); that the delivery of services include stationery, signs, and advertising in Irish and the right of customers to be answered in the language of their choice; that public bodies be obliged to publish documents such as policy and strategy proposals, annual reports, financial statements, and other documents of public importance, in Irish and English; that the Office of Official Languages Commissioner be established in order to monitor and ensure compliance (including the right of compensation to those whose language rights are infringed), investigate complaints and failures, and provide advice and help to the public and public bodies, about the legislative provision.

It is of course as yet too early to know the effect of the legislation and in the end it might simply operate to protect the rights of an ever-dwindling number of Irish speakers rather than to act as an instrument for the effective promotion of the language; that has to be the choice of the Irish people themselves. And although the legislation is in many respects weak and conservative in its short-sighted application to only

---

[22] In a Supreme Court case in 2001 (Ó Beoláin v Fahy) the State was stringently criticized for its failure to uphold the constitutional status of Irish by not having all acts and statutory instruments available in English and Irish.

the two official languages (rather than the languages of minorities such as Travellers, or the immigrant languages which will increasingly become part of Irish reality) the principle which lies behind it is a significant one both for those who will benefit from it and for the nation itself.[23] Better that than the pretence of a language policy formulated on a conception of the cultural nation which has long since disappeared.

What of the current situation in Northern Ireland? In the 1970s prospects for Irish language work were bleak with the outbreak of the war and the sustained violence of the early part of that decade providing an unpropitious background to that type of cultural activity. Where the language was taught, it was in a handful of adult classes or in schools on the same terms as Latin or Greek. One study commented in 1979 that,

> the study of the language has certainly been a claim to characteristic identity by the minority Roman Catholic group . . . Irish has been taught—sometimes with inadequate textbooks and methods—as another subject on the timetable, studied for reasons of cultural heritage, possibly, but from the viewpoint of the learners, not useful for everyday communication . . . (Alcock, cited in Maguire 1991: 75).

Nonetheless the founding of the Shaw's Road Gaeltacht Community and the opening of its self-funded Bunscoil in 1971 were acts of self-confidence and determined, not to say defiant, expressions of identity. In fact peculiarly, after the suspension of Unionist Home Rule and the introduction of British direct rule, the Department of Education in Northern Ireland issued a teachers' guide to primary education in 1974 which appeared to recognize Irish as part of the cultural heritage of Northern Ireland:

> In dealing with the teaching of Irish in the primary school, consideration can be given to certain environmental factors which bear on the subject in Ireland. Unlike other languages, Irish does have immediate historical relevance for school pupils here. Surnames, Christian names, names of towns, counties, rivers, fields and numerous other geographical features are in most cases derived directly from Irish (Maguire 1991: 47).

But recognition of historical significance did not stretch as far as funding for the Irish language. British direct rulers in the 1970s,

---

[23] Though the Irish government's commitment in *The Belfast Agreement* to 'demonstrate its respect for the different traditions in the island of Ireland' (*The Belfast Agreement* 1998: 18) is contradicted by its refusal to sign the European Charter for Regional or Minority Languages.

committed to their 'Ulsterization' policy, proved as hostile in practice as the Unionists had been for fifty years: notwithstanding a vigorous campaign for state recognition, Bunscoil Phobal Feirste remained dependent on parents and local people for thirteen years.[24]

Despite the inauspicious circumstances, however, it is a remarkable fact that in Northern Ireland in the past thirty years, based at first in West Belfast and then spreading to nationalist areas across the country, an Irish language revival has taken place which even its most ardent advocates could not have imagined. In the 2001 census some 167,490 respondents (10.35 per cent of the population) claimed some knowledge of Irish. The growth of the Irish-medium schools is one factor in this development, with the establishment of infant or primary schools in all six counties and a secondary school, Méanscoil Feirste, in Belfast. Other Irish language initiatives in Belfast include the Council for Irish medium education, Gaeloiliúint, a development agency, Forbairt Feirste, an e-tech organization, An Telelann, a daily newpaper, *Lá*, and an arts centre, Cultúrlann McAdam Ó Fiaich. The cumulative effect of such activities and achievements has been that Irish, viewed as a somewhat eccentric practice pursued by a tiny minority of mainly middle class people in the early 70s, has risen to the centre of political and cultural debate. To trace how this change has developed it is necessary to turn first to the political situation in the late 70s.

There is no doubt that the Shaw's Road Gaeltacht community and the Bunscoil provided an inspiration for the Irish language movement both in West Belfast and the rest of Northern Ireland. But there is also no disputing the fact that the real interest in, and fostering of, the language in the late 70s and early to mid 80s in Northern Ireland was directly linked to the Republican struggle, particularly in the prisons. One crucial component of the British policy of 'Ulsterization', treating the war in Northern Ireland as though it were a criminal campaign by gangsters, was the stripping of Republican and Loyalist prisoners of the 'special category' rights which had effectively given them the status of political prisoners. Republican opposition to the British policy led to the dirty protest and in 1981 to the Hunger Strikes; as part of the prison campaign, the prisoners engaged in the learning and use of the Irish

---

[24] The story of the founding and campaign for state recognition of the Bunscoil is rendered in Maguire 1991: 76–81.

language and deployed it both as an expression of their identity and as an anti-British symbol. A Sinn Féin pamphlet, *The Role of the Language in Ireland's Cultural Revival*, later stressed the historical shift in perception which occurred:

At the start of the present IRA campaign, people began thinking again of their Irish identity. At that time Sinn Féin left the language work to the various organisations involved with the revival. But as time went by Sinn Féin realised they were obliged to make a greater contribution. Republicans understood also that an Irish revival and the freedom struggle went hand in hand. They began then giving proper attention to the jewel in our heritage. In the prisons and in the clubs Irish classes started (Sinn Féin 1986: 18).

There is an element of revisionism here, since it is doubtful whether many nationalists at the start of the 1970s saw their plight primarily in terms of Irish cultural identity. What is historically correct, however, is the sense that for Republican activists, over a period of time, the Irish language came to be understood as part of their struggle. The prisons were the particular focus of language activity and commonly became known as the Jailtacht:

When the men in the H-Blocks of Long Kesh jail and the women in Armagh prison were stripped of everything, they realised that the most Irish thing they had was their Irish language. Learning it, speaking it all day, was a way of resisting, of asserting your identity, of crying out your defiance against a system that sought to rob you of all identity, and break in you all spirit of defiance (Sinn Féin 1986: 9).

Such rhetoric belonged to what O'Reilly calls 'decolonising discourse' and in its cruder versions it led to claims of a sort which had mostly been disavowed in mainstream nationalist ideology in the Republic and which borrowed heavily from the Fanon-inspired rhetoric of national liberation struggles in Africa in particular.[25] For example, the assertion that children learning Irish in Belfast would 'not feel the alienation of Irish people with only the language imposed on them by imperialism in their mouths' (Sinn Féin 1986: 8), or that learning the language would weaken

---

[25] O'Reilly's very useful analysis of the history of the Irish language in Northern Ireland over the past thirty or so years cites the emergence of three principal discourses around the language: 'decolonizing discourse', 'cultural discourse and 'rights discourse'. These are useful analytical tools but as she indicates, it is often difficult to separate these discourses and the same individual or institution may employ more than one discourse at the same time. See O'Reilly 1999: chapters three–seven.

British rule 'because it would show them that the people of this nation are returning to their real identity once again' (Sinn Féin 1986: 19). A slightly more sophisticated version of such discourse was deployed by Gerry Adams, President of Sinn Féin, in *The Politics of Irish Freedom*, in which he aligned the contemporary situation in Northern Ireland with that of Ireland in its pre-independence phase. Using a combination of the type of cultural nationalist rhetoric employed by the Gaelic League and socialist polemic, Adams presented the language as central to Republican strategy. Mairtín Ó Cadhain, writer, IRA activist, and TCD Professor of Irish, provided Adams with a useful slogan: 'Tosóidh athghabháil na hÉireann le hathghabháil na Gaeilge.' (The reconquest of Ireland will begin with the reconquest of the Irish language) (Adams 1986: 144)[26].

The most significant turning point in Northern Ireland came with the Hunger Strikes in 1981. Though in one sense a defeat, for Republicans it acted as an enormous boost both with regard to active support and in terms of a rethinking of strategy, particularly the realization that politics offered a way out of an increasingly deadlocked war. But for the language revival too the Hunger Strikes provided a real impetus, as one activist recalled:

At the time of the Hunger Strikes it was a political reaction with me, because Irish was the language I should be speaking and it's the least I could do for those men who were dying. I wanted to make it clear that I supported them standing up for their civil rights and human rights. If this hadn't happened I don't think that the Irish language would be as strong as it is today (O'Reilly 1999: 58).

Politicized by the mass mobilization of the Hunger Strike campaign, some joined Sinn Féin and helped set up the Cultural Department which was largely concerned with language issues. Many others, however, saw in the language revival a way of expressing their identity and their political antagonism to British rule which was, crucially, non-violent and culturally based (rather than political in a narrow sense of the term). And it was members of that group, some of whom were republicans, many of whom were not (there were often tensions between the two wings), who eventually took on the leadership of the language movement in Northern Ireland.

In fact as the 80s wore on and the political and military situation seemed stagnant, the decolonizing discourse of Republicanism began to

---

[26] One of the long-standing objects of the IRA constitution is 'to promote the revival of the Irish language as the everyday language of the people' (Moloney 2003: 503).

be replaced by a more 'culturalist discourse'. There were two principal reasons for this change. First, the concern was voiced by a number of people in the language movement that an overt connection between the language and Republicanism was doing the language harm. This may have been a lesson gained from reflecting on the disastrous results of the association of the language with a very narrow version of nationalism in the Republic after independence; it was clear to many that the more linguistic nationalists had declared Gaelic to be central to Irish identity, the more it had been rejected by those who were excluded by that claim. But the reaction was often also a form of genuine cultural nationalism which viewed the language as a thing of beauty in its own right. The second impulse behind cultural discourse was the state's response to the growing popularity and influence of the language movement, with its close links with nationalism and Republicanism. Cultural discourse has been a means to 'depoliticize' the language issue (that is decouple it from nationalist or republican ideology) by constructing it in terms of tradition, heritage, and reconciliation; though of course tradition, heritage, and reconciliation are all politically loaded concepts.

State sponsorship of cultural discourse was demonstrated by the formation of the Cultural Traditions Group in 1988 as a sub-committee of the Community Relations Council, a government-funded body. Two important conferences staged by the group, 'Varieties of Irishness' and 'Varieties of Britishness' in 1989 and 1990, concluded that Irish was too closely associated with Republicanism, that this was 'a distortion of its true cultural significance', and that it 'alienated those who wanted to retain their Britishness' from the language. The Cultural Traditions Group therefore sought 'to confer a new legitimacy on its use' (Cultural Traditions Group 1994: 24–5). Of course to its users the idea that the language needed legitimacy from the state was puzzling at best (given the state's hostility to the language for more than seventy years) and offensive at worst. But in 1989 the Cultural Traditions Group's objectives were embodied in the founding of Iontaobhas Ultach/Ultach Trust (funded by a large grant from the British government in 1991). One of the aims of the trust is 'to make [Irish] classes available in areas in which people from the Protestant community will not feel threatened and help create an environment in which they can comfortably learn and use the language' (Cultural Traditions Group 1994: 25). In one sense such a development was welcome since for the first time the British government recognized and indeed funded an organization to promote the

Irish language. But there were those too who argued that the state's real objective was to gain ideological and financial control of the Irish language movement and in doing so to undermine Republicanism. The clumsy and arbitrary way in which the government withdrew funding from the highly successful West Belfast Irish language group Glór na Gael in the same year that it set up the Ultach Trust lent much credence to this view.

One effect of culturalist discourse was to draw attention to the important fact that in the past the Irish language had not 'belonged' to just one section of the community. Interestingly, such a rejection of the nationalist community's ownership of Irish had been made previously in an unlikely place. In *Combat*, a journal issued by the Ulster Volunteer Force in 1974, 'Uliad' commented that

> The truth of the matter is, Ulster Protestants have as much claim, if not more in some cases, to the Gaelic culture as the Roman Catholic population. Someone once said that the Irish language was stolen from the Protestant people by the Papists; it would be more correct to say that the Protestant people gave their culture away to the Roman Catholics (Ó Glaisne 1981: 39).

The reclamation of Protestant association with the Irish language was also the aim of Ó Snodaigh's *Hidden Ulster* (originally published in 1973), but such revisionism was largely confined to the historical margins before the interest which was stimulated by the heritage and cultural traditions perspective of the 1990s. Examples of this later work include the proceedings of an Ultach-sponsored seminar at the Ulster People's College in 1992 on 'The Irish Language and the Unionist Tradition' (Mistéil 1994), the re-publication of *Hidden Ulster* (in 1995 with the aid of Ultach), and Blaney's *Presbyterians and the Irish Language* (1996, co-published by the Ulster Historical Foundation and Ultach). A visible sign of the extent to which such a perspective has become legitimate (if not widespread) in ways previously inconceivable was the mural on the loyalist Shankhill Road in July 2003; a large Red Hand (the traditional symbol of Ulster) was accompanied by the slogan 'Lámh Dearg Abú Ulster to Victory'.

The Cultural Traditions Group's model stressed recognition and respect for two distinct cultural formations: the Catholic, nationalist tradition with its Gaelic culture and language, and the Protestant, unionist tradition with its (Ulster-) English culture and language. As many critics pointed out, however, such a view was both simplistic and dangerous. Simplistic in that it tended to assume a certain rigidity and insularity to the traditions; dangerous in that such an assumption could lead to the prolongation of precisely such characteristics. Beginning in the 60s and 70s, however, though only really becoming significant in the 90s, there was another element whose appearance disrupted the model and led to a further complication of the cultural map of Northern Ireland; this was the campaign for recognition and respect for another of Ireland's languages and cultural traditions, Ulster Scots. The first academic study proper of this language arose out of the establishment of the Ulster Dialect Archive at the Ulster Folk Museum in 1960 (the material had been gathered since 1951 by the Folklore and Dialect Section of the Belfast Naturalists' Field Club) and a symposium at the museum in 1961. The publication arising from the seminar, *Ulster Dialects: An Introductory Symposium* (1964), contained a seminal essay in which G. B. Adams asserted that 'Ulster English consists essentially of two primary dialects: the north-eastern or Ulster-Scots dialect, and the central or mid-Ulster dialect, together with a number of marginal contact dialects' (Adams 1964: 1). The identification of Ulster-Scots may have remained of interest to linguists, folklorists and literary historians only but for the fact that it was taken up and given a central place in the work of a unionist intellectual and politician, Ian Adamson.[27] Adamson's *The Identity of Ulster: The Land, the Language and the People* (1982) was the beginning of an ideological challenge to received notions of language and cultural identity in the island of Ireland which may yet have influential political effects.

In tacit dialogue with Irish cultural nationalism, Adamson adopted the tactic of identifying the earliest inhabitants of Ulster:

Similar British people such as the 'Brigantes' lived in both Britain *and* Ireland in early times. The two islands were known to the ancient Greeks as the 'Isles of the Pretani'. From 'Pretani' are derived both the words 'Cruthin' and 'Briton' for the inhabitants of these islands. The ancient British Cruthin or 'Cruithne' formed the bulk of the population of both Ulster and North Britain in early Christian times and they are therefore the earliest recorded ancestors not only of the people of Ulster but those of Scotland as well (Adamson 1982: 1).

---

[27] In *Rhyming Weavers and other Country Poets of Antrim and Down* (1974) the influential poet and critic John Hewitt had given an account of the Ulster-Scots literary tradition but this was largely neglected.

There are two crucial ideological assertions here: first the claim to primary possession, since origins lend legitimacy to appeals for cultural recognition. Second, the claim that the Cruthin were the common ancestors of the peoples of both Ulster and Scotland, since it posits an ancient and enduring kinship. From a linguistic perspective Adamson went on to make an even more striking proposition:

The oldest Celtic language, however, spoken in Ireland as well as Britain, was Brittonic (Old British) and this has survived as Breton, Cornish and Welsh. Gaelic did not arrive until *even later*, at a time when the ancient British and Gaels thought of themselves as distinct peoples (Adamson 1982: 1).

Politically this is a far-reaching claim, since it revised Irish nationalism's received version of history and undermined one of its crucial grievances. Rather than Gaelic simply being the victim of colonial usurpation, it was in fact itself once the instrument of conquest: 'Old British was displaced in Ireland by Gaelic just as English later displaced Gaelic'. What Adamson achieved with this model is the neat trick of challenging one form of cultural nationalism (Irish) with another (Ulster). Thus in the same way that Irish cultural nationalists ground the authenticity of their cultural identity in an appeal to Gaelic ancestors, Adamson likewise represented Ulster identity:

Today we must evolve in Ulster a cultural consensus, irrespective of political conviction, religion or ethnic origin, using a broader perspective of our past to create a deeper sense of our belonging to the country of our ancestors. For this land of the Cruthin is our Homeland and we are her children. We have a right to her name and her nationality . . . Only in the complete expression of our Ulster identity lies the basis of that genuine peace, stamped with the hallmarks of justice, goodness and truth, which will end at last the War in Ireland (Adamson 1982: 108).

Adamson's position reflected that of the political wing of the Ulster Defence Association in the early 1980s, and was grounded in what became a growing disenchantment amongst Ulster Loyalism and Unionism with the British authorities. For the UDA the future lay with an independent or devolved state of Ulster (whose cultural and linguistic heritage was threatened by British and Irish nationalisms alike) with close ties to Scotland within a politically reconstituted United Kingdom.

Though Ulster-Scots was considered a dialect (even Adamson referred to it as a variety of the English language), its prominence as the
core element of a new form of Ulster nationalism in the 90s meant that it
was elevated to the status of a language both in the works of its
supporters and eventually by the British government.[28] During the past
decade the interest in Ulster-Scots, and the political significance
accorded to it, have been remarkable. In 1992 the Ulster-Scots Language
Society was founded to gain recognition for a language claimed to
have more than 100,000 speakers. A year later it began publication of
its annual journal *Ullans*, dedicated to reprinting Ulster-Scots literature
and fostering writing in the language as well as including articles of
general Ulster-Scots interest; the Society also publishes *Kintra Sennicht*
(Country Week), a news-sheet entirely in Ulster-Scots. 1994 saw Belfast
City Council give recognition to the linguistic and cultural diversity of
the city and afford equal recognition to both Ulster-Scots and the Irish
language. And in the same year the Ulster-Scots Heritage Council was
formed as an umbrella group to advance Ulster-Scots culture in general.
1995 saw the publication of the first dictionary of the language, James
Fenton's *The Hamely Tongue*, and the production of the first sound
recordings; the Cultural Traditions Group also funded a development
officer for the Ulster-Scots Heritage Council that year. 1996 witnessed
important practical recognition for Ulster-Scots as Michael Ancram, a
Minister of State in Northern Ireland, stated that government policy was
to treat Ulster-Scots in the same way in Northern Ireland as Scots in
Scotland; in addition Ards Borough Council erected street signs
in Ulster-Scots in Greyabbey, and began to use bilingual English
Ulster-Scots stationery. 1997 was marked by the publication of Philip
Robinson's *Ulster-Scots Grammar*. And in 2000 the British government
formally recognized Ulster-Scots as a variety of Scots when it signed the
European Charter for Lesser Used Languages.[29]

The most significant recognition for Ulster-Scots, however, came in
the most important document in the history of the island of Ireland in
the past seventy-five years, *The Belfast Agreement* (1998). In the section of

[28] Adamson refers to Ulster Lallans and Ulster English as 'two varieties of the English
language' (Adamson 1982: 78). Billig offers an interesting exploration of the political significance of the difference between dialects and languages (Billig 1995: chapter two).
[29] Ulster-Scots was recognized under part two of the Charter while Irish was given
recognition under part three. Provisions made under part two offer a lower level of status
and protection than those given under part three.

the agreement which deals with rights, safeguards, and equality of opportunity, particularly with reference to economic, social, and cultural issues, the text declared that:

All participants recognise the importance of respect, understanding and tolerance in relation to linguistic diversity, including in Northern Ireland, the Irish language, Ulster-Scots and the languages of the various ethnic minorities, all of which are part of the cultural wealth of the island of Ireland (*Belfast Agreement* 1998: 19)

As a matter of fact, the recognition given to Ulster-Scots in the Agreement was something of a surprise to the Ulster-Scots Language Society as they had not been informed that their political representatives were negotiating on the issue (*Ullans* 1998: 4). Despite this, and the fact that the text did not refer to Ulster-Scots as a language, the acknowledgement of Ulster-Scots in the Agreement's agenda was an important breakthrough. It was certainly a defence against the sneering dismissal of some Republicans that Ulster-Scots was 'a DIY language for Orangemen' (*Ullans* 1999: 4).

But if *The Belfast Agreement* offered respect and tolerance to Ulster-Scots, it offered far more for the Irish language. Notwithstanding the proviso that such measures would be introduced 'where appropriate and where people so desire it', the British government declared that it would:

- take resolute action to promote the language;
- facilitate and encourage the use of the language in speech and writing in public and private life where there is appropriate demand;
- seek to remove, where possible, restrictions which would discourage or work against the maintenance or development of the language;
- make provision for liaising with the Irish language community; representing their views to public authorities and investigating complaints;
- place a statutory obligation on the Department of Education to encourage and facilitate Irish medium education in line with current provision for integrated education;
- explore urgently with the relevant British authorities, and in co-operation with the Irish broadcasting authorities, the scope for achieving more widespread availability of Teilifís na Gaeilige (sic) in Northern Ireland;
- seek more effective ways to encourage and provide financial support for Irish language film and television production in Northern Ireland; and

- encourage the parties to secure agreement that this commitment will be sustained by a new Assembly in a way which takes account of the desires and sensitivities of the community.
  (*The Belfast Agreement* 1998: 19–20)

Given the overt hostility of the British state to the Irish language over hundreds of years (including its activities in the early 1990s) this is a remarkable and radical, if at first sight somewhat puzzling, turnaround. Why, after all, would tolerance and respect for languages play such an important role in the agreement designed to bring an end to a particularly bitter and divisive period of a conflict which was centuries-old?

The answer lies in the negotiations which prepared the way for the eventual settlement. The basic principles of the agreement, set out by the British and Irish Governments in the Downing Street Declaration (1993) and the Framework Document (1995), consisted of the non-negotiable principle of consent with regard to the border question, new constitutional arrangements between Britain, the Republic of Ireland and Northern Ireland, and a negotiated internal settlement within Northern Ireland. Necessary to that internal settlement were 'full respect for the rights and identities of both traditions in Ireland' (*Joint Declaration* 1993: para. 4), and an emphasis on 'parity of esteem, and on just and equal treatment for the identity, ethos and aspirations of both communities' (*New Framework* 1995: para. 20). Rights, identity and parity of esteem were to be central to the negotiated settlement and given the historical context, this meant that language issues (which have both civil and cultural implications) were thrust to the fore. This was hardly surprising so far as nationalists were concerned. For cultural nationalists the demand for rights for Irish language users side-stepped the question of either 'politicizing' the language (which usually meant any association with Republicanism) or treating it as in some sense apolitical (the state's preferred option) by insisting that such rights formed part of the larger complex of civil rights, which were political only in the sense of being the concern of everyone. For political nationalists, language rights were crucial because Irish had become a cipher for the question of identity and since the beginning of the all-Irish schools movement in Northern Ireland it had also been the focus of demands for equal treatment and recognition from the state. What is more striking, however, was the way in which Ulster-Scots was placed on the agenda by Unionist politicians. This is notable because it marks a shift away from traditional Unionist ideological concerns with questions of citizenship and legal rights, towards the more cultural nationalist perspective of a section of Loyalism.[30] Whether such a shift has long-term implications remains to be seen.

Under the terms of the Good Friday Agreement, the North/ South Ministerial Council was established in December 1999 in order to facilitate regular consultation and cooperation on matters of mutual interest within the competence of both governments on the island of Ireland. Six North/South Implementation Bodies were also introduced, including The North/South Language Body which reports to the Ministerial Council but consists of two separate and autonomous agencies: Foras na Gaeilge, which incorporated Bord na Gaeilge, An Gúm (the state publishing body), and An Coiste Téarmaíochta (the Terminology Committee), has the responsibility for the promotion of the Irish language throughout the island of Ireland (including funding, publications, and support for Irish language education); and Tha Boord o Ulstèr-Scotch/Ulster-Scots Agency, which is responsible for propagating greater awareness of Ulster-Scots language and cultural issues both in Northern Ireland and the Republic.

Perhaps more significant, at least with regard to the language situation in Northern Ireland, was the commitment made by the British Government in the Belfast Agreement to establish a Northern Ireland Human Rights Commission (NIHRC) which would be charged with drafting a Bill of Rights (supplementary to the European Convention on Human Rights) 'to reflect the particular circumstances of Northern Ireland, drawing as appropriate on international instruments and experience' (*The Belfast Agreement* 1998: 17). The purpose of the bill is to guarantee and regulate the relationship between state and citizen, ensure equality for all under the law, and 'in a divided and multi-cultural society like Northern Ireland . . . establish and guarantee the rights of members of each community to equality and fair treatment', including 'parity of treatment and esteem for members of the two communities' and all others (NIHRC 2003). Consultation for the bill was started in 2002 and NIHRC is expected to submit proposals in 2005 with a view to legislation in 2006.

---

[30] For a discussion of this shift and the related 'politicized linguistic consciousness' see Nic Craith 2001.

The move to legislate is important because without it declarations of tolerance and respect might remain as effective as the 1937 Irish Constitution's assertion of the primacy of the Irish language. As with the *Official Languages Act* in the Republic, the Commission's proposals on language will enshrine in law both the rights of language users and the obligations of the state with regard to the provision of services. The proposals note that 'all of the languages and dialects used here contribute to the cultural richness of the whole community' but argue that,

Rather than provide for 'official' or 'national' languages and for 'second' or 'other' languages, the consultation document asserts rights for *all* language users and makes the extent of those rights dependent on the extent to which each language is used and understood in the community. The proposals in the Bill aim to combine the principle of respect for linguistic diversity with that of special recognition for the Irish language and Ulster-Scots (*NIHRC* 2003).

The proposals also recommend that ordinary legislation should cover the detailed implementation of rights such as:

• the right to use any language privately and when accessing essential public or state services;
• the right to display signs (including street signs) and names in any language; and
• the right to education in one's own language where sufficient demand exists.
(*NIHRC* 2003).

Sufficient demand is defined in part as the number of users of the language and available public expenditure, but in a significant gain for the Irish language movement such criteria are already deemed to have been met for Gaelic in Northern Ireland.

As the summary of responses to the Bill of Rights consultation documents indicates, the language proposals are unsurprisingly contentious (21 per cent of the submissions are concerned with them). For example POBAL, an umbrella organization for Irish language groups in Northern Ireland, argues that the NIHRC approach is minimalist and contravenes the United Kingdom's obligations under the European Charter for Regional or Minority Languages (on the basis that Irish is indigenous to Northern Ireland). It also contends that 'all languages are not entitled to the same protection or promotion' and that Irish should be made an official working language of Northern Ireland and treated equally with English (*NIHRC* 2003: Submission 122). The submission from the Ulstèr-Scotch Heirskip Cooncil/Ulster-Scots Heritage Council and Ulstèr-Scotch Leid Society on the other hand protests the fact that the NIHRC documents do not at any stage recognize Ulster-Scots as a language in its own right, and in fact treat it implicitly as a dialect. And it argues that 'the approach of equality for all should be applied to the language section' with no privileges for any particular language (*NIHRC* 2003: Submission 204). The precise measures with regard to language rights are yet to be determined, but as with the Republic of Ireland's *Official Languages Act* they will amount to a specific view of the social order in terms of inclusiveness, equality, and respect. Meanwhile the debates have raised significant questions which will no doubt continue to be addressed. Examples include: is Northern Ireland a society of two, three, or more traditions which are rigidly discreet and which the law must seek to protect (thereby possibly maintaining the divisions)? Do any of the traditions have claim to protection simply on the basis that they are older, or indigenous? Are all languages to be treated equally or do some language-users deserve more respect than others? What rights should the speakers of ethnic community languages have (there are some 8,000 native Chinese speakers in Northern Ireland)? What effect will the fact that the Irish Republic has implicitly recognized that the Irish language is not the essence of Irish identity have on the nationalist movement in Northern Ireland? Is an Ulster identity based on the distinctiveness of Ulster Gaelic, Ulster English, and Ulster-Scots possible? Are Ulster Unionism or Loyalism to be reconstituted on a cultural rather than political basis and what might be the political implications of such a shift?

The answers to these and many other pertinent questions are as yet unknown. Which is to say of course that the war of words will go on ... The war of words covered by this history started in 1537 with an act of legislation which attempted to proscribe the words of one group of speakers and prescribe those of another. And now, strangely enough, the history closes with two further legal acts. But these latest two pieces of legislation seek to play out the war of words *in words*. And although words are powerful weapons, as weapons they are infinitely preferable to the weapons with which this war has been fought in the past: dispossession, impoverishment, starvation, arbitrary violence, assassination, ignorance, prejudice, and division. There is no such thing as free speech, because there are always costs; but then there are costs and costs. Words embody cultural and political differences, but they also embody the means of negotiating them. Precisely because language is so central to our social being, it is therefore subject to all sorts of domination, restriction, and narrowing. But in the end languages are open-ended, flexible, and creative systems for our own use in making our own histories; subject to the forces of history, language is yet a creative force within it.

# CHAPTER EIGHT

# Post-Agreement Script: writers and the language questions

'a new language | is a kind of scar' (Eavan Boland, 'Mise Eire', 1986).

All languages are kinds of scars; at one and the same time they embody a history of injury and healing, reminding us of past pain and the possibilities of recovery. It is unsurprising, given Ireland's history, that contemporary writers have shown themselves to be sensitive to language both as the repository of difference and antagonism, and as a creative and innovative force. Contemporary poets in particular, writing from a variety of perspectives, have addressed the language questions. For some the English language has appeared at times to be simply too laden with historical difficulty; what Tom Paulin calls a sense of 'language as historical struggle, language heavy with violence, atavism, the memory of later invasions and pitched battles' (Paulin 1998: ix). Biddy Jenkinson, for example, has forbidden translation of her work 'as a small rude gesture to those who think that everything can be harvested and stored without loss in an English-speaking Ireland' (de Paor 1996: 1141). Michael Hartnett bade farewell to English and went 'with meagre voice | to court the language of my people'.[1] In the face of an Ireland open to the forces of international capital and its ways, 'the world of total work', he chose instead to write in Irish as a protest against the forces of commercial levelling and cultural homogeneity:

> .... All that reminds us
> that we are human and therefore not a herd
> must be concealed or killed or slowly left

---

[1] Hartnett renounced English in *A Farewell to English* in 1978 and published three volumes in Irish. The critical reception, largely one of indifference, caused him to wonder: 'do thréig mé an Béarla - | ar dhein mé tuaiplis?' (I have deserted the English tongue | have I made a mistake?) (Bartlett 1988: 114). In 1985 he rescinded his decision and began publishing in English again.

to die, or microfilmed to waste no space.
For Gaelic is our final sign that
We are human, therefore not a herd.
(Hartnett 1978: 66).

The fact that Nuala Ní Dhomhnaill's work uses Gaelic to present an informed social and political sensibility, combined with a rude scepticism towards traditional pieties, has sometimes provoked surprise. Reflecting on a question made of her work by a fellow-Irish citizen ('and is there a word for sex in Irish?'), Ní Dhomhnaill comments: 'here I was in my own country, having to defend the official language of the state from a compatriot who obviously thought it was an accomplishment to be ignorant of it. Typical, and yet maybe not so strange' (Nic Craith 1996: 190–1). But despite the fact that her use of the language conveys a modern, secular, and playful consciousness, characterized as much by feminism as by Gaelic mythology, she is also aware that the language in which she writes has yet a precarious future. It is beautifully set out in 'Ceist na Teangan' (translated by Paul Muldoon as 'The Language Issue'):

Cuirim mo dhóchas ar snámh
i mbáidín teangan
faoi mar a leagfá naíonán
i gcliabhán
a bheadh fite fuaite
de dhuilleoga feileastraim
is bitiúman agus pic
bheith cuimilte lena thóin

I place my hope on the water
in this little boat
of the language, the way a body might put
an infant

in a basket of intertwined
iris leaves,
its underside proofed
with bitumen and pitch

ansan é a leagadh síos
i measc na ngiolcach
is coigeal na mban sí
le taobh na habhann,
féachaint n'fheadaraís
cá dtabharfaidh an sruth é
féachaint, dála Mhaoise,
an bhfóirfidh iníon Fhorainn?

then set the whole thing down amidst
the sedge
and bulrushes by the edge
of a river

only to have it borne hither and thither,
not knowing where it might end up;
in the lap, perhaps,
of some Pharoah's daughter.

(Ní Dhomhnaill 1990: 154–5).

Other writers have chosen to write in English but to record the feelings of difficulty and alienation which that entails from an Irish nationalist perspective. 'A Severed Head', section four of John Montague's *The Rough Field* (1972), is a prolonged meditation on the linguistic consequences of colonialism: 'And who ever heard | Such a sight unsung | As a severed head | With a grafted tongue?'[2] The poem, in part an account of the conquest of Ulster and the Flight of the Earls, is structured by representations from John Derricke's series of woodcuts, *The Image of Irelande: With a Discoverie of Woodkarne* (1581), and comments from colonial and native sources such as Sir John Davies, George Carew, Chichester, Mountjoy, and the Annals of the Four Masters. The aftermath of the conquest, including the destruction of Gaelic culture, is recorded in the 'shards of a lost tradition', place names which represent 'memory defying cruelty', 'The whole landscape a manuscript | We had lost the skill to read' (Montague 1972: 35). The pain of the loss of the language is figured as a comparison between a colonial decapitated head, an Irish child in the nineteenth century learning English, and the stuttering child of Montague's own youth:

> Dumb,
> bloodied, the severed
> head now chokes to
> speak another tongue.

The Irish child, weeping, repeats its 'garbhbhéarla' (Ó Bruadair's term meaning 'rough English') under threat of punishment, slurring, and stumbling 'in shame | the altered syllables | of your own name'. The acquisition of English brings alienation from parents and home since 'in cabin and field' (the 'rough field' of the poem's title is a translation of 'garbh faiche', or Garvaghey, the name of the poet's birth-place),

> they still
> speak the old tongue.
> You may greet no one.

> To grow
> a second tongue, as
> harsh a humiliation
> as twice to be born
> (Montague 1972: 39).

Yet Montague's poem also celebrates the uniqueness of Ulster English in its divergence from the standard form: 'even English in these airts |

---

[2] As noted earlier, both Ó Bruadair and Joyce expressed this feeling; see Chapter three, page 60 and Chapter six, page 160.

'Took a lawless turn' ('airts' from the Scottish Gaelic 'àird', Irish 'aird', meaning areas or districts). Place names in particular twine 'braid Scots and Irish | Like Fall Brae, springing native | As a whitethorn bush' ('Fall' from the Gaelic 'fál', hedge, 'Brae' from the Scots, hillside or steep road). And this link to the important Gaelic tradition of dinnseanchas is also explored in Seamus Heaney's place name poems ('Anahorish', Toome', 'Broagh'), which acknowledge this function of language as the storehouse of the past. In 'Traditions' Heaney provides in miniature a linguistic history of Ireland in which he remarks approvingly on the retention of archaic features in Ulster English (a characteristic of Hiberno-English in general which Stanihurst, Edgeworth, and Joyce also noted):

> We are to be proud
> of our Elizabethan English:
> 'varsity', for example,
> is grass-roots stuff with us;
>
> we 'deem' or we 'allow'
> when we suppose
> and some cherished archaisms
> are correct Shakespearean.
> (Heaney 1980: 68).[3]

In a much later poem Heaney offers an unusually forthright view of the colonial language question, even if it is cloaked in the persona of the spirit of James Joyce:

> The English language
> belongs to us. You are raking at dead fires,
> rehearsing the old whinges at your age.
> That subject people stuff is a cod's game,
> Infantile.
> (Heaney 1990: 193).

Such characteristically Joycean brusqueness and confidence (expressed here in the use of the Hiberno-English 'cod', fool or humbugger) link back to Joyce's own annoyance at discovering that 'tundish' was good old English. Yet in 'Traditions' Heaney is also careful to acknowledge another of the linguistic consequences of colonial rule: 'the furled | consonants of lowlanders', 'obstinately' inhabiting Ulster.

---

[3] For the comments of Stanihurst, Edgeworth, and Joyce on this see respectively Chapter two, note 85; Chapter four, page 10; Chapter one, page 8.

Ulster-Scots has a long literary tradition, consisting of the 'unselfconscious' writing of the plantation period (from the late sixteenth to the mid seventeenth centuries) and the 'selfconscious' writing of the early eighteenth to the late nineteenth centuries (Robinson 1997: 7–11).[4] As noted in the last chapter, part of the recent resurgence of interest in Ulster-Scots has been the attempt by the Ulster-Scots Language Society to encourage new writing in its magazine *Ullans*. An example is 'The Gaelic Archipeligo' by Philip Robinson (author of the grammar of Ulster-Scots), which compares those opposed to the Belfast Agreement to Paineites, Gandhi, Anne Frank, Martin Luther King, and Soviet dissidents. The difference being that the latter are remembered and celebrated whereas the anti-Agreement dissenters are castigated:

> Scrievin
> Sic puzhin in oor Papers
> Skailin dissent
> Like oul dung on that Green Paice
> Dinosaurs fae *These Islanns*
> Tha *Gaelic* Archipeligo
> Brave an guid New Warl
> (*Ullans* 2001: 37).

(Writing such poison in our papers, scattering dissent like old dung on that Green Peace. Dinosaurs from *These Islands*, the *Gaelic* Archipeligo. Brave and good New World).

'Whit richt hae they', the poem asks, to keep on saying 'Na'? 'Nane ava', is the reply, none at all.

If as the ghost of Joyce claims, the English language now belongs to the Irish in the form of Hiberno-English, then what these brief selections from the work of contemporary writers demonstrates is that Gaelic, Ulster-English, and Ulster-Scots also belong to the peoples of the island of Ireland as viable vehicles for the differing voices which need to be heard. There are of course other voices and languages (there are more than thirty language communities in Northern Ireland alone) which also require recognition. And given the patterns of emigration and immigration in the Republic and Northern Ireland which are occurring and which will continue, the interrelations between the spoken languages of modern Ireland are likely to become more complex rather than less. In that sense the island of Ireland today and tomorrow

---

[4] For a discussion of the literary history of Ulster-Scots see Robinson 1997: 7–11.

may well be a more complicated version of the Ireland of yesterday. For as has been argued, 'multilingualism and translation did not arrive on Irish shores with the European Economic Community in 1973' (Cronin 1996: 39), but were features of medieval Ireland. What the effects of this new set of peoples, languages, cultures, and differences will be is of course unknown. But it is unlikely in the long term that cultural models which are conceived in terms of one, two, or even three traditions will survive; to adapt Brian Friel's metaphor in *Translations*, they will become maps which no longer match the landscape of fact (Friel 1981: 43). Of course there already has been one literary representation of a utopian multilingual and multicultural Ireland in *Finnegans Wake*'s dizzying refusal to be tied to any single language, nationality, or system of belief. But that is literature, and in the social realm the problems and answers are always harder. The difficulties are real enough and it is more than likely that only wars of words (subject to the rider made at the end of the last chapter) and the commitment of significant resources will resolve them. But a good place to start in tackling the problems is the simple but radical acknowledgement which massive majorities in both the Republic of Ireland and Northern Ireland made by voting for *The Belfast Agreement*: that the languages of the island of Ireland form part of its cultural wealth. All forms of wealth can be a source of division or common good; it's a choice.

# Bibliography

## Primary Texts

Adams, G. B. (1964) 'Ulster Dialects' in *Ulster Dialects: An Introductory Symposium*, Belfast: Ulster Folk Museum.

Adams, Gerry (1986) *The Politics of Irish Freedom*, Dublin: Brandon.

Adamson, Ian (1982) *The Identity of Ulster: The Land, the Language and the People*, Belfast: Pretani Press.

*An Claidheamh Soluis* (1899–1932) vol. 1, Dublin: Gaelic League.

*Ancient Irish Histories: the Works of Spencer, Campion, Hanmer, and Marleburrough* (1809) 2 vols, Dublin.

Anderson, Christopher (1818) *A Brief Sketch of Various Attempts which Have Been Made to Diffuse a Knowledge of the Holy Scriptures through the Medium of the Irish Language*, Dublin.

Anon (1598) *The Supplication of the Blood of the English Most Lamentably Murdered in Ireland, Cryeng Out of the Yearth for Revenge*, ed. Willy Maley (1995) *Analecta Hibernica*, 36, 1–77.

Anon [?G. Peele] (1605) *The Life and Death of Captain Thomas Stukeley* in *The School of Shakspere* (1878) R. Simpson, New York.

Anon (1843*a*) 'English Schools and Irish Pupils', *The Nation*, 26, Dublin.

Anon (1843*b*) 'The Irish Language', *The Nation*, 31, 35, Dublin.

Anon (1858) 'A Dialogue in the Ulster Dialect', *Ulster Journal of Archaeology*, 6, 40–8.

*Athbheochan na Gaeilge/The Restoration of the Irish Language* (1965), Baile Átha Cliath: Oifig an tSoláthair.

Barron, P. (1835*a*) *Ancient Ireland. A Weekly Magazine Established for the Purpose of Reviving the Cultivation of the Irish Language and Originating an Earnest Investigation Into the Ancient History of Ireland*, I–V, Dublin.

—— (1835*b*) *Irish Sermons with Translations*, Dublin.

Begly, Conor and Hugh MacCurtin (Conchobar ÓBeaglaoich agus Aodh Buidhe MacCruitín) (1732) *The English-Irish Dictionary. An Focloir Bearla Gaoidheilge*, Paris.

*Belfast Agreement, The: An Agreement Reached at the Multi-Party Talks on Northern Ireland* (1998) London: The Stationery Office.

Berkeley, Bishop George (1837) 'The Querist' (1750) in *The Works of George Berkeley*, London: Daly.

Bord na Gaeilge (1983) *Action Plan for Irish 1983–86*, Dublin: Bord na Gaeilge.

—— Advisory Planning Committee (1988) *The Irish Language in a Changing Society: Shaping the Future*, Dublin: Bord na Gaeilge.

Bourke, U. J. (1856) *The College Irish Grammar*, 5th edn., (1868) Dublin.

Bowers, Fredson (1966) ed., *The Dramatic Works in the Beaumont and Fletcher Canon*, Cambridge: Cambridge University Press.

Brooke, Charlotte (1789) *Reliques of Irish Poetry; Consisting of Heroic Poems, Odes, Elegies, and Songs Translated into English Verse*, Dublin.

*Bunreacht na hÉireann. Constitution of Ireland* (1999) Dublin: The Stationery Office.

Burke, Edmund (1790) *Reflections on the Revolution in France*, ed. Conor Cruise O'Brien (1969), Harmandsworth: Penguin.

Butler, Mary E. L. (1901) *Irishwomen and the Home Language*, Dublin: Gaelic League.

*Calendar of Ancient Records of Dublin* (1889–95) vols. i–v, 1172–1692, ed. J. T. Gilbert, Dublin.

*Calendar of the Carew Manuscripts preserved in the Archiepiscopal library at Lambeth* (1867–73), 1515–74 [etc.] 6 vols., London.

*Calendar of the Patent and Close Rolls of Chancery in Ireland 18th to 45th of Queen Elizabeth* (1862), ed. J. Morrin, Dublin.

*Calendar of the State Papers Relating to Ireland* (1860–1912), 1509–1573 [etc.] 24 vols., London.

Campion, Edmund (1633) *A Historie of Ireland* (1571) in *The Historie of Ireland Collected by Three Learned Authors* (1633), ed. James Ware, Dublin.

Carsuel, Seon (John Carswell) (1873) *Foirm na nUrrnuidheadh agus Freasdal na Sacramuinteadh, The Book of Common Order Commonly Called John Knox's Liturgy* (1567), ed. T. McLaughlan, Edinburgh: Edmonston and Doug.

Cawdry, Robert (1604) *A Table Alphabeticall*, London.

Céitinn, Seathrún (Geoffrey Keating) (1902–14) *Foras Feasa ar Éirinn (A Basis of Knowledge about Ireland)* (1634), 4 vols. ed. and trans. D. Comyn and P. S. Dinneen, London: Irish Texts Society.

Collins, Michael (1922) *The Path to Freedom*, Dublin: Talbot Press.

*Committee on Irish Language Attitudes Research/An Coiste um Thaighde ar Dhearcadh an Phobail I dtaobh na Gaeilge* (1975), Dublin: The Stationery Office.

Committee on Irish Language Attitudes (1975) *Report*, Dublin: The Stationery Office.

Coneys, Rev. (1842) 'The Irish Language', *The Nation*, 5, Dublin.

Connellan, Owen (1834) *A Dissertation on Irish Grammar*, Dublin.

Connellan, Thaddeus (1814) *An English-Irish Dictionary, Intended for the Use of Schools*, Dublin.

—— (1822) *The King's Letter, In Irish and English*, Dublin.

Corcoran, Fr. T. J. (1925) 'The Irish language in the Irish Schools', *Studies*, xiv, 377–88.

Cox, Sir Richard (1689–90) *Hibernia Anglicana, or the History of Ireland from the Conquest thereof by the English to this Present Time*, 2 Pts, London.

Cultural Traditions Group (1994) *Giving Voices: the Work of the Cultural Traditions Group 1990–1994*, Belfast: Community Relations Council.

Curran, W. H. (1882) *The Life of John Philpott Curran*, ed. R. Shelton Mackenzie, Chicago.

D'Alton, R. (1862) *An Fíor Éirionnach*, Tipperary.

Daniel, William, see Ó Domhnaill, Uilliam.

Daunt, W. J. O'Neill (1848) *Personal Recollections of the Late Daniel O'Connell, M. P.*, Dublin.

Davies, Sir John (1890) *A Discovery of the True Causes Why Ireland Was Never Entirely Subdued*, in *Ireland Under Elizabeth and James I* (1619) ed. J. Morley, London: Routledge.

Davis, Thomas (1843) 'Our National Language', *The Nation*, 25, Dublin.

—— (1844) 'Repeal Reading Rooms', *The Nation*, 97, Dublin.

—— (1914) *Essays Literary and Historical*, Dundalk: Dundalga Press.

De Bhaldraithe, T. (1979) *The Diary of Humphrey O'Sullivan*, Dublin: Mercier.

Dekker, Thomas (1600) *The Pleasant Comedie of Old Fortunatus*, London.

Delvin, Lord (Christopher Nugent) (1882) *Primer of the Irish Language* (*c*.1584–5) in *Facsimiles of the National Manuscripts of Ireland* (1874–84) 4 vols., vol. IV, i, ed. J. T. Gilbert, Dublin.

Dewar, D. (1812) *Observations on the Character, Customs and Superstitions of the Irish*, London.

Dinneen, Rev. P. S. (1904) *Lectures on the Irish Language Movement*, Dublin: Gill.

—— (1904, second edn. 1927) *Foclóir Gaedhilge agus Béarla (An Irish-English Dictionary)*, Dublin: Irish Texts Society.

Donlevy, Andrew (1742) *An Teagasg Críosduidhe do réir agus ceasda agus freagartha. The Catechism, or Christian Doctrine by way of Question and Answer*, Paris.

Edgeworth, Maria (1833) *Forgive and Forget, a tale and Rosanna, a tale*, trans. [into Irish] T. Feenachty, Belfast and Dublin.

Edgeworth, Maria and Richard (1802) *Essay on Irish Bulls*, London.

*Fáinne an Lae* (1898–1900) 5 vols., Dublin: Gaelic League.

Fenton, James (1995) *The Hamely Tongue. A Personal Record of Ulster-Scots in County Antrim*, Newtownards: Ulster-Scots Academic Press.

Ferguson, Samuel (1834) 'Hardiman's Irish Minstrelsy No.II', *Dublin University Magazine*, vol. 4, 20.

Fichte, J. G. (1968) *Addresses to the German Nation* (1808), ed. G. Armstrong Kelly, New York: Harper.

Flaherty, Donal (1884) 'Practical Hints Towards Preventing the Decay of Irish in the Irish Speaking Districts', *Proceedings of the [Society for the Preservation of the Irish Language] Congress Held in Dublin*, Dublin.

Flood, Henry (1795) 'Henry Flood's Will' in *Ancient Ireland* (1835) no. 5, ed. Philip Barron, Dublin.

Forde, Rev. Patrick (n.d.?1901) *The Irish Language Movement: Its Philosophy*, Dublin: Gaelic League.

Friel, Brian (1981) *Translations*, London: Faber.

—— (1989) *Making History*, London: Faber.

Gaelic League (1901–2) *The Irish Language and Intermediate Education*, 11–20 Dublin: Gaelic League.

Gaelic Society of Dublin (1808) *Transactions*, ed. E. O'Reilly, Dublin: Barlow.

Gaelic Union (1882) *Irisleabhear na Gaedhilge/ The Gaelic Journal*, vol.1, Dublin.

Gallagher, James (1736) *Sixteen Sermons in an Easy and Familiar Style on Useful and Necessary Subjects*, Dublin.

Gallduf, Teabóid (Theobald Stapleton) (1639) *Catechismus seu Doctrina Christiana Latino-Hibernica*, Brussels.

Gerrard Papers (1931) 'Lord Chancellor Gerrard's Notes of his Report on Ireland', 1577–8, ed. Charles McNeill, in *Analecta Hibernica*, 2, 93–291.

Gilbert, J. T. (1859) *A History of the City of Dublin*, 3 vols., Dublin.

Giraldus Cambrensis (Gerald of Wales) (1188), *The History and Topography of Ireland* (1982), trans. J. J. O'Meara, Dublin: Dolmen.

*Gramadach na Gaeilge agus litriú na Gaeilge: an Chaighdeán Oifigiúil* (2001), Baile Átha Cliath: Oifig an tSoláthair.

Grattan, Henry (1812) 'Letter to the Secretary of the Board of Education', 14th Report, Commission of the Board of Education, Ireland, October 1812, appendix 3, 336, *House of Commons Papers*.

Gregory, Lady (1901) *Ideals In Ireland*, London: Unicorn.

—— (1902) *Cuchulain of Muirthemne: the Story of the Men of the Red Branch of Ulster*, London: Murray.

—— (1974) *Seventy Years: Being an Autobiography of Lady Gregory*, ed. Colin Smythe, Gerrards Cross: Colin Smythe.

Haliday, William (1808) see Edmond O'Connell.

Hamilton, Hugo (2003) *The Speckled People*, London: Fourth Estate.

Hardiman, James (1831) *Irish Minstrelsy, Or Bardic Remains of Ireland; with English Poetical Translations*, London.

Hartnett, Michael (1978) *A Farewell to English*, Dublin: Gallery Press.

Heaney, Seamus (1980) *Selected Poems 1965–75*, London: Faber.

—— (1990) *New Selected Poems 1966–1987*, London: Faber.

Historical Manuscripts Commission (1885) 'Archives of the Municipal Corporation of Waterford' in *Historical Manuscripts Commission Report*, 10, appendix v, Dublin.

Holinshed, R. (1587) *The Chronicles of England, Scotland and Ireland* ed. John Hooker et al, 3 vols., 1587; ed. Henry Ellis, 6 vols., 1807–8, London.

Humboldt, William Von (1836) *On Language: The Diversity of Human Language Structure and Its Influence on the Mental Development of Mankind*, trans. P. Heath, 1988, Cambridge: Cambridge University Press.

Hutchinson, Francis (1722) *The Church Catechism in Irish, with the English Placed over it in the Same Karacter*, Belfast.

Hyde, Douglas (1889) *Leabhar Sgeulaigheachta*, Dublin.

—— (1890) *Beside the Fire*, London.

—— (1892) 'The Necessity for De-Anglicising Ireland', in B. Ó Conaire, ed. (1986) *Language, Lore and Lyrics: Essays and Lectures of Douglas Hyde*, Dublin: Irish Academic Press.

—— (1893) *Abhráin Grádh Chúige Connacht Or, The Love Songs of Connacht* (1969) Shannon: Irish University Press.

—— (1899) *A Literary History of Ireland. From Earliest Times to the Present Day*, London: Fisher Unwin.

—— (1899) 'Irish as a Spoken Language' in *A Literary History of Ireland From Earliest Times to the Present Day* (1967) new ed. and intro. B. Ó Cuív, London: Benn.

—— (1900) *A University Scandal*, Dublin: Gaelic League.

Irish Archaeological Society (1843), 'The Statute of Kilkenny' (1366) in *Tracts Relating to Ireland*, Dublin: Irish.

Irish National Teachers Organisation (1941) *Report of the Committee of Inquiry into the Use of Irish as a Teaching Medium to Children whose Home Language is English*, Dublin: Cahill.

—— (1947) *A Plan for Education*, Dublin: INTO.

*Irisleabhar na Gaedhilge (Gaelic Journal)* (1882–1909) Dublin: Gaelic Union.

*Joint Declaration by An Taoiseach, Mr. Albert Reynolds, T. D., and The British Prime Minister, The Rt. Hon. John Major, M. P.* (1993) <http://www.irlgov.ie/iveagh/angloirish/jointdeclaration/default.htm>

Jonson, Ben (1941) *The Irish Masque at Court* (1613) in *Works*, vol.VII (1941) ed. C. H. Herford, Percy and Evelyn Simpson, Oxford: Clarendon.

—— (1947) *Timber, or Discoveries* (1641), in *Works*, vol VIII ed. C. H. Herford, Percy and Evelyn Simpson, Oxford: Clarendon.

Joyce, James (1939) *Finnegans Wake*, London: Faber and Faber.

—— (1992) *A Portrait of the Artist as a Young Man* (1916) ed. Seamus Deane, Harmondsworth: Penguin.

—— (1992) *Ulysses* (1922) ed. Declan Kiberd, London: Penguin.

Kavanagh, Rev. P. F. (1902) *Ireland's Defence—Her Language*, Dublin: Gaelic League.

Keenan. P. J. (1856) 'Twenty-second Report of the Commissioners of National Education in Ireland', ii, 75, pt 2, 81, *House of Commons Papers*, London.

—— (1857–8) 'Twenty-third Report of the Commissioners of National Education in Ireland', i, 143–4, *House of Commons Papers*, London.

Keogh, John (1748) *A Vindication of the Antiquities of Ireland*, Dublin.

Ledwich, E. (1790) *Antiquities of Ireland*, Dublin.

Lewis, John (1712) *The Church Catechism. Explain'd By Way of Question and Answer; Caitecism na Heaglaise, Ar Mhodh Cheiste agus Fhreagra*, trans. John Richardson, London.

Lhuyd, Edward (1707) *Archaeologia Britannica, Giving Some Account Additional to What Has Hitherto Been Published, of the Languages, Histories, and Customs of the Original Inhabitants of Great Britain*, Oxford.

—— (1707) 'Focloir Gaoidheilge-Shagsonach', preface trans. in W. Nicolson, *The Irish Historical Library* (1724) Dublin.

Lynch, John [T. Lucius, Gratianus] (1662) *Cambrensis Eversus*, trans. as *Cambrensis Refuted* (1795) T. O'Flanagan, Dublin.

Lynch, P. (1795) *Bolg an tSaolair: Or, Gaelic Magazine*, Belfast.

MacAingil, Aodh (1618) *Sgáthán Shacramuinte na hAithridhe*, Louvain.

MacCruitín, Aodh (Hugh MacCurtin) (1717) *A Brief Discourse in Vindication of the Antiquity of Ireland*, Dublin.

—— (1728) *The Elements of the Irish Language, Grammatically Explained in English*, Louvain.

—— (1732) *The English-Irish Dictionary. An Focloir Bearla Gaoidheilge*, Paris, see Begly.

MacDonagh, Thomas (1920) *Literature in Ireland*, Dublin: Talbot Press.

McDonald, D. W. (1874) trans. Richard Conway, 'An Account of the Decrees and Acts ... in the Year 1611 in Dublin', *Irish Ecclesiastical Record*, 203–7.

MacHale, Bishop John (1844) *An tIliad*, Dublin.

—— (1861) *An Irish Translation of the Holy Bible from the Latin Vulgate*, vol.1, Tuam.

—— (1871) *A Selection of Moore's Melodies; translated into the Irish language by the Most Rev. John MacHale*, Dublin.

MacNeill, Eoin (1909) *Irish in the National University of Ireland*, Dublin: Gaelic League.

MacPherson, James (1760) *Fragments of Ancient Poetry Collected in the Highlands of Scotland and translated from the Gaelic or Erse Language*, Edinburgh.

McSweeny, Conor (1843) *Songs of the Irish*, Dublin.

Maley, Willy (1995) ed. *The Supplication of the Blood of the English Most Lamentably Murdered in Ireland, Cryeng Out of the Yearth for Revenge*, *Analecta Hibernica*, 36, 1–77.

Martyn, E. (n.d.? 1901) *Ireland's Battle for her Language*, Dublin: Gaelic League.

Mason, H. M. (1829) *Facts Afforded by the History of the Irish Society*, Dublin.

—— (1844) *The History of the Origin and Progress of the Irish Society*, Dublin.

'Memo of Commissioners of National Education to the Chief Secretary' (1884) in *Irisleabhar na Gaedilge. Gaelic Journal*, 15, Dublin.

Montague, John (1972) *The Rough Field*, Portlaoise: Dolmen.

Moore, George (1901) 'Literature and the Irish Language' in Lady Gregory, ed., *Ideals In Ireland*, London: Unicorn.

Moran, D. P. (1901) 'The Battle of Two Civilisations' in Lady Gregory, ed., *Ideals In Ireland*, London: Unicorn.

—— (1905) *The Philosophy of Irish Ireland*, Dublin: Duffy.

Morris, Henry (1898) 'The Loss of the Irish Language and Its Influence on the Catholic Religion in Ireland', *Fáinne An Lae*, I, 13, Dublin.

Moryson, Fynes (1903) *Shakespeare's Europe. Unpublished Chapters of Fynes Moryson's Itinerary* (1617) ed. C. Hughes, London: Sherratt and Hughes.

—— (1907–8) *An Itinerary Containing his Ten Yeeres Travell through the Twelve Dominions of Germany, Bohmeland, Sweitzerland, Netherland, Denmarke, Poland, Italy, Turky, France, England, Scotland and Ireland* (1617) Glasgow: Maclehose.

Muldoon, Paul (1987) *Meeting the British*, London: Faber.

*The Nation* (1842–8), 8 vols, Dublin.

Neilson, Rev. W. M. (1808) *An Introduction to the Irish Language*, Dublin. New *Framework for Agreement* (1995) <http://www.irlgov.ie/iveagh/angloirish/frameworkdocument/default.htm>

Ní Dhomhnaill, Nuala (1990) *Pharoah's Daughter*, Oldcastle: Gallery Press.

Nicholson, E. (1715) 'Letter to the Secretary, Society for Promoting Christian Knowledge', in *Analecta Hibernica* (1931) 2, Dublin: Historical Manuscripts Commission.

Nicolson, Lord Bishop William (1724) *The Irish Historical Library*, Dublin.

Northern Ireland Human Rights Commission (2003) 'Bill of Rights Consultation', <http://www.nihrc.org.>

Nolan, John (1877) *Irish Grammar in Prose and Verse*, Dublin.

O'Brien, Dr. John (1768) *Focalóir Gaoidhilge-Sax-Bhéarla, Or, an Irish-English Dictionary*, Paris.

Ó Bruadair, Dáibhí (David O'Bruadair) (1910–17) *Duanaire Dhábhidh Uí Bhruadair, The Poems of David Ó Bruadair*, part I, 1910, part II, 1913, part III, 1917, ed. and trans. J. C. MacErlean, London: Irish Texts Society.

Ó Cearnaigh, Seán (John Kearney) (1571) *Aibidil Gaoidheilge & Caiticiosma* Dublin.

Ó Cléirigh, Michéul (Michael O'Clery) (1643) *Foclóir na Sanasán Nua. A New Vocabulary or Glossary* in *Révue Celtique*, vol. IV (1879–80) trans. A. Miller, Paris.

Ó Conaire, B. ed. (1986) *Language, Lore and Lyrics: Essays and Lectures of Douglas Hyde*, Dublin: Irish Academic Press.

O'Connell, Edmond [William Haliday] (1808) *Uraicecht na Gaedhilge. Grammar of the Gaelic Language*, Dublin.

O'Connor, Frank (2000) 'The Future of Irish Literature' (1942) in *Irish Writing in the Twentieth Century A Reader*, ed. David Pierce, Cork: Cork University Press.

O'Conor, Charles (1753) *Dissertations on the Antient History of Ireland*, Dublin.

O'Curry, Eugene (1861) *Lectures on the Manuscript Materials of Ancient Irish History*, Dublin.

Ó Domhnaill, Uilliam (William Daniel) (1602) *Tiomna Nuadh ar dTighearna agus ar Slánaightheora Iosa Críosd* Dublin.

Ó Domhnaill, Uilliam (1608) *Leabhar na nUrnaightheadh gComhchoidchiond*, Dublin.

O' Donnell, F. H. (1902) *The Ruin of Education in Ireland and the Irish Fanar*, 2nd edn., London: Nutt.

O'Donovan, John (1845) *A Grammar of the Irish Language*, Dublin.

O'Farrelly, A. (1901) *The Reign of Humbug*, Dublin: Gaelic League.

Ó Fathaigh, P (2000) *Pádraig Ó Fathaigh's War of independence Recollections of a Gaelic Leaguer*, ed. T. G. McMahon, Cork: Cork University Press.

O'Flanagan, T. (1795) *Cambrensis Refuted*, trans. of *Cambrensis Eversus*, T. Lucius, Gratianus [John Lynch] (1662) Dublin.

———— ed. (1808) *Transactions of the Gaelic Society of Dublin*, Dublin.

Ó Glaisne, Risteárd (1966) *Language Freedom*, Longfort: Éire Nua.

O'Growney, Rev. Eugene (1894) *Simple Lessons in Irish giving the Pronunciation of Each Word*, Pt 1, Dublin.

Ó hEigceartaigh, P. S. (1918) 'Politics and The Language', *Samhain*, Dublin: Curtis.

Ó hEódhasa, Giolla Brighde (Bonaventura Hussey) (1611) *An Teagasg Críosdaidhe*, Antwerp.

O' Hickey, Rev. M. P. (1900) *The True National Ideal*, Dublin: Gaelic League.

———— (nd. ?1901) *The Future of Irish in the National Schools*, Dublin: Gaelic League.

Ó Maoil Chonaire, Flaithrí (Florence Conry) (1616) *Sgáthán an Chrábhaidh*, Louvain.

O'Meara, J. J. (1982) trans. *The History and Topography of Ireland*, Giraldus Cambrensis (Gerald of Wales) (1188), Dublin: Dolmen.

Ó Rathaille, Aodhagáin (Egan O'Rahilly) (1911) *Dánta Aodhagáin Uí Rathaille. The Poems of Egan O'Rahilly*, 2nd edn., ed. and trans. P. S. Dinneen and T. O'Donoghue, London: Irish Texts Society.

O'Reilly, E. (1817) *Sanas Gaoidhilge Sagsbeurla. An English Irish Dictionary*, Dublin.

O'Reilly, Rev. John M. [n. d. ?1901] *The Threatening Metempsychosis of a Nation*, Dublin: Gaelic League.

Orpen, Dr. Charles (1821) *The Claims of Millions of our Fellow Countrymen or Present and Future Generations To Be Taught In Their Own and Only Language; the Irish. Addressed to the Upper Classes in Ireland and Great Britain*, Dublin.

O'Sullivan Beare, P. (1903) *Ireland under Elizabeth . . . being a Portion of the History of Catholic Ireland by Don Philip O'Sullivan Beare*, ed. and trans. M. J. Byrne, Dublin: Sealy, Bryers and Walker.

Ó Tuama, Seán and Kinsella, Thomas (1981) *An Duanaire 1600–1900: Poems of the Dispossessed*, Portlaoise: Dolmen Press.

Paulin, Tom (1984) 'A New Look at the Language Question', in *Ireland and the English Crisis*, Newcastle: Bloodaxe.

—— (1998) 'Foreword', *A Dictionary of Hiberno-English*, T. Dolan, ed., Dublin: Gill and Macmillan.

Pearse. P. H. (1899) 'The "Irish" Literary Theatre', (letter) *An Claidheamh Soluis*, I, 10, Dublin.

—— (1952) *Political Writings and Speeches*, Dublin: Talbot.

Peele, George (1605) *The Life and Death of Captain Thomas Stukeley*, in Richard Simpson (1878) *The School of Shakespere*, New York.

Petty, William (1691) *The Political Anatomy of Ireland*, London.

Peyton, V. J. (1771) *The History of the English Language*, London.

Puttenham, G. (1936) *The Arte of English Poesie* (1589) G. D. Willcock and A.Walker, eds. Cambridge: Cambridge University Press.

Rialtas na hÉireann/Government of Ireland (1926) *Gaeltacht Commission: Report*, Baile Áthat Cliath: Oifig an tSolátháir.

—— (2002) *Bille na dTeangacha Oifigiúla (Comhionannas)/ The Official Languages (Equality) Bill*, Dublin: Stationery Office.

—— (2002) *Bille na dTeangacha Oifigiúla/ The Official Languages Bill*, Dublin: Stationery Office.

—— (2003) *Acht na dTeangacha Oifigiúla/ The Official Languages Act*, Dublin: Stationery Office.

Richardson, John (1712) *A Proposal for the Conversion of the Popish Natives of Ireland to the Established Religion: With the Reasons upon which it is Grounded: And an Answer to the Objections made to it* 2nd. edn., corrected and enlarged, London.

—— (1712) *A Short History of the Attempts that Have Been Made to Convert the Popish Natives of Ireland, to the Established Religion: With a Proposal for their Conversion*, London.

Robinson, Philip (1997) *Ulster-Scots: A Grammar of the Traditional Written and Spoken Language*, Belfast: Ullans Press.

—— (2001) 'The Gaelic Archipelago', *Ullans*, 8, 33–8.

*Royal Charter for Erecting English Protestant Schools in the Kingdom of Ireland* (1733) in T. Corcoran, ed. (1916) *State Policy in Irish Education 1536 to 1816*, Dublin: Fallon.

Ruadh, Donnchadh (1899) 'Irish in County Wexford', *An Claidheamh Soluis*, I, 29, Dublin.

Schlegel, F. von (1847) *The Philosophy of Life and Philosophy of Language in a Course of Lectures by Friedrich von Schlegel*, trans. A. J. W. Morrison, London: Bohn.

Scurry, James (1827) *Remarks on the Irish Language*, Dublin.

Shakespeare, William (1623) *Comedies, Histories and Tragedies*, London.

Shaw, George Bernard (1962) *The Matter with Ireland*, ed. D. H. Greene and D. H. Laurence, London: Rupert Hart-Davis.

Sheridan, Thomas (1754) *The Brave Irishman*, Dublin.

—— (1756) *British Education: or, the Source of the Disorders of Great Britain*, London.

—— (1780) *A General Dictionary of the English Language*, London.

Sidney, Henry (1585) 'A Discourse for the Reformation of Ireland' in *Calendar of the Carew Manuscripts preserved in the Archiepiscopal library at Lambeth* (1868) vol. ii, London.

Sigerson, George [Erionnach] (1860) *The Poets and Poetry of Munster*, 2nd series, Dublin.

Sinn Féin (1986) *The Role of the Language in Ireland's Cultural Revival*, Belfast: Sinn Féin.

Society for the Preservation of the Irish Language (1877) *An Cheud Leabhar Gaedhilge. The First Irish Book*, Dublin.

—— (1880) *Transactions 1877–79*, Dublin.

—— (1878–1914) *Reports*, Dublin.

—— (1884) *Proceedings of the Congress Held in Dublin 1882*, Dublin.

Spenser, Edmund (1633) *A View of the State of Ireland* (1596) in Ware, Sir James (1633) *The Historie of Ireland Collected by Three Learned Authors*, Dublin.

Stanihurst, James (1633) 'The Oration of James Stanihurst, Speaker of the Parliament' (1570), in Campion's *A Historie of Ireland*, in Ware, Sir James (1633) *The Historie of Ireland Collected by Three Learned Authors*, Dublin.

Stanihurst, Richard (1587) *A Treatise Containing a Plain and Perfect Description of Ireland* (1577) in R. Holinshed, *The Chronicles of England, Scotland and Ireland* (1587) ed. John Hooker et al, 3 vols., 1587; ed. Henry Ellis, 6 vols., 1807–8, London.

—— (1584) 'De Rebus in Hibernia Gestis' in Colm Lennon, ed. (1981) *Richard Stanihurst the Dubliner 1547–1618*, Dublin: Irish Academic Press.

*State Papers, Henry VIII*, 11 vols. (1830–52), London.

*The Statutes at Large Passed in the Parliaments Held in Ireland* (1786–1801) 1310–1800, 20 vols., Dublin.

Stephens, James (1922) 'The Irish Past is the Irish Language', *The Century Magazine*.

Stokes, Whitley (1799) *Projects for Re-Establishing the Internal Peace and Tranquility of Ireland*, Dublin.

Swift, Jonathan (1712) *Proposal for Correcting, Improving and Ascertaining the English Language*, London.

—— (n.d. ?1735) 'A Dialogue in Hibernian Style Between A and B', in *Prose Writings*, vol. IV (1973) ed. Herbert Davis with Louis Landa, Oxford: Blackwell.

—— (n.d ?1740) 'On Barbarous Denominations in Ireland', in *Prose Writings*, vol. IV (1973) ed. Herbert Davis with Louis Landa, Oxford: Blackwell.

—— (n.d.) 'A Discourse to Prove the Antiquity of the English Tongue', in *Prose Writings*, vol. IV (1973) ed. Herbert Davis with Louis Landa, Oxford: Blackwell.

Synge, J. M. (1979) *The Aran Islands* (1907) Oxford: Oxford University Press.

—— (1966) 'Can We Go Back Into Our Mother's Womb?' (1907), *Collected Works* vol.2 ed. A. Price, London: Oxford University Press.

Taylor, J. S. (1817) *Reasons for Giving Moral Instruction to the Native Irish, Through the Medium of their Vernacular Language*, London.

Thomas, Daniel (1787) *Observations on the Pamphlets Published by the Bishop of Cloyne, Mr. Trant, and Theophilus, On One Side, and Those by Mr. O'Leary, Mr. Barber, and Dr. Campbell On the Other*, Dublin.

*Transactions of the Gaelic Society of Dublin* (1808) ed. Theophilus O'Flanagan, Dublin.

Trench, D. C. (1912) *What is the Use of Reviving Irish?* Dublin: Maunsel.

*Ullans. The Magazine for Ulster-Scots* (1993– ) nos.1–8.

Ulster Folk Museum (1964) *Ulster Dialects: An Introductory Symposium*, Belfast: Ulster Folk Museum.

Vallancey, Charles (1772) *An Essay on the Antiquity of the Irish Language. Being a Collation of the Irish with the Punic Language*, Dublin.

—— (1773) *A Grammar of the Iberno-Celtic or Irish language* (1782) 2nd ed., Dublin.

Walker, J. C. (1786) *Historical Memoir of the Irish Bards*, Dublin.

Walsh, Rev. Paul (1918) *Gleanings from Irish Manuscripts Chiefly of the Seventeenth Century*, Dublin: Dollard.

Ware, Sir James (1633) *The Historie of Ireland Collected by Three Learned Authors*, Dublin.

Williams, N. J. A. (1981) ed. *Pairlement Chloinne Tomáis* (1615) Dublin: Dublin Institute for Advanced Studies.

Wilson, Thomas (1553) *The Arte of Rhetorique*, London.

Yeats, W. B. (1902) *Samhain*, 2, Dublin: Sealy, Bryers and Walker.

—— (1902) *Cathleen ni Hoolihan*, London: Chiswick.

—— (1955) *Autobiographies*, London: Macmillan.

—— (1957) *The Varorium Edition of the Poems of W. B. Yeats*, ed. P. Allt and R. K. Alspach, New York: Macmillan.

—— (1975) 'Letter to *The Leader*' (1900) in *Uncollected Prose*, vol. 2, ed. J. Frayne and C. Johnson, London: Macmillan.

Young, Arthur (1780) *A Tour in Ireland, with General Observations on the State of that Kingdom*, 2 vols., Dublin.

## Secondary Texts

Adams, G. B. (1975) 'Language Census Problems 1851–1911', *Ulster Folklife*, 21, 68–73.

Akenson, D. H. (1970) *The Irish Education Experiment: The National System of Education in the Nineteenth Century*, London: Routledge & Kegan Paul.

—— (1975) *A Mirror to Kathleen's Face: Education in Independent Ireland 1922–1960*, London: McGill–Queen's University.

Akenson, D. H. (1996) 'Pre-University Education, 1870–1921' in W. E. Vaughan, ed. (1996) *A New History of Ireland*, vol.VI, 'Ireland Under the Union', II, Oxford: Clarendon.

*Analecta Hibernica, including the Reports of the Irish Historical Manuscripts Commission* (1930–) Dublin: Irish Historical Manuscripts Commission.

Anderson, Benedict (1983) *Imagined Communities: Reflections on the Origin and Spread of Nationalism*, London: Verso.

Andrews, Liam (1997) '*The very dogs in Belfast will bark in Irish* The Unionist Government and the Irish Language 1921–43' in MacPóilin, Aodán, ed. (1997) *The Irish Language in Northern Ireland*, Béal Feirste/Belfast: Iontaobhas ULTACH/ULTACH Trust.

Arnold, Matthew (1867) *On the Study of Celtic Literature*, London.

Barker, Ernest (1915) *Mothers and Sons in War Time and Other Pieces*, London: Humphreys.

Barnard, T. C. (1993) 'Protestants and the Irish Language, c.1675–1725', *Journal of Ecclesiastical History*, vol. 44, 2, 242–73.

Bartlett, Thomas, C. Curtin, R. O' Dwyer, G. Ó Tuathaigh, eds. (1988) *Irish Studies. A General Introduction*, Dublin: Gill and Macmillan.

Bergin, O. ed. (1970) *Irish Bardic Poetry*, re-edited D. Greene and F. Kelly, Dublin: Dublin Institute for Advanced Studies.

Billig, M (1995) *Banal Nationalism*, London: Sage.

Blaney, R (1996) *Presbyterians and the Irish Language*, Belfast: Ulster Historical Foundation/Ultach Trust.

Bliss, A (1976) 'The English Language in Early Modern Ireland', in Moody et al., *A New History of Ireland*, vol III, 'Early Modern Ireland, 1534–1691', Oxford: Clarendon.

—— (1979) *Spoken English in Ireland 1600–1740*, Dublin: Dolmen.

Boyce, D. G. and O'Day, Alan (1996) *The Making of Modern Irish History: Revisionism and the Revisionist Controversy*, London: Routledge.

Bradshaw, Brendan (1978) 'Sword, Word and Strategy in the Reformation in Ireland', *Historical Journal*, 21, 475–502.

—— (1994) 'The Bardic Response to Conquest and Colonisation', *Bullán: An Irish Studies Journal*, v.1.1, 119–22.

—— 'Geoffrey Keating: Apologist of Irish Ireland', in Brendan Bradshaw, A. Hadfield and W. Maley, *Representing Ireland: Literature and the Origins of Conflict, 1534–1660*, Cambridge: Cambridge University Press 1993.

Braidwood, John (1964) 'Ulster and Elizabethan English' in *Ulster Dialects: An Introductory Symposium*, Belfast: Ulster Folk Museum.

—— (1975) The Ulster Dialect Lexicon, Belfast: The Queen's University.

Breatnach, R. A. (1956) 'Revival or Survival? An Examination of the Irish Language Policy of the State', *Studies*, 45, Dublin.

—— (1961) 'The End of a Tradition: A Survey of Eighteenth Century Gaelic Literature', *Studia Hibernica*, i, 28–50.

—— (1965) 'Two Irish Scholars: J. C. Walker and Charlotte Brooke', *Studia Hibernica*, v, 88–97.

Brennan, M. (1964) 'The Restoration of Irish', *Studies*, 53, 263–77.

Brown, Terence (1985) *Ireland A Social and Cultural History 1922–1985*, London: Fontana.

Burke, Rev. William (1896) 'The Anglo-Irish Dialect', *Irish Ecclesiastical Review*, 3rd Series, XVII, 694–704, 777–89.

Caball, M (1993) 'Pairlement Chloinne Tomáis I: A Reassessment', *Éigse*, xxvii, 47–57.

—— (1998) *Poets and Politics Continuity and Reaction in Irish Poetry 1558–1625*, Notre Dame: University of Notre Dame University in association with Field Day.

Cahill, E. (1935) 'The Irish National Tradition', *The Irish Ecclesiatical Record*, 5th Series, 46: 2–10, Dublin.

—— (1938) 'Norman French and English Languages in Ireland 1170–1540', *The Irish Ecclesiastical Record*, 5th Series, 51: 159–73, Dublin.

—— (1939) 'The Irish Language and Tradition, 1540–1691', *The Irish Ecclesiatical Record*, 5th Series, 54: 123–42, Dublin.

—— (1940*a*) 'The Native Schools of Ireland in the Penal Era', *The Irish Ecclesiastical Record*, 5th Series, 55: 16–28, Dublin.

—— (1940*b*) 'The Irish Language in the Penal Era', *The Irish Ecclesiastical Record*, 5th Series, 55: 591–617, Dublin.

Canny, Nicholas (1982) 'The Formation of the Irish Mind: Religion, Politics and Gaelic Irish Literature 1580–1750', *Past and Present*, 95, 91–116.

—— (1987) 'Identity Formation in Ireland: The Emergence of the Anglo-Irish', in N. Canny and A. Padgen, eds., *Colonial Identity in the Atlantic World 1500–1800*, Princeton: Princeton University Press.

—— (1988) *Kingdom and Colony. Ireland in the Atlantic World 1560–1800*, London: Johns Hopkins University Press.

—— (2001) *Making Ireland British 1580–1650*, Oxford: Oxford University Press.

Clery, Arthur (1919) 'The Gaelic League, 1893–1919', *Studies*, viii, 398–407.

Corcoran, T. ed. (1916) *State Policy in Irish Education 1536 to 1816*, Dublin: Fallon.

Corkery, D. (1925) *The Hidden Ireland: A Study of Gaelic Munster in the 18th Century*, Dublin: Gill and Macmillan.

—— (1954) *The Fortunes of the Irish Language*, Cork: Mercier.

Cosgrove, A. ed. (1987) *A New History of Ireland*, vol.II, 'Medieval Ireland 1169–1534', Oxford: Clarendon.

Coughlan, Patricia (1989) "'Some secret scourge which shall by her come unto England": Ireland and incivility in Spenser' in Patricia Coughlan, ed., *Spenser and Ireland: an interdisciplinary perspective* (Cork: Cork University Press, 64–70).

Crane Bag (1981) *Irish language and Culture: An tEagrán Gaelach*, 5.

Croghan, M. J. (1990) 'Swift, Thomas Sheridan, Maria Edgeworth and the Evolution of Hiberno-English', *Irish University Review*, vol. 20., 1, 19–34.

Cronin, M. (1996) *Translating Ireland; Translation, Languages, Cultures*, Cork: Cork University Press.

Cronin, S. (1978) 'Nation-Building in the Irish Language Revival Movement', *Éire-Ireland*, vol 6, 7–14.

Crowley, Tony (1991) *Proper English? Readings in Language, History, and Cultural Identity*, London: Routledge.

——(1996) *Language in History: Theories and Texts*, London: Routledge.

——(2000) *The Politics of Language in Ireland 1366–1922 A Sourcebook*, London: Routledge.

Cullen, L. M. (1969) 'The Hidden Ireland: Re-Assessment of a Concept', *Studia Hibernica*, ix, 7–47.

Cunningham, B. (2000) *The World of Geoffrey Keating. History, myth and religion in seventeenth-century Ireland*, Dublin: Four Courts Press.

Curtis, Edmund (1919) 'The Spoken Languages of Medieval Ireland', *Studies*, viii, 234–54.

de Brún, Pádraig (1982–3) 'The Irish Society's Bible Teachers, 1818–27', *Éigse*, xix, 281–332.

——(1983) 'Scriptural Instruction in Irish: A Controversy of 1830–1', in Pádraig de Brún, Seán Ó Coileáin, Pádraig Ó Riain, eds., *Folia Gadelica. Essays presented by former students to R. A. Breatnach*, Cork: Cork University Press.

de Fréine, S. (1965) *The Great Silence*, Dublin: Foilseacháin Náisiúnta Teoranta.

——(1977) 'The Dominance of the English Language in the Nineteenth Century' in D. Ó Muirithe, ed., *The English Language in Ireland*, Cork: Mercier.

de Paor, Louis (1996) 'Disappearing Language: Translations from the Irish' in David Pierce, ed., (2000) *Irish Writing in the Twentieth Century A Reader*, Cork: Cork University Press.

Deane, Seamus (1997) *Strange Country: Modernity and Nationhood in Irish Writing since 1790*, Oxford: Clarendon.

Derricke, John (1581) *The Image of Irelande: With a Discouerie of Woodkarne*, ed. J. Small (1883), Edinburgh.

Dolan, T. (1998) *A Dictionary of Hiberno-English*, Dublin: Gill and Macmillan.

Dowling, P. J. (1968) *The Hedge Schools of Ireland*, Dublin: Mercier.

Draper, J. (1919) 'Spenser's Linguistics in "The Present State of Ireland"', *Modern Philology*, 17.8, 471–86.

Dunne, T. J. (1980) 'The Gaelic Response to Conquest and Colonisation: The Evidence of the Poetry', *Studia Hibernica*, 20, 7–30.

Eagleton, Terry (1998) *Crazy John and the Bishop and Other Essays on Irish Culture*, Notre Dame: Notre Dame University Press/Field Day.

Edgeworth, Maria (1800) *Castle Rackrent. An Hibernian Tale*, London.

Edwards, Ruth Dudley (1977) *Patrick Pearse The Triumph of Failure*, London: Victor Gollancz.

Ellis, S. (1998) *Ireland in the Age of the Tudors 1447–1603 English Expansion and the End of Gaelic Rule*, London: Longman.

Farquhar, George (1703) *The Twin Rivals*, London.

Farren, Sean (1995) *The Politics of Irish Education 1920–65*, Belfast: Queen's University Institute of Irish Studies.

Fitzsimons, J. (1949) 'Official Presbyterian Irish Language Policy in the 18th and 19th Centuries', *Irish Ecclesiastical Record*, 5th Series, 72, 255–64.

Fogarty, Anne (1989) 'The Colonisation of Language: Narrative Strategy in *A View of the Present State of Ireland* and the *Faerie Queene*, Book VI', in P. Coughlan, ed, *Spenser and Ireland an interdisciplinary perspective*, Cork: Cork University Press, 75–108.

Foster, R. (1989) *Modern Ireland: 1600–1972*, Harmondsworth: Penguin.

French, R. B. D. (1966) 'J. O. Hannay and the Gaelic League', *Hermathena*, cii, 26–52.

Garvin, Tom (1987) *Nationalist Revolutionaries in Ireland 1858–1928*, Oxford: Clarendon.

—— 'The Politics of Language and Literature in Pre-Independence Ireland', *Irish Political Studies*, 2, 49–63.

Görlach, M. (2000) 'Ulster Scots: A language?', in *Language and Politics in Northern Ireland, the Republic of Ireland, and Scotland*, ed J. Kirk and D. Ó Baoill, Belfast: Cló Ollscoil na Banríona.

Gray, Thomas (1757) *Odes: The Progress of Poesy and the Bard*, Strawberry Hill.

Greenblatt, Stephen (1990) *Learning to Curse: Essays in Early Modern Culture*, London: Routledge.

Greene, David (1966) *The Irish Language*, Dublin: Cultural Relations Committee.

—— (1970) 'The Irish Language Movement', in M. Hurley, ed. *Irish Anglicanism 1869–1969*, Dublin: Allan Figgis.

—— (1972) 'The Founding of the Gaelic League', in Ó Tuama, *The Gaelic League Idea*, Cork: Mercier.

Hadfield, A. (1993) 'Briton and Scythian: Tudor representations of Irish origins', *Irish Historical Studies*, xxviii, 112, 390–408.

—— and J. McVeagh (1994) *Strangers to that Land: British Perceptions of Ireland from the Reformation to the Famine*, Gerrards Cross: Colin Smythe.

Hayes-McCoy, G. A. (1976) 'The royal supremacy and ecclesiastical revolution, 1534–47', in Moody, T. W., F . X. Martin and F. J. Byrne, eds. *A New History of Ireland*, vol. III, 'Early Modern Ireland, 1534–1691', Oxford: Clarendon.

Hewitt, John (1974) *Rhyming Weavers and other Country Poets of Antrim and Down*, Belfast: Blackstaff Press.

Hindley, R. (1990) *The Death of the Irish Language: A Qualified Obituary*, London: Routledge.

Hogan, J. J. (1927) *The English Language in Ireland*, Dublin: Educational company of Ireland.

Hume, A (1858) 'The Irish Dialect of the English Language', *Ulster Journal of Archaeology*, 6, 47–55.

Hutchinson, John (1987) *The Dynamics of Cultural Nationalism: The Gaelic Revival and the Creation of the Irish Nation State*, London: Allen and Unwin.

Jackson, D. (1973) 'The Irish Language and Tudor Government', *Éire-Ireland*, vol. 8: 1, 21–8.

Jones, Rev. F. M. (1953) 'The Congregation of Propaganda and the Publication of Dr. O'Brien's Irish Dictionary', *Irish Ecclesiastical Record*, lxxvii, 29–37.

Jones, R. F. (1953). *The Triumph of the English Language*, Oxford: Oxford University Press.

Joyce, P. W. (1910) *English as we Speak it in Ireland*, Dublin.

Kelly, A. (2002) *Compulsory Irish: Language and Education in Ireland 1870s–1970s*, Dublin: Irish Academic Press.

Kiberd, Declan (1979) *Synge and the Irish Language*, London: Macmillan.

—— (1981) 'Editorial: the Irish Language', *The Crane Bag*, 5, 4–6.

—— (1996) *Inventing Ireland: The Literature of the Modern Nation*, London: Vintage.

Kidd, Colin (1999) *British Identities before Nationalism. Ethnicity and Nationhood in the Atlantic World, 1600–1800*, Cambridge: Cambridge University Press.

Kirby, Peadar, Luke Gibbons and Michael Cronin (2002) *Reinventing Ireland. Culture, Society and the Global Economy*, London: Pluto.

Kirk, J., Ó Baoill, D. (2000) *Language and Politics in Northern Ireland, the Republic of Ireland, and Scotland*, ed J. Kirk and D. Ó Baoill, Belfast: Cló Ollscoil na Banríona.

Lee, Joseph (1979) ed., *Ireland 1945–70*, Dublin: Gill and Macmillan.

—— (1989) *Ireland 1912–1985 Politics and Society*, Cambridge: Cambridge University Press.

Leerssen, Joep (1986) 'On the edge of Europe: Ireland in search of Oriental roots, 1650–1850', *Comparative Criticism*, 8, 91–112.

—— (1996) *Mere Irish and Fiór Ghael: Studies in the Idea of Irish Nationality, Its Development and Literary Expression prior to the Nineteenth Century*, Cork: Cork University Press in association with Field Day.

Lennon, Colm (1981) *Richard Stanihurst the Dubliner 1547–1618*, Dublin: Irish Academic Press.

Lyons, F. S. L. (1979) *Culture and Anarchy in Ireland 1890–1939*, Oxford: Clarendon.
—— (1985) *Ireland Since the Famine*, London: Fontana.

MacAdam, Robert (1858–62) 'Six hundred Gaelic proverbs gathered in Ulster', *Ulster Journal of Archaeology*, 6, 172–83, 250–67, 7, 278–87, 9, 223–36.

Macafee, C. I. (1996) *A Concise Ulster Dictionary*, Oxford: Oxford University Press.

Macardle, Dorothy (1968) *The Irish Republic*, London: Gollancz.

McCartney, D. (1973) 'MacNeill and Irish Ireland', in F. X. Martin and F. J. Byrne (eds.), *The Scholar Revolutionary: Eoin MacNeill and the Making of the New Ireland*, Shannon: Irish University Press.

McCaughey, T. P. (1967–8) 'Muiris Ó Gormáin's English-Irish Phrase Book', *Éigse*, xii, 203–27.

McCormack, W. J. (1985) *Ascendancy and Tradition in Anglo-Irish Literary History from 1789 to 1939*, Oxford: Clarendon.

McCoy, G., C. O'Reilly (2003) 'Essentialising Ulster? The Ulster-Scots Language Movement' in M. Tymoczko and C. Ireland, eds., *Language and Tradition in Ireland Continuities and Displacements*, Boston: University of Massachussets Press and American Conference for Irish Studies.

MacNamara, John (1966) *Bilingualism and Primary Education*, Edinburgh: Edinburgh University Press.

MacPóilin, Aodán, ed. (1997*a*) *The Irish Language in Northern Ireland*, Béal Feirste/Belfast: Iontaobhas ULTACH/ULTACH Trust.

—— (1997*b*) 'Aspects of the Irish Language Movement', in MacPóilin, Aodán, ed. (1997) *The Irish Language in Northern Ireland*, Béal Feirste/Belfast: Iontaobhas ULTACH/ULTACH Trust.

Maguire, Gabrielle (1991) *Our Own Language: An Irish Language Initiative*, Clevedon: Multilingual Matters.

Mahony, R. (1989) 'Yeats and the Irish Language', *The Irish University Review*, vol. 19, 2.

Martin, F. X. and F. J. Byrne, eds. (1973) *The Scholar Revolutionary: Eoin MacNeill and the Making of the New Ireland*, Shannon: Irish University Press.

Mercier, Vivien (1996) 'Literature in English, 1891–1921' in W. E. Vaughan (1996) *A New History of Ireland*, vol. VI, 'Ireland under The Union', II, Oxford: Clarendon.

Mistéil, Pilib (1994) *The Irish Language and the Unionist Tradition*, Belfast: Ulster People's College/Ultach Trust.

Moloney, Ed (2003) *A Secret History of the IRA*, London: Penguin.

Moody, T. W, F. X. Martin (2002) *The Course of Irish History*, Cork: Mercier Press.

Moody, T. W., F. X. Martin and F. J. Byrne, eds.(1976) *A New History of Ireland*, vol. III, 'Early Modern Ireland, 1534–1691', Oxford: Clarendon.

Moody, T. W and W. E. Vaughan, eds. (1986) *A New History of Ireland*, vol. IV, 'Eighteenth Century Ireland, 1691–1800', Oxford: Clarendon.

Mooney, Rev. C. (1944) 'The Beginnings of the Irish Language Revival', *Irish Ecclesiastical Record*, 5th Series, 64, 10–18.

Morash, C. (1995) *Writing the Irish Famine*, Oxford: Clarendon.

Myers, J. P. (1983) *Elizabethan Ireland*, Connecticut: Archon.

Nic Craith, Máiréad, ed. (1996) *Watching One's Tongue: Issues in Language Planning*, Liverpool: Liverpool University Press.

—— (1999) 'Irish Speakers in Northern Ireland and the Good Friday Agreement', *Journal of Multilingual and Multicultural Development*, 20: 6, 494–507.

—— (2000) 'Contested Identities and the Quest for Legitimacy', *Journal of Multilingual and Multicultural Development*, 21: 5, 1–15.

—— (2001) 'Politicised linguistic consciousness: the case of Ulster-Scots', *Nations and Nationalism*, 7, 21–37.

Ó hAilin, Tomás (1969) 'Irish Revival Movements', in Brian Ó Cuív (1969a) ed., *A View of the Irish Language*, Dublin: Stationery Office, 91–101.

Ó Buachalla, Breandán (1968) *I mBéal Feirste Cois Cuain*, Dublin: An Chlochomhar Teo.

—— (1992) 'Poetry and Politics in Early Modern Ireland', *Eighteenth Century Ireland Iris an Dá Chultúr*, 7, 149–75.

Ó Buachalla, Séamas (1981) 'The Language in the Classroom', in *The Crane Bag*, 5.

Ó Cadhain, Máirtín (1973) *The Language Movement: A Movement Astray*, trans. Seósamh Ó Díochan, Dublin: Communist Party of Ireland.

Ó Cassidy, Séamus (Séamus Ó Casaide) (1930) *The Irish Language in Belfast and County Down 1601–1850*, Dublin: Gill.

Ó Catháin, L. (1996) 'The Irish Language: Administrative and Legal Status' in Nic Craith, Máiréad, ed. (1996) *Watching One's Tongue: Issues in Language Planning*, Liverpool: Liverpool University Press.

Ó Ciosáin, Niall (1997) *Print and Popular Culture in Ireland, 1750–1850*, Macmillan: Houndmills.

O'Connell, Maurice (1968) *A History of the Irish Teachers' Organisation*, Dublin: Irish University Press.

Ó Cuív, Brian (1951) *Irish Dialects and Irish-Speaking Districts*, Dublin: Dublin Institute for Advanced Studies.

—— (1969a) ed, *A View of the Irish Language*, Dublin: Stationery Office.

—— (1969b) 'The Changing Form of the Irish Language' in Brian Ó Cuív, ed., *A View of the Irish Language*, Dublin: Stationery Office.

—— (1976) 'The Irish Language in the Early Modern Period' in Moody, T. W., F. X. Martin and F. J. Byrne, eds. *A New History of Ireland*, vol. III, 'Early Modern Ireland, 1534–1691', Oxford: Clarendon.

—— (1986) 'Irish Language and Literature, 1691–1845' in Moody, T. W. and W. E. Vaughan, eds., *A New History of Ireland*, vol. IV, 'Eighteenth Century Ireland, 1691–1800', Oxford: Clarendon.

—— (1996) 'Irish Language and Literature 1845–1921' in W. E. Vaughan, ed., *A New History of Ireland*, vol.VI, 'Ireland Under the Union', II, Oxford: Clarendon.

Ó Cuív, Shán (1936) *The Problem of Irish in the Schools*, Dublin: Talbot Press.

O'Driscoll, R. (1971) 'Ferguson and the Idea of an Irish National Literature', 6:1, *Éire/Ireland*, 82–95.

Ó Fearaíl, P. (1975) *The Story of Conradh na Gaeilge. A History of the Gaelic League*, Dublin.

Ó Fiaich, Tomás (1969) 'The Language and Political History' in Brian Ó Cuív, ed., *A View of the Irish Language*, Dublin: Stationery Office.

—— (1972) 'The Great Controversy' in Seán Ó Tuama, ed., *The Gaelic League Idea*, Cork: Mercier.

Ó Glaisne, Risteárd (1981) 'Irish and the Protestant Tradition', *The Crane Bag*, 5.2, 33–44.

Ó hAodha, Mícheál (1969) 'Introduction', Douglas Hyde, *Abhráin Grádh Chúige Connacht: The Love Songs of Connacht*, Shannon: Irish University Press.

Ó Hualacháin, Fr. Colm (1994) *The Irish and Irish – a Sociolinguistic Analysis of the Relationship Between a People and their Language*, Baile Átha Cliath: Irish Franciscan Office.

O'Leary, Philip (1994) *The Prose Literature of the Gaelic Revival, 1881–1921 Ideology and Innovation*, Pennsylvania: Pennsylvania University Press.

Ó Loingsigh, P. (1975) 'The Irish Language in the Nineteenth Century', *Oideas*, 14, 5–21.

Ó Muirithe, D. ed. (1977) *The English Language in Ireland*, Cork: Mercier.

Ó Murchú, M. (1985) *The Irish Language*, Dublin: Government Publications.

Ó Néill, S. (1966) 'The Hidden Ulster: Gaelic Pioneers in the North', *Studies*, 55, 60–6.

O'Rahilly, T. F. (1932) *Irish Dialects Past and Present* (1972) Dublin: Dublin Institute for Advanced Studies.

O'Reilly, C. (1999) *The Irish Language in Northern Ireland. The Politics of Culture and Identity*, Houndmills: Macmillan.

Ó Riagáin, P. (1997) *Language Policy and Social Reproduction in Ireland 1893–1993*, Oxford: Clarendon.

O' Riordan, Michelle (1990) *The Gaelic Mind and the Collapse of the Gaelic World*, Cork: Cork Uuniversity Press.

Ó Snodaigh, Padraig (1995) 2nd edn. *Hidden Ulster. Protestants and the Irish Language*, Belfast: Lagan Press.

Ó Tuama, Seán, ed. (1972) *The Gaelic League Idea*, Cork: Mercier.

Ó Tuama, Seán, (1988) 'Gaelic Culture in Crisis: The Literary Response 1600–1850' in T. Bartlett et al., *Irish Studies A General Introduction*, Dublin: Gill and Macmillan.

—— (1995) *Repossessions: Selected Essays on the Irish Literary Heritage*, Cork: Cork University Press.

Ó Tuathaigh, Gearóid (1979) 'Language, Literature and Culture in Ireland since the War' in J. Lee ed., *Ireland 1945–70*, Dublin: Gill and Macmillan.

Palmer, Patricia (2001) *Language and Conquest in Early Modern Ireland. English Renaissance Literature and Elizabethan Imperial Expansion*, Cambridge: Cambridge University Press.

Parkes, Susan (1996) 'Higher Education, 1793–1908', in W. E. Vaughan ed. (1996) *A New History of Ireland*, vol VI, 'Ireland under The Union', II, 1870–1921, Oxford: Clarendon.

Pierce, David (2000) *Irish Writing in the Twentieth Century A Reader*, Cork: Cork University Press.

Reynolds, J. A. (1954) *The Catholic Emancipation Crisis in Ireland 1823–9*, New Haven: Yale University Press.

Risk, M. H. (1966) 'Charles Lynegar, Professor of the Irish Language 1712', *Hermathena*, cii, 16–25.

Sheehan, Catherine (1953) 'The Contribution of Charles O'Conor of Belangare to Gaelic Scholarship in Eighteenth Century Ireland', *Journal of Celtic Studies*, vol. 2.1, 219–37.

Tovey, Hilary (1993) 'Re-Imagining the Language Question', *The Irish Reporter*, 11, 14–16.

———, D. Hannan, H. Abramson, (1989) *Why Irish? Language and Identity in Ireland Today*, Dublin: Bord na Gaeilge.

Tymoczko, M., and C. Ireland, (2003) *Language and Tradition in Ireland Continuities and Displacements*, Boston: University of Massachussets Press and American Conference for Irish Studies.

Vance, Norman (1981) 'Celts, Carthaginians, and constitutions: Anglo-Irish literary relations 1780–1820', *Irish Historical Studies*, 22, 87, 216–38.

Vaughan, W. E., ed. (1989) *A New History of Ireland*, vol. V, Ireland Under the Union, I, 1801–1870, Oxford: Clarendon.

—— ed. (1996) *A New History of Ireland*, vol.VI, 'Ireland Under the Union', II, 1870–1921, Oxford: Clarendon.

Wall, Maureen (1969) 'The Decline of the Irish Language', in Brian Ó Cuív, ed., *A View of the Irish Language*, Dublin: Stationery Office.

Wall, T. (1943) 'Doctrinal Instruction in Irish: The Work of Theobald Stapleton', *Irish Ecclesiastical Record*, 5th series, vol. lxii, 101–12.

Walsh, John (2002) *Díchoimisiúnú Teanga: Coimisiún na Gaeltachta 1926*, Baile Átha Cliath: Cois Life.

Walsh, Fr. P. (1918) *Gleanings from Irish Manuscripts*, Dublin: Dollard.

—— (1920) 'The Irish Language and the Reformation', *Irish Theological Quarterly*, vol.15, 242–53.

Walsh, T. J. (1973) *The Irish Continental College Movement: the Colleges at Bordeaux, Toulouse and Lille*, Dublin: Golden Eagle.

Watt, J. A. (1961) 'English law and the Irish Church: the Reign of Edward I', in *Medieval Studies Presented to A. Gwynn*, ed. J. A. Watt, J. B. Morrall, F. X. Martin, Dublin: Three Candles.

—— (1987*a*) 'Approaches to the history of fourteenth-century Ireland', in A. Cosgrove, ed., *A New History of Ireland*, vol.II, 'Medieval Ireland 1169–1534', Oxford: Clarendon.

—— (1987*b*) 'Gaelic Polity and Cultural Identity' in A. Cosgrove, ed. *A New History of Ireland*, vol. II, 'Medieval Ireland 1169–1534', Oxford Clarendon.

—— (1987*c*) 'The Anglo-Irish Colony Under Strain 1327–99' in A. Cosgrove, ed., *A New History of Ireland*, vol.II, 'Medieval Ireland 1169–1534', Oxford: Clarendon.

Zeuss, Johann Kaspar (1853) *Grammatica Celtica*, Leipzig.

# Index